MARKETING SUCCESSES
Historical to Present Day: What We Can Learn

MARKETING SUCCESSES
Historical to Present Day: What We Can Learn

Robert F. Hartley
Cleveland State University

John Wiley & Sons, Inc.
New York Chichester Brisbane Toronto Singapore

Library of Congress Cataloging in Publication Data:

Hartley, Robert F.
Marketing successes, historical to present day.

Includes index.
1. Marketing—Case studies. I. Title.
HF5415.H2432 1985 658.8 84-17227
ISBN 0-471-84221-4

Printed in the United States of America

10 9 8 7 6 5 4 3

CONTENTS

CHAPTER 1

What Role for History?

A historical treatment of marketing—of its instruments, its institutions, its strategies—has developed spasmodically and not systematically. It has been of tertiary, not even of secondary, concern to both marketing practitioners and marketing academicians. Perhaps this lack reflects the relative immaturity of marketing as a discipline, at least in comparison with economics or management, in which histories of economic thought and management philosophies have existed for decades. But after all, even the term *marketing* dates back not much more than half a century. In general, an acquaintance with the past becomes more important as a discipline ages. Perhaps marketing is now old enough for this.

The major effort to develop some notion of marketing evolution has been Bartels' classic work, *History of Marketing Thought*. This focuses primarily on philosophies and personalities of marketing-thought development, and the writings, since the turn of the century. A few scattered books have traced certain historical precedents in specialized areas of marketing, such as retailing and advertising. *The Great Merchants* by Mahoney and Sloan, for example, has provided background on some of the major retailers of today, particularly the department store moguls. And a massive book by Presbrey traces the early *History and Development of Advertising*. Books have depicted the histories of certain major retail and manufacturing firms, such as Rich's, Coca-Cola, and General Motors. But generally these have been descriptive and of some popular interest rather than bases for furthering the discipline of marketing.

So perhaps we are left with a feeling of inadequacy, a sense that we have failed to look back enough to determine what if anything might be gleaned from the past. Failure to fully consider the past may be myopic in its assumption that nothing can be learned from the past and that the past can make no contributions to present-day endeavors.

THE VARIETIES OF HISTORY

Marketing history can be studied from several vantage points. We can examine how marketing thought has evolved, as Bartels has done. We can look at statistical growth of various marketing activities, such as advertising, packaging, and marketing research—and these are impressive, indeed. We can examine how marketing texts and writings have evolved, and here again Bartels has done an admirable job. We can examine the changing sociolegal relations of marketing, which is intriguing and has received sporadic attention in an age of consumerism, environmental concern, and governmental insistence on fair treatment for all.

But another aspect of marketing history has received little attention, and perhaps it should. Cases of historical marketing successes should give us some practical learning experiences as well as other benefits. We focus on this aspect of marketing history in this book: entrepreneurial studies. However, this is hardly a comprehensive record, a definitive treatment of the historical background of marketing entrepreneurial activities; rather, we have tried to give a sense of the past, not so much history as events along its way. Detailed examples of notable marketing successes are covered chronologically, from the turn of the century to the present. We have tried to identify the key factors of these successes and, further, to assess their relevance to today's problems and opportunities—in other words, their transferability.

Individuals shape history and are intimately involved in its machinations and consequences. These "shape makers," of course, are present in all histories, and are certainly major participants in marketing history. In this book, we describe some of the influential individuals—such as James Cash Penney, Robert Woodruff, George Washington Hill, Harry Cunningham, Frank Perdue, Joel Hyatt, and many others—and try to humanize them as space permits. They have shaped enterprises in the past, been innovators, and can show the way for others to come.

CONTRIBUTIONS OF HISTORY

Unless something can be gained that has relevance and application to the present, the study of history is merely an academic exercise, of some interest to the scholars of that particular field and perhaps even to those members of the general public who tend to look backward rather than forward (more characteristic of age than of youth), but certainly of no importance to most of us who are striving in the present and the future. But *if* history has some relevance to the present, then we have reason to consider it and maybe even become familiar with the strivings, the victories, and the defeats of the past. I believe that history has relevance to the present and the future in at least these aspects, which we will discuss in more detail:

History can provide an important learning experience at the micro level.

History engenders interest and inspiration.

History can be an important ingredient in the development of marketing theory. If a theory is achieved, we will have advanced far in our ability to predict future roles and directions for marketing and its institutions and techniques.

A Learning Experience. For history to provide a learning experience, several questions must be answered in the affirmative:

Does the past have any similarities to the present and the future?

Would what worked then (or did not work then) have relevance for today?

Are the opportunities of the past gone forever, or do they still exist in the same or similar form today?

Human nature being as it is, it is foolish to conclude that the past was unique and has no similarities to the future. We know that in the international arena, bickering and bloodshed between groups of different religions is as commonplace today as it was millenia ago. And turning to marketing, the public's desire for want-satisfying products and services has hardly lessened through the years. Even the means of satisfying such wants remain little changed: offering good values and empathetic service. Although we may have developed somewhat more sophisticated tools for our marketing arsenal today than at the turn of the century—such as marketing research, more diversity in and media for advertising, better understanding of consumer behavior (although far from complete), and computer-based analytical tools—the basic thrust of marketing efforts today still requires creativity and judgment in translating such inputs into a marketing success. Here we have one of the fascinating characteristics of marketing: despite all the mathematical and sophisticated tools and techniques, marketing remains more of an art than a science.

Although many aspects of marketing decision making—the manipulation of the controllable elements of price, product, promotion, distribution, and public image—represent an art rather than a science, with many combinations possible, and more than one combination or blend likely to result in success, we would still do well to have some acquaintance with what worked or did not work in the past with other firms and other situations. The present may be somewhat different, with different competitors and different customers, but previous successes or failures at least can trigger ideas for modifications or new adaptations if different strategy seems to be needed. And sometimes no modification is really needed:

> For example, the early success of the J. C. Penney Company was due to offering customers better values than competitors, better service through the personal commitment of managers to their community, the formula for rapid growth in a highly motivated trainer-trainee interface, and the avoidance of face-to-face confrontation with larger, more powerful competitors—in other words, through finding a target market that was not being adequately served by other marketers. All these elements of success back in the first few decades of this century are applicable today. What worked in the formative years with Penney's, or with Coca-Cola, or with Spry, or McDonald's, is certainly relevant with other firms in other situations.

The third question, "Are the opportunities of the past gone forever?" can hardly be answered in the negative, or there would be no new businesses achieving success, no new millionaires, and entrepreneurship would be unattractive to the able and ambitious. Such a position is ludicrous and flies in the face of all known facts. Later in this book we examine some of the more recent successes: Joel Hyatt of Hyatt Legal Services, Mark McCormack of International Management Group, Steven Jobs of Apple, and Frank Perdue and his chickens. These are just a few examples of the opportunities that still exist today, opportunities awaiting the innovator or simply the person alert to potential customers' needs that are not being fully met by present firms.

Interest and Inspiration. The formative years of great corporations can be of signal interest to observers. We are all intrigued by the paths of success followed by the fortunate and the talented. We can gain inspiration from such examples, even though the probability of any one of us achieving such success is remote—*but not impossible.* In reading about the success patterns of what seem like ordinary people, sometimes with most humble backgrounds, one can ponder the thought that "nothing is impossible, even for me." And this is the theme of David J. Schwartz's 2 million copy best seller, *The Magic of Thinking Big.*

As you read the following cases, place yourself in the role of the main character, the Jim Penney, Harry Cunningham, Frank Perdue, or other notable characters you will encounter. Try to see from their perspectives in the early formative days of their enterprises. Imagine their thoughts, their shifting goals, their feelings of ultimate satisfaction of accomplishment. For example, in the first case we examine, Jim Penney's early aspirations were to have 6 stores; before long he raised this to 25 stores. Less than ten years later he was to raise his sights to having 500 stores. Eventually, he wound up with over 1600 stores.

Toward Developing Marketing Theory. If we are ever to develop definitive and useful approaches to marketing theory and eventually even to principles and laws, marketing history will have to play a significant part. At such a point, if it can be reached, we will have come a long way toward predicting the future role of marketing, its tools and techniques, its most promising strategies, and its most effective contribution to society. In the quest for developing a theory of some consequence, we need to:

Identify commonalities and important classifications of events and situations.

Gain some insights as to probable cause and effect relationships. In this regard, we will have come a long way if we can attach probabilities of certain events occurring from certain inputs.

Of course, the challenge is great given the many interrelated variables that affect most marketing outcomes. But a historical study may prove the best approach since it provides us with known outcomes from certain inputs, despite the ever-present uncontrollable and hardly identifiable contaminating variables that may be called fortuitous. The alternative to historical analysis is experimentation. Here the problem of uncontrollable and barely identifiable variables may be lessened, but the sterile and unrealistic setting thwarts the quest of developing marketing theory and arriving at some predictive power for real-world situations. I firmly believe that if we are to make any progress toward developing such a theory or theories, this must come from a greater concentration on historical inputs and outcomes. I hope this book will be a small step toward such a goal.

PART One

THE EARLY DECADES OF THIS CENTURY: STRATEGIES GEARED TO GREAT GROWTH

The first three decades of the twentieth century saw the emergence of marketing strategies geared to a time of rapid growth on a scale never encountered before. These strategies had great impact in those days because they were innovative and also because competition, although growing in strength, was in no way as intensive and sophisticated as today. These successful early strategies showed clearly the great potential that aggressive and well-targeted marketing efforts could have in any age.

In the first case, the Penney Company demonstrated a simple strategy: be concerned with customers' needs and wants and cater to those who are not being well taken care of by competing firms. Penney's sought to give customers honest values at fair prices, prices that were lower and quality that was better than what could be found elsewhere. In its formative years it directed its efforts to small towns in the rural West. But Penney also was an early pioneer in furthering the chain concept that was to become dominant in retailing from the 1920s to the present day. Growth was achieved by opening hundreds of new stores. This was a tremendous growth challenge for that day when transportation and communication were primitive by today's standards and, of course, long before the computer was available as an important management tool for controlling far-flung operations.

A major achievement of the Penney Company during its geometric early growth was finding the qualified managers to run its stores. This was achieved through a unique profit-sharing program in which both new managers and the experienced managers who trained them received a share of the profits of the new stores. In the 1920s, after almost 30 years of operation, Penney's changed to a more conventional and centralized organization, but the strong foundation had been laid. Penney's was the bellwether of the general merchandise chain movement, far surpassing the latecomers into retail stores—the mail-order houses of Sears and Montgomery Ward. Even by 1927, Sears had only 27 retail stores and Ward had 37, while Penney had about 800 and was doing well over $100 million in sales.

Advertising was in its youth in these decades. Its effectiveness, however, was increasing as more and better media developed and as the art of advertising became more sophisticated. To capture this potential, of course, a firm had to make a financial commitment to advertising, even to spending an undreamed-of sum for mass-media advertising—that is, undreamed of a few short years before. And these expenditures for advertising, though they undoubtedly had great impact on sales, could never be fully evaluated or planned as to their specific effectiveness per dollar invested. The push by the more aggressive marketers still continued to increase their advertising budgets. Table 1 compares the total advertising expenditures in the early decades in the United States with total expenditures in recent years. You can see that this powerful marketing tool was still embryonic in the early decades. But two cases, Coca-Cola and American Tobacco Company, illustrate its power for those who were bold and had the resources to match this aggressiveness.

The Coca-Cola case illustrates the emergence of more than the powerful use of advertising. Its early days

Table 1 Trend of Advertising Expenditures in the United States

Year	*Expenditures (Billions of Dollars)*
1880	$ 0.2
1890	0.4
1900	0.5
1909	1.1
1919	2.3
1925	3.1
1929	3.0
1940	2.1
1950	5.9
1960	11.9
1970	19.6
1979	49.8
1981	61.5 (est.)

Sources: U.S. Department of Commerce, Bureau of the Census, Historical Statistics of the United States, Colonial Times to 1957; Statistical Abstract of U.S., 1982.

marked the introduction of such powerful marketing tools as dealer promotions, distinctive packaging, point-of-purchase displays, and the great effectiveness of product differentiation, even if such differentiation was more psychological than real. Coca-Cola also popularized a rather new distribution concept for those days: franchising. The use of franchised bottlers hastened the growth of the Coca-Cola Company and proved to be a precursor to the important role of franchising today, when some 30 percent of all retail and service revenues in this country are generated by franchised outlets of a great diversity of products, services, and operations.

CHAPTER 2

J. C. Penney Co.: Running with the Chain Concept

Penney's was not the originator of the chain concept. But James Cash Penney embraced the idea of horizontal integration for small dry goods stores and gave it a special twist to foster growth. He became one of the great successes in the early decades of this century, laying the groundwork for the $12 billion company of today. The beginnings were very humble: management sophistication consisted mainly of willingness to work hard and long, coupled with concern for giving customers honest values and employees (mostly small-town boys) an opportunity to participate in growth and self-fulfillment.

THE BEGINNING

At sunrise on a spring morning in 1902, a young man, Jim Penney, opened a tiny dry goods store in Kemmerer, a frontier town in the southwest corner of Wyoming. He called the store the Golden Rule, remembering his father's admonitions to deal with people according to the Biblical injunction: "Therefore all things whatsoever ye would that men should do to ye, do ye even so to them." The opening day was advertised by handbills distributed throughout the town. Penney remained open that day until midnight, and his sales were $466.59. After that he opened at 7 A.M. on weekdays and 8 A.M. on Sundays, and remained open as long as there was a miner or shepherd on the street. Sales for the first year were $28,898.11.[1]

[1]Tom Mahoney, *The Great Merchants* (New York: Harper & Row, 1955), p. 255.

Penney faced a tough competitor in Kemmerer. The town was dominated by a mining company, and a company-owned store had practically a local monopoly with most business done on credit or with the scrip issued by the mining company. Penney did not offer any credit, nor could he accept the scrip. What he did offer was such good values that customers were willing to pay cash and carry home their purchases. He had no fancy fixtures—all the merchandise was piled on tables where customers could see and touch, and there was one price for all. Penney also had a return-goods policy: if customers were not satisfied, they could return the purchase and get their money back.

Jim Penney had not always been successful in his business dealings. He was born on a farm in Missouri in 1875 into the big family of a poor Baptist minister. Upon graduating from high school he worked as a clerk in a local dry goods store. His salary was $2.27 a month. But poor health forced him to resign and move west. (In 1923, Penney was to buy this store of his first employer, and he reopened it as the five hundredth store in the Penney chain.)

Not wanting to work for someone else, he scraped up enough money to open a butcher shop in Longmont, Colorado. He soon lost this, however, along with all his savings. His first venture into entrepreneurship had failed. The second venture was not to fail; the little store in the small mining town in Wyoming became the seed of the J. C. Penney Company.

THE RETAIL ENVIRONMENT IN 1900

In colonial days, small specialized shops, such as cobblers', candlemakers', and tailors' shops characterized the retail environment. On the frontier were trading posts. These were established along main routes of travel and were major goals of wagon trains as they crossed a sparsely populated and often hostile land. Later the trading posts evolved into general stores that featured a wide variety of goods. Though crude compared to present-day stores, these served the needs of their communities.

By the last decades of the nineteenth century, retailing was becoming more sophisticated, especially in the larger cities. The population had grown, and much of this growth was concentrated in cities. Growth and concentration of markets created burgeoning opportunities. By 1900, practically all the department stores now in existence had made their appearances. Most of these had started as small shops in big cities. For example, Macy's started in 1858 as a small dry goods store with an 11-foot front; Marshall Field had started in 1852, also as a quite modest undertaking. The development of urban transportation systems, notably the trolley car, stimulated the growth of department stores. The main Marshall Field store, at that time the "largest store in the world," was built in 1907. The trolley cars made downtown easily accessible from all parts of the city and greatly enlarged the "draw" of a big store.

The mail-order houses of Ward and Sears date back to 1872 and 1886, respectively. These found their opportunity in the rapidly expanding farm market west of the Mississippi. This market was composed mostly of farmers living on scattered and often isolated farms, and of small-town dwellers in a vast hinterland. Tapping this market became feasible with the building of railroads, which made shipping possible, and with the increase in public education, which increased literacy and the ability to read catalogs and follow ordering directions. But improvement in postal service also played a major role. It was now possible to distribute catalogs and advertising cheaply; orders could be received by a penny postcard or a 2-cent letter.

The early chains also started about this time. George Huntington Hartford began what was to become A&P in 1859 when he was 26. Frank W. Woolworth, a farm boy, established $350 for a credit line, and opened his first "5 and 10" in 1879. The chain concept grew slowly, but by 1900 the early vestiges of what were destined to become large and important firms had appeared not only in the grocery and variety areas but also in the drug, tobacco, and shoe trades. By 1900 it was estimated that there were about 700 chains with a total of 4500 stores.[2] Growth continued slowly in the early twentieth century, and it was estimated that chain organizations comprised no more than 4 percent of total retail trade even up to 1918.[3] In the 1920s, with Penney's leading the way among general merchandise stores, all chains experienced a growth spurt.

Thus, the market was beginning to be tapped by powerful retailers at the time Penney made his move. However, retailing in the rural small towns of the West was still far less sophisticated than in the big cities. And although mail order was tapping the rural consumer, this was not quite as appealing to many as being able to see and handle the goods and obtain needed items immediately.

THE EARLY GROWTH YEARS

Penney was not content to run just one store. As the store in Kemmerer prospered he thought of opening other stores. By 1905 he had two stores with total sales just under $100,000. In 1910, Penney changed his company's name from the Golden Rule to the J. C. Penney Company.

Still, Penney had modest ambitions; he hoped to have a chain of six stores. More than financial problems, he saw the biggest challenge was to find capable men—partners—to run such stores. He interviewed 50 candidates before finding what seemed to him one suitable partner, Earl Corder Sams, from a small town in Kansas. As we will describe later, Sams was destined to succeed Penney as head of a by-then flourishing enterprise.

[2] H. H. Maynard and T. N. Beckman, *Principles of Marketing,* 4th ed. (New York: Ronald, 1948), p. 46.

[3] C. F. Phillips and D. J. Duncan, *Marketing Principles and Methods* (Chicago: Irwin, 1948), p. 213.

As more stores were opened, Penney kept to the same strategy that had worked well in Kemmerer. He tried to give his customers honest values, which usually meant the lowest possible prices; he stayed with a cash-only policy, and he had no fancy fixtures or high overhead expenses. Thus, he could offer low prices and still make money. Not the least of the success factors at this time was the environment Penney had chosen for his business. He confined his stores to small towns where the Penney managers could be well known, friendly, and respectable members of the community.

A few years later, Penney raised his aspirations. He then had 14 stores, with eight partners, all small-town men who had started with him as clerks. Now he dreamed of 25 stores, and—audaciously—even more. But how could such growth be achieved, given the still limited resources of the fledgling enterprise? Where could Penney possibly find the trained, competent, and honest managers to run more new stores? And almost as important, where could he find the financial resources to open such new stores in a short period of time and stock them with sufficient merchandise?

To foster such an expansion, he now devised a scheme that was to pave the way for the phenomenal growth of the Penney Company. In one move he both financed and created the managerial resources needed by taking in "partner associates." As each store manager was able to accumulate enough capital out of his store's earnings, he could buy a one-third partnership in a new store, *if* he had trained one of his employees to the point where he could go out and effectively manage such a new store. Here we have the great incentive to provide the resources needed by such a growing company: motivation by each store manager to find the best qualified employees and give them the best possible training. And profits were often plowed back into the company to pay off partnership interests or to back new outlets.

By 1914, the chain had grown to 48 stores, with sales well over $3 million. A central buying office was established in New York City that year, and Jim Penney raised his sights to a national chain with perhaps as many as 500 stores. In only two years, the 48 stores had grown to 127, and sales had increased almost threefold. In 1917, Sams became president while Jim Penney moved up to chairman. And the headquarters was moved from Salt Lake City to New York City.

THE GREAT GROWTH YEARS

By 1924 there were 570 stores and partners. But financial constraints were becoming more and more apparent. During World War I, the government had imposed heavy taxes on business. These, and the burgeoning demands of rapid growth, forced president Sams to seek new sources for borrowing. New York investment bankers did not approve of the organizational structure, and in order to win them over Sams and Penney had to form the partnerships into a corporation under which the stores became company owned. The days of managers getting one-third shares of stores was over, and the complexion of the company changed dramatically.

Up to this time, store operations had been highly individualized, with each manager making his own decisions within rather general policies. Such looseness of organization now gave way to more centralized policies and activities, a trend that continued in the decades to come. Operations were made more uniform, with strict budgeting systems, improved operational methods, store arrangements, merchandise, and promotions planned by experts and followed by all stores. Central buyers had more authority over managers as to what goods and prices they would carry. And the performance of a store manager was now evaluated against that of other managers; promotions to better stores or to the home office went to the better producers. Penney's was beginning to shape itself into a unified and efficient organization.

INFORMATION SIDELIGHT

The Deadly Parallel

The organizational arrangement that leads to the so-called deadly parallel, or intrafirm competition, can be a powerful motivating and control factor. This requires establishing operating units of comparable characteristics, and the chain organization with its many store outlets is well geared to the promulgation of the deadly parallel. Sales, expenses, and profits can be readily compared, and strong as well as weak performances can be identified and appropriate action taken. Besides providing control and performance evaluation, the deadly parallel with its fostering of internal competition can stimulate best efforts.

For the deadly parallel to be used effectively, the operating units must be as equal as possible in sales potential. But this is not difficult to achieve with retail units, because departments and stores can be divided into various sales volume categories—often designated as A, B, and C stores—and operating results of stores within the same volume category can then be compared. Although the deadly parallel is particularly effective in chain store organizations, it can also be used with sales territories and certain other operating units in which sales and applicable expenses can be allocated so that profit contributions can be directly measured and compared with similar units.

Later in the decade of the 1920s, expansion was accelerated by acquisition of some smaller chains. From the F. S. Janes and Company, 54 stores were purchased; 20 from Johnson-Stevens Company, and 113 stores from the J. B. Byars Company and the J. N. McCracken Company. By this time the wildest dreams of Jim Penney had been surpassed. His chain by the end of 1929 consisted of 1395 stores, with

Table 2.1 Growth of the J. C. Penney Company by Stores and Sales

Year	*Number of Stores*	*Sales (Dollars)*
1902	1	28,898
1905	2	97,653
1912	34	2,050,641
1919	197	28,783,965
1926	747	115,957,865
1933	1,466	178,773,965
1940	1,586	302,539,325

Source: Norman Beasley, Main Street Merchant (New York: McGraw-Hill, 1948), p. 222.

sales of $209 million, and profits of more than $12 million. Penney stock was listed on the New York Stock Exchange—unfortunately, this was just six days before the stock market crashed and the Great Depression began.

The Depression years of the 1930s until practically the beginning of World War II devastated the U.S. economy and most businesses. But the Penney Company proved far more resilient than most firms. Although sales dropped to a low of $155 million in 1932, even then earnings did not fall below $5 million, and the company recovered the next year and continued its expansion, with profits more than doubling in 1933 to $14,235,638. By the end of the decade there were 1586 stores, with sales of over $300 million. Table 2.1 shows the growth trend by stores and sales.

In these years, however, regulatory and environmental threats posed a greater threat than the economy to the Penney Company as well as other chains.

ANTICHAIN THREATS

A great growth of chains of all kinds occurred in the 1920s. To be specific,

> In 1918, chains were estimated to comprise 4 percent of the total retail trade.
>
> In 1929, the first census of distribution found 159,638 stores in 7061 chain organizations, accounting for 21 percent of total retail trade.[4]

Such a growth created devastating concerns among conventional business firms. It was only logical that they would seek to defend their traditional positions against the inroads of aggressive and iconoclastic competitors. Such defense was most easily accomplished by seeking governmental protection and condemnation of the

[4]Roland S. Vaile, E. T. Grether, and Reavis Cox, *Marketing in the American Economy* (New York: Ronald, 1952), p. 206.

interlopers. The situation worsened in the 1930s with harsh economic conditions. Now the established firms could point to the chains as the cause of their difficulty because of their unreasonable power and unfair methods of competition. Thus was posited the antichain sentiments that were prominent in the late 1920s and through the decade of the 1930s. Although such aggressively negative sentiments had an impact on all chains, they posed the most dangers to Penney's, A&P, Woolworth, and Kroger—the largest chains in number of units.

The agitation against chains culminated in a "death sentence" antichain bill introduced by Representative Wright Patman of Texas. This would have imposed additional taxes of $63,912,000 on the Penney Company at a time when its earnings were $13,739,160 a year.

As the first opposition witness to the subcommittee considering the bill, president Sams asked for defeat of the measure for the following reasons:

1. It would destroy the Penney Company and all other similar companies.
2. It would destroy the finest field of opportunity that has ever existed in retailing for ambitious young persons without family means.
3. It would add to the cost of living for every American family of limited means and would lower the American standard of living.
4. It would deal a staggering blow to the economic life of the entire country and would be especially destructive to smaller cities and towns to the benefit of larger cities.
5. It would hurt and tax the entire nation for the protection and enrichment of a minority group of self-interested middlemen and another minority of ill-advised marginal retailers.[5]

Scores of other witnesses from farm, labor, and consumer groups supported Sams, and the Patman bill was killed in committee. Although a number of states passed antichain legislation in the 1930s, the agitation was dying out, and by 1940 some of these measures had been repealed. Chains had weathered the most protracted environmental pressures against them.

THE INGREDIENTS OF SUCCESS

When Jim Penney opened his first store in Kemmerer, Wyoming, the term *marketing* was unknown; certainly its essence of profitability through customer satisfaction was hardly embraced by most businesses of the day. The time was little removed from the traditional era of caveat emptor, "let the buyer beware." The days of the robber barons and intense business self-interest at consumers' and competitors' expense were hardly over. The Yankee horse trader symbolized this era. One won-

[5]Godfrey M. Lebhar, *Chain Stores in America 1859–1950* (New York: Chain Store Publishing Corporation, 1952), pp. 240–276.

ders how many sorry nags wound up in unsure hands. In an age when one's livelihood might depend on the horse, and even one's very life hinge on a dependable means of transportation, the risks for consumers were not matters for light concern.

Jim Penney, and a few other enlightened early merchants, thought there must be a better way to serve their customers and still find satisfactory profits. And the secret was very simple:

> Make your customers happy. Provide for their unmet needs. Give them better values, more to choose from. In other words, gear a business to customer satisfaction.

Nothing arcane or mysterious about this! Today, it may be a bit more difficult to achieve relative to competitors, but business success is still based on this simple principle. In Penney's day, of course, the opportunity and the need were greater.

How did Penney achieve this customer satisfaction, far beyond that offered by competitors? He offered honest values. He wanted to save his customers money on everything they bought. Merchandise that appealed to general customer demand was piled on tables where customers could see and touch it. There was one price for all—no one could drive a harder bargain than a neighbor through shrewder negotiating. Furthermore, if customers were not satisfied after they had taken their purchases home, they could return the merchandise and get their money back, with no hassle. Penney prices in 1910 were unbelievably low. Children's underwear could be bought for 7 cents, women's coats for $2.99, and men's suits for from $4.98 to $6.90.

In the early decades of the Penney Company, almost all the stores were located in small rural towns west of the Mississippi. This area of the United States was virtually ignored by the larger retailers, such as department stores. Penney brought to such people an assortment of goods, a consistency of quality and value, that could hardly be dreamed of by these rural consumers. Mail-order firms were beginning to tap this hinterland market, but the local Penney store provided the opportunity to see and feel and have instant gratification.

Customers sometimes actually petitioned the company to locate a store in their neighborhood. For example, one unit was opened in National City, California, in response to a petition circulated by Mrs. A. H. Bolen, who had been a customer of Penney before moving to California.

Not the least of the ingredients of success of the Penney Company was the extent to which tremendous growth could be fostered and controlled. The increase in the number of stores in the first three decades of the company almost defied imagination. Even today with computer technology, better communication, and more sophisticated management techniques, a firm would have great difficulty in matching the growth of the Penney Company 50 years ago without losing control of the operation or diluting the quality of performance and personnel.

One of the widely noted drawbacks of multiunit operations is the decreased motivation of the hired manager in contrast to the independent entrepreneur. To some extent this is true, but Penney found the way to overcome such deficiencies. Another major problem commonly presented as hindering rapid multiunit growth is the lack of trained labor to staff the ever more numerous and widely scattered units. Accordingly, the critics are quick to point out that more and more marginal people have to be employed, and the overall effectiveness of the operation is bound to suffer. Penney also found the way to overcome these limitations during the crucial early decades of the company—the idea of partnerships, with each store manager buying one third of a new store if he had trained a subordinate sufficiently well to manage that store. The motivation of profit sharing, not only of present stores but of stores still to come was bound to be a powerful incentive for motivating manager and trainee alike.

In later years, when eastern bankers practically forced the company to adopt a more common organizational and ownership form, another motivational tool was employed (by no means unique to Penney's, but widely used today by all chains), that of the deadly parallel, or intrafirm or internal competition.

WHAT CAN BE LEARNED?

The historical development of Penney's graphically shows the great growth opportunity of geographical expansion and expanding the number of units. But this must be controlled growth. Resources, controls, and labor motivation must not be sacrificed for growth at any cost. Recent examples of marketing mistakes exemplify the dangers of letting growth get out of hand: Korvette, W. T. Grant, Burger Chef.[6]

It is practically axiomatic today that successful businesses are close to their customers, concentrate on satisfying customer needs, and stress enhancement of customer relations. Virtually all firms today espouse this view, of course, but the degree to which they achieve this goal is often disappointing. As Peters and Waterman note in their book, *In Search of Excellence,* "the excellent companies *really are* close to their customers. That's it. Other companies talk about it; the excellent companies do it."[7] In the early years of this century, such a customer orientation was by no means universal thinking. Jim Penney was in the vanguard; catering to customers, keeping their best interests in mind, offering money-back guarantees—these were strong inducements for business in those days. And they are far from outmoded today.

Related to the firmly adhered-to customer-first policy, Penney initiated the

[6]These are described in detail in Robert F. Hartley, *Marketing Mistakes,* 2nd ed. (Columbus, Ohio: Grid Publishing, 1981).

[7]Thomas J. Peters and Robert H. Waterman, Jr., *In Search of Excellence* (New York: Harper & Row, 1982), p. 156.

notion of value as a fuel for growth. He saw that by giving customers honest values, business success and growth was more assured. Do not customers want the same treatment today, the same assurance of value?

Environmental problems, the threat of regulation, and even punative enactments are not unique to today. Businesses must be concerned about their public image. Such matters may make the job of managing more difficult and distracting from operational commitments. But firms can still defend themselves from unjustified attacks, as Penney's did in the 1930s. More and more we have to recognize that businesses do not operate in a vacuum.

A final point to learn from the early success of the Penney Company concerns competitive confrontation. Remember, Penney's in its period of most rapid growth stayed with small rural communities in the sparsely settled country west of the Mississippi. This meant less competition. Penney's for many years (practically five decades) shunned the populous eastern cities. For almost 50 years it feared to beard the department stores and other aggressive merchants who dominated those markets. But let us recognize the early rationale: a prudent marketing strategy avoids severe competitive confrontation, if at all possible, until a firm is large enough and has ample experience and resources to counter such competition. This suggests that any emerging firm should seek relatively untapped markets and segments rather than go head to head against a strong and entrenched competitor. In Penney's case, it was easier to gain experience and develop marketing effectiveness in these more insulated markets. Only when success had been achieved here, and resources and experience built up, did it become prudent to attack strong competitors. But in Penney's case, did it take 50 years to build up these resources and experience?

INCIPIENT FLAWS IN THE PROVEN PATTERN OF SUCCESS

Although we must admire, and have something to learn from, the success of the Penney Company in its early decades, its later performance evinced serious flaws. It is almost axiomatic that success does not guarantee future success. The long delay in entering the more competitive big city markets seems ill-advised in retrospect. One suspects that Penney's top management lacked confidence.

The Penney Company was guilty of several other serious flaws of omission in later years.[8] For example, consumer credit—Penney's did not even begin testing the feasibility of offering credit to its customers until 1958, long after almost all major retailers had found 50 percent and more of their total sales volume typically coming from charge sales. Not providing credit, of course, badly hindered the ability to offer higher priced items, such as appliances and furniture, and higher priced clothing and accessories. Not until 1962 did Penney's begin diversifying its

[8]For much more detail on the later mistakes of the Penney Company, see Hartley, *Marketing Mistakes,* pp. 35–47.

merchandise beyond strictly "soft goods" such as hosiery, sheets and blankets, coats and dresses, work clothes, and men's furnishings.

The company began changing its traditional mode of operation by the middle and late 1960s, but one can only speculate on how much the reliance on traditional policies had cost in lost sales potential.

Questions

1. Can you think of other less drastic incentives for store managers to develop trainees than that practiced by the Penney Company in its early years of growth?
2. Evaluate the deadly parallel, considering both pros and cons.

Invitation to Role Play

Place yourself in the position of a new store manager shortly after the organization had been changed from partnerships to a corporation. The days of managers getting one-third shares of store profits were over. Discuss what impact this change might have on

(a) Your motivation.
(b) Your income.
(c) Your initiative.
(d) Your incentive to train new managers.

Discuss how the Penney Company might seek to minimize negative impacts.

CHAPTER 3

Coca-Cola: Initiating Mass Marketing

Coca-Cola is virtually a century-old firm, one of the few such in the United States. Although its great growth came decades after its humble start, it was one of the first firms to use truly mass marketing techniques, and it showed the world the potency of marketing for a firm that used it effectively. Undreamed-of growth, not only in the United States, but throughout the world, was achieved in perhaps the greatest example of single-product popularity the world had ever seen. The product's evolution from an "elixir," for which wild curative claims abounded, into a reputable and popular product illustrates the evolution of marketing since the turn of the century.

THE ELIXIR YEARS

Coca-Cola was invented by a cavalry general for the Confederates during the Civil War. John Styth Pemberton was a pharmacist, and he settled in Atlanta after the war and began putting out patent medicines such as Triplex Liver Pills and Globe of Flower Cough Syrup. In 1885 he registered a trademark for French Wine Cocoa, "an Ideal Nerve and Tonic Stimulant." In 1886 Pemberton unveiled a modification of French Wine Cocoa which he called Coca-Cola, and began distributing this to soda fountains in used beer bottles. He looked on the concoction less as a refreshment than as a headache cure, especially for people who had overindulged in food or drink. By chance, one druggist discovered that the syrup tasted better when mixed with carbonated water.

As his health failed and Coca-Cola failed to bring in sufficient money to meet his financial obligations, Pemberton sold the rights to Coca-Cola to a 39-year-old pharmacist, Asa Griggs Candler, for a paltry $2300. The destitute Pemberton died in 1888 and was buried in a grave that went unmarked for the next 70 years.

Candler, a small-town Georgia boy born in 1851 (and hence too young to be a hero in the Civil War), had planned to become a physician, but he changed his mind after observing that druggists made more money than doctors. He struggled along for almost 40 years until he bought Coca-Cola, but then his fortunes changed dramatically. In 1892 he organized the Coca-Cola Company, and a few years later downgraded the therapeutic qualities of the beverage and began emphasizing its pleasure-giving qualities. At the same time, he developed the bottling system that still exists, and for 25 years he almost single-handedly guided the drink's destiny.

THE EARLY GROWTH YEARS

In the spring of 1894, the first plant outside of Atlanta was established in Dallas, Texas. In the summer of that year, the first Coca-Cola bottler, A. Biedenharn, started operations. By 1895 Candler could announce that "Coca-Cola is now sold and drunk in every state and territory in the United States." In 1898 he said that "Coca-Cola is now sold in some cities in Canada and Honolulu, and arrangements are on foot for its introduction into the Republic of Mexico."[1]

The infatuation with elixirs in that era was hard to dispel. At about the time that Asa Candler bought Coca-Cola, he also acquired some other proprietaries, chief among them Botanic Blood Balm, a blood purifier. For a while he alternately brewed Coca-Cola and BBB, as the balm was called, in the same copper kettle, and in its early ads, Coca-Cola shared space with these other products. But gradually Asa turned more and more attention to Coca-Cola, and the faith was justified. "Candler, who had come to Atlanta with exactly one dollar and seventy-five cents, amassed a fortune of around fifty million dollars, and his name was to be immortalized in the city through a hotel, a park, a street, an airfield, and the city's first skyscraper."[2] In 1916 he was elected mayor of Atlanta and stepped down as president of the company.

THE PRODUCT

The Formula

The secret ingredient in Coca-Cola syrup was often referred to as "Merchandise 7X." In the beginning, the formula for 7X was mixed by Candler and his bookkeeper and kept in a safe which only they were permitted to enter. Candler himself

[1] "Facts About Coca-Cola," a pamphlet published by the Coca-Cola Company, n.d., p. 6.
[2] E. J. Kahn, Jr., *The Big Drink: The Story of Coca-Cola* (New York: Random House, 1950), p. 59.

ordered the ingredients and meticulously checked to be sure that the correct quality and quantity were received and that they had the proper care and storage. Invoices were also locked up so as to maintain the tightest security. Even today the utmost secrecy is still maintained, with the formula housed in a vault at the Trust Company of Georgia Bank with only a handful of people having access to it.

At the turn of the century the question arose as to whether or not Coca-Cola contained any cocaine, which had the connotation of a habit-forming drug. But Candler had authorized an analysis of the drink, and in 1901 it had been found to contain only a minute trace of cocaine originating from the cola leaves. This trace had been removed by 1905, thereby thwarting criticism and investigations.

As the product gained ever-wider popularity, numerous imitators appeared. In the early 1900s, as many as 153 imposters were competing, with such similar names as Fig Cola, Candy Cola, Cold Cola, Cay-Ola, Hoca-Nola, Kel Kola, and Kaw-Kala. The name *Coca-Cola,* which was first suggested by Frank Robinson, a bookkeeper of Dr. Pemberton, came from two of its ingredients, the coca leaf and the kola nut, spelled with a ''c'' to look better in advertisements. This has proven to have great memorability and esthetic qualities, ''much like that of a familiar and beloved melody,'' as one musician described it.[3] Candler was forced to spend thousands of dollars in legal fees to defend his product's good name, and he was generally successful.

The Bottling Strategy

In the first several years after his acquisition of Coca-Cola, Candler had a rather dim view of the prospects for bottling. The stopper used on the bottles at the time was a cumbersome device that caused a foul odor if the product was not used within ten days. Furthermore, the bottling process was tediously slow and there was always the possibility of damage suits over bottles exploding.

These problems led Candler to sell the rights of bottling Coca-Cola, allowing for independent bottling plants that would buy the syrup from the company and substitute nothing else for it. Coca-Cola agreed to sell the syrup exclusively to these bottlers, to grant them sales rights to use the trademark, and to furnish labels and advertising materials. By the end of 1910, Coca-Cola was bottled in 379 plants across the United States.

The Bottle

Before 1916 Coca-Cola was bottled in nondistinctive generic bottles, which resulted in Coca-Cola looking little different from its imitators. The need to develop a standard, distinctive bottle had become increasingly evident.

The bottle was invented by two employees of the Root Glass Company of

[3]Ibid., p. 6.

Terre Haute, Indiana, who were inspired by a drawing of the cacao bean, which had bulged sides and parallel longitudinal ridges with tapered ends. The owner of the Root Glass Company charged Coca-Cola nothing for developing the design but was paid a royalty for every bottle produced. The bottle was patented in 1923 and became a trademark of the Coca-Cola Company in 1960.

PROMOTION OF COCA-COLA

Asa Candler, as noted before, had difficulty deciding on advertising objectives for his new product. Should its taste be extolled or its alleged curative properties? Early advertising reflected this ambiguity. It was marketed both as a temperance drink that was delicious, exhilirating, refreshing, and invigorating and as a valuable cure for all nervous afflictions.

In the very early days, Frank Robinson headed a sales force of three other men. As early as 1891, they were moving the syrup far beyond Atlanta, getting it into drugstores all over the south. In the south, the soda-fountain season was from May 1 to November 1, and it was the mission of these first three salesmen to push Coca-Cola as the alternative to sodas.

By 1891 the sales force began the heavy use of fountain signs and free-sample tickets. To further encourage customers to increase purchases, the company offered premiums of decorative clocks, porcelain fountain urns, prescription cabinets, and showcases. In addition, newspaper advertisements, outdoor posters, painted wall and barn signs, blotters, calendars, serving and change trays, Japanese fans, bookmarkers, and paperweights were used to make Coca-Cola famous throughout the country.

A free sampling ticketing scheme was a highly effective ''push'' technique to motivate dealers to carry and promote Coca-Cola. (See the following Information Sidelight for a perspective of push and pull techniques for gaining market entry.) The company offered a 5-gallon keg of syrup for $8.75. Then it sent $5.00 worth of coupons to people on a mailing list provided by the fountain owner. When the coupons were returned to the company, the store would be sent $5.00. Thus, the net investment was $3.75. The $5.00 worth of coupons used only 1 gallon of syrup. Thus, for an investment of $3.75, the soda fountain owners made $25.00 ($5.00/gallon $\times$ 5 gallons). Also, when customers came in to redeem the coupons, the owner was likely to sell them other goods as well.

INFORMATION SIDELIGHT

Pushing and Pulling Strategies for Gaining Market Entry

Most firms have some difficulty in gaining the support of dealers for new products, primarily because new products involve additional investment, handling efforts, and shelf space. In order to gain dealer cooperation, a manufacturer has two strategies: (1) pushing or (2) pulling. Figure 3.1 lists the more important push and pull techniques.

A *pushing strategy* is directed to dealers and usually involves some incentives to get the dealer to stock the product, give it adequate display, and recommend it to customers. Free goods, advertising allowances, and other techniques, as listed in Figure 3.1, may be needed to get the desired dealer cooperation. Sometimes these dealer incentives can be quite ingenious as were those of Coca-Cola at the dawn of sophisticated marketing.

A *pulling strategy,* as shown in Figure 3.1, is directed at the consumer rather than the dealer and most often involves samples or heavy advertising, or both. The objective is to induce customers to demand the product from dealers as well as to convince dealers of the heavy commitment of the manufacturer to demand-arousal.

The ability of large firms to both push and pull simultaneously gives them a powerful advantage over smaller firms—who may not be able to afford much pull efforts—in getting their new products quickly into the channel system, and thus gaining market entry.

The sales force was particularly important in the early days of Coca-Cola. Some of the most effective salesmen were cotton brokers who sold Coca-Cola during their off-season. By 1899, the company was holding training meetings of several weeks each year in the late winter. Each salesman was provided with a fiber trunk to carry advertising on trains. The company paid travel expenses but not an overly generous salary. The Coca-Cola salesman, when calling on a new customer, also showed the soda fountain help how to mix a proper Coca-Cola. Further, he contracted with a local billposter in each town to select locations to put up advertising displays. Advertising and display material was so abundant that the salesmen often had difficulty in getting it all distributed.

Additional dealer push was obtained by offering them a high profit incentive to increase Coca-Cola sales. In 1899 customers were given a 2 percent discount for an order if they paid within ten days. The company paid freight costs on orders of 35 gallons of syrup. At the end of the year, it paid rebates of 5 cents a gallon to those who had bought 100 gallons, and an additional 5 cents for the next 100 gallons, on up to 25 cents a gallon for the large users. The salesmen also sold accessory items such as Coca-Cola glasses.

By 1900, company revenues had risen to $400,000, and by 1902 the ad budget was over $120,000, and Coca-Cola was the best known product in America. The first national magazine advertisement came in 1904. By 1908 the company had hung Coca-Cola signs on 2.5 million square feet of walls and buildings in every major city. By 1908 the company spent well over half a million dollars on advertis-

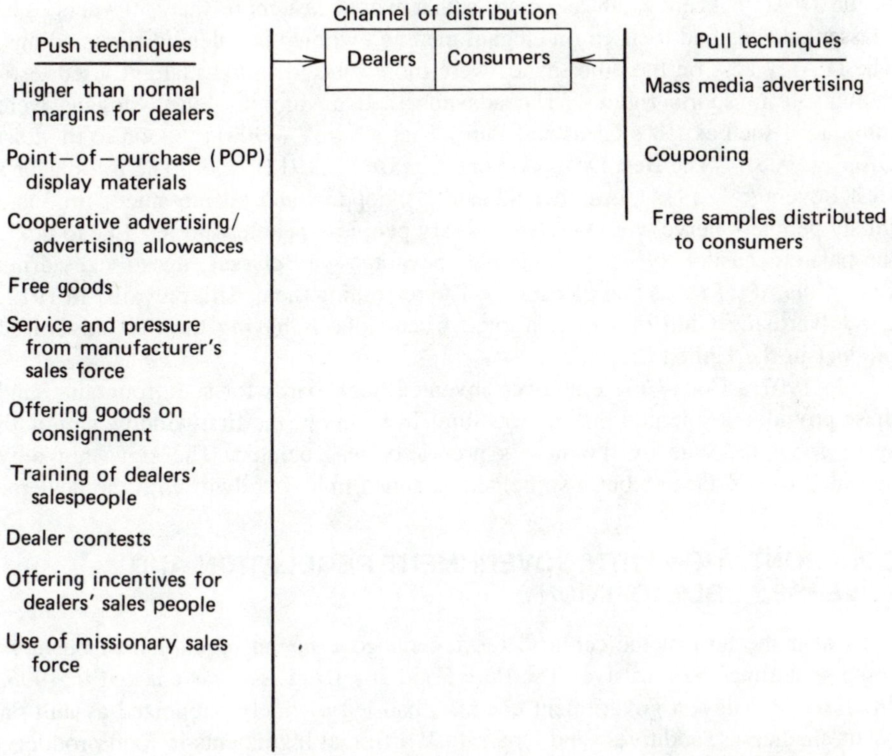

Figure 3.1. Pushing and pulling techniques for gaining market entry. [*Source:* Robert F. Hartley, *Sales Management* (Boston: Houghton Mifflin, 1979), p. 54. Used with permission.]

ing, and 10,000 window displays were also erected in that year. In 1911 the ad budget hit $1 million—this was at a time when total advertising expenditures in the United States were barely $1 billion.

The diversity of promotional efforts was unparalleled. In 1913 alone, over 120 million novelties were distributed, including eight-day clocks, paper napkins, matches, pocket knives, pencils, mirrors, baseball cards, and the first in a long line of trays and calendars illustrated with bathing beauties.[4]

As bottling became more important, the advertising changed. Slogans began to be used such as "from a bottle, through a straw," with pictures of bottles and the soda fountain glasses. The new distinctive bottles were also portrayed in ads from 1916 on. Bottlers carried on their own local advertising. The company subsidized bottler advertising at rates based on the number of gallons each bottler used.

In 1904 the advertising account was transferred from the Massengale Agency

[4] Some of this information is compiled from J. C. Louis and Harvey Z. Yazijian, *The Cola Wars* (New York: Everest House, 1980), pp. 35–36.

to the D'Arcy Agency, an association that would last more than 50 years. The Massengale ads had focused on elegant men and women in splendid surroundings. The D'Arcy ads, on the other hand, were more relaxed and casual and used testimonials from sports figures. The ads now had a vigorous tone. Slogans were introduced such as "It's Clear and Pure, That's Sure" (1909), "Good to the Last Drop" (1908), "The Best Drink Anyone Can Buy" (1913), and "The Ballplayer's Best Beverage" (1914). Another ad said: "Shoppers and businessmen, tired and thirsty people—nerve worn and brain weary people—people who just like to tickle the palate occasionally with a delicious beverage—all classes, ages, sexes drink Coca-Cola, it refreshes and pleases."[5] The refreshing theme still prevails. In 1912, the Advertising Club of America cited Coca-Cola as having the best advertised product in the United States.

In 1907 a Coca-Cola employee invented backboards for soda fountains, and these provided a splendid display medium. In addition, the first window sign with space for a message by the store's proprietor was painted. The signs not only appealed to consumers, but also helped establish more goodwill with the dealers.

CONFRONTATION WITH GOVERNMENT REGULATION AND ADVERSE PUBLIC OPINION

Even near the turn of the century, the federal government regulation of business could sometimes be intrusive. The Pure Food and Drug Act was enacted in 1906. Dr. Harvey Wiley, a government chemist, had led a widely publicized assault on patent medicines, additives, and "harmful" artificial ingredients in food products. In 1909, a shipment of Coca-Cola syrup was seized and in a celebrated case, Wiley contended that caffeine was not an essential ingredient but an additive, which the new law prohibited. The case dragged on for almost ten years in southern courts and then went to the Supreme Court. But although Coca-Cola eventually lost the case, the judgment was binding only for the particular lot of goods seized, which meant that the federal government would have to bring suit for each violation in the future. This essentially made the law toothless as far as Coca-Cola was concerned.

During Prohibition, Coca-Cola became the target of such temperance groups as the Women's Christian Temperance Union. In the 1920s, such groups attacked Coke as catering to the degeneracy of modern society. Coca-Cola was also assailed as contributing to the promotion of idleness.

But such criticisms and governmental scrutiny were of little consequence as Coca-Cola continued its growth, notwithstanding even the Great Depression of the 1930s. Not until Pepsi-Cola emerged as an aggressive competitor in the 1950s did the growth and prosperity of Coca-Cola slow. (We will analyze the Pepsi-Cola invasion of Coca-Cola's market dominance in a later case.)

[5]Kahn, *The Big Drink,* p. 152.

ROBERT WOODRUFF AND THE MATURING OF THE COCA-COLA COMPANY

In 1916, Candler left Coca-Cola to run for mayor of Atlanta. The company was left in the hands of his relatives who after only three years sold it to a group of Atlanta businessmen for $25 million. Asa was not consulted, and he was profoundly distraught. The company was then netting $5 million. By the time of his death in 1929, annual profits were approaching the $25 million sales price. The group who bought Coca-Cola was headed by Ernest Woodruff, an Atlanta banker. Coke today still remains in the hands of the Woodruff family. Under the direction of the son, Robert Winship Woodruff, Coca-Cola became not only a household word within the United States, but one of the most recognized symbols the world over.

Robert Woodruff grew up in affluence. His father had made a fortune by consolidating small, related companies into large profitable concerns. Robert grew up among some of the most prominent men and families in Atlanta.

He believed in the virtues of personal achievement and effort. As a young man, Robert ignored his father's orders to return to Emory College to complete the remaining years of his education. He wanted to earn his keep in the real world, and not "waste" three years in school. Eventually, in 1911 he joined one of his father's firms, the newly organized Atlantic Ice & Coal Company, as a salesman and a buyer. But he and his father violently disagreed again, this time over the purchase by Robert of trucks from White Motors, to replace the horse-drawn carts and drays of the day. Ernest fired his son and told him never to return home again. So Robert promptly joined White Motors. At the age of 33, he had become the nation's top truck salesman and was earning $85,000 a year. But then he heeded the call to come home.

Robert assumed the presidency of Coca-Cola in 1923. Things were not going well for the company. An untimely purchase of sugar, just before prices plummeted, had resulted in a staggering amount of borrowing to keep the company afloat. Bottler relations were at an all-time low because the company had wanted to raise the price of syrup, thus violating the original franchise contracts in which the price had been permanently fixed.

Woodruff appealed to a unity of interest with the bottlers, and was able to cement the relations. He stressed his conviction that he wanted everyone connected with Coca-Cola to make money. The sales department was reorganized into a service department that stressed quality control and the servicing of soda fountain accounts rather than simply filling orders. By 1926, there were 1250 domestic bottlers and 2200 jobbers who served over 900,000 retail outlets. Innovations that fostered dealer support included top-loading coolers that were sold to dealers at cost—$12.50 versus $90 for competing models—and the six-pack. The latter was conceived in 1924 with the objective of increasing in-home sales and furthering wholesaling cost-efficiency, and it proved an instant success and became the indus-

Table 3.1 Sales and Profits for Coca-Cola, 1892–1930

	Sales	*Profits*
1892	$ 49,676	
1900	400,000	
1919	6,737,630	$ 988,640
1921	28,464,599	2,345,990
1926	30,107,272	8,402,658
1930	41,284,500	13,513,535

Sources: Compiled from miscellaneous sources, including Moody's for the more recent years.

try standard. In 1926 a Foreign Department was established to facilitate production overseas. By 1930, there were 64 bottlers in 28 countries, and the quest for foreign markets was expanded with the formation of the Coca-Cola Export Corporation.

Advertising for the 1920s stressed the following themes: "Nature's purest and most wholesome drink" (1926); "A drink of natural flavors" (1928); "Enjoy the sociable" (1925); and "The sociability of thirst." These evolved into such slogans as "The pause that brings friends together," and "Friend for lift." In 1929, only months before the Great Depression, the slogan "The pause that refreshes" was unveiled. This was to be the theme for Coca-Cola for the next 30 years and was heralded as the greatest product slogan ever coined.[6]

Woodruff molded the company to his own image and ideas and so it was to stay for 30 years, until the middle 1950s, when mounting pressures from competition, Pepsi in particular, cracked the mold slightly and brought in some new methods of operation. Woodruff was an aloof and often unpredictable executive. He kept a tight hold. Although this type of autocratic leadership was commonplace at that time, it did serve to drive one of the Coca-Cola executives, Alfred Steele, to defect to Pepsi, where he was instrumental in directing a resurgence of Pepsi, the chief rival of Coca-Cola. Table 3.1 shows the trend of sales and profits for Coca-Cola for selected years from 1892 to 1930.

INGREDIENTS OF SUCCESS

Coca-Cola was a trailblazer in the use of a mass marketing strategy. This strategy intensified from the 1950s on, but it was virtually unheard of in the early days of Candler and Robert Woodruff. The success of Coca-Cola showed other firms the power of a comprehensive and well-coordinated marketing strategy.

[6]Louis and Yazijian, *The Cola Wars*, p. 45.

The ingredients of success were not very different 80 years ago from today. Only the level of effective competition was less. Consequently the impact of the strategy was awesome. This strategy embodied most of the elements of what we think of as the marketing mix: the product, promotional efforts, and the method of distribution and the leadership (or captaincy) of that distribution.

The Product

Most of the success of Coca-Cola is attributed to the product, the unique formula so carefully safeguarded, that was appealing and inimitable. But was this *the* magic ingredient of Coke's success? Not entirely. Consider the following:

We know that in the early days numerous imitators sought to ride on the coattails of Coca-Cola. Certainly the two main ingredients, the kola nut and the cocoa leaf were readily available and the subtleties of taste being as they are, minor flavor differences should not have prevented successful market entry of similar products. We know that the name ''Coca-Cola'' had an instant appeal and recognition value. The name proved to be easily imitated, and certainly part of the success of the firm can be attributed to the zealousness of Candler in legally defending the name against a host of imposters and close imitators. He saw the need to develop a product somehow distinctive from competing products, and used everything in his power to safeguard that uniqueness, even though it was more psychological than real.

Promotional Efforts

Coca-Cola was virtually the first firm to invest heavily in mass media advertising. Although at first the advertising followed the elixir claims of the era, this was changed to a theme not too different from that of today. The powerful advertising thrust, coupled with a product that was readily identifiable through its catchy name and distinctive bottle, found a broad appeal, not only in this country but throughout the world. Let us note here, however, that as powerful as massive advertising efforts can be in influencing people to try a product, unless the product matches expectations, repeat business will be lacking and the advertising mitigated. This did not happen to Coca-Cola, of course; the product met the expectations and repeat business is still flourishing almost a century later.

The push-type promotional efforts directed to dealers were a rather unusual strategy at that time. Now, it is commonplace. The effectiveness at that time was clearly evident in enthusiastic dealers who readily pushed this profitable new product. Success was virtually ensured, with dealer push, massive advertising, and a product that merited repeat business and customer loyalty. The thousands of window displays and the hundreds of thousands of signs on walls and buildings attests to the assiduousness of the company sales force. But these were also instrumental in building a loyal and eager network of dealers. This could only be enhanced by the premiums and coupons that brought customers into dealer premises where as often as not they would buy other merchanidse as well. Such wooing of dealers was virtually unheard of in those days, and proved amazingly effective in vastly increasing the distribution to the point where it was available in every city and hamlet of the United States and much of the rest of the world in only a few decades.

Distribution

Coca-Cola virtually pioneered the franchising concept between manufacturer and wholesaler. See the Information Sidelight for a wider perspective of franchising.

INFORMATION SIDELIGHT

Types of Franchising Arrangements

Manufacturer (Franchisor) and Wholesalers (Franchisees)
A manufacturer may franchise independent wholesalers. This arrangement is most common in the soft-drink industry. Most national manufacturers of soft-drink syrups—Coca-Cola, Pepsi-Cola, Seven-Up, Royal Crown—franchise independent bottlers, who then serve the retail markets.

Manufacturer (Franchisor) and Retailers (Franchisees)
A manufacturer may franchise a number of retail outlets to sell its particular brands and products. This is one of the oldest franchise arrangements and is particularly prevalent among outlets for cars and trucks, farm equipment, shoes, paint, and petroleum. Virtually all new cars and trucks are sold through franchised dealers, and an estimated 90 percent of gasoline is sold through franchised independent retail service stations.

Service Sponsor (Franchisor) and Retailers (Franchisees)
Rather than a product, the major component of these arrangements is a service. Although the franchisor may provide some manufacturing and wholesaling functions, the major contribution is a carefully developed, promoted, and controlled format. This is the most common type of franchise today. Examples are many, including Holiday Inn, McDonald's, Hertz, Kelly Girl (employment franchises), and H & R Block (income tax preparation).

Following the example of Coca-Cola, most soft drink firms have found it practical to be in the business only of manufacturing syrup concentrates. These concentrates are then wholesaled to independent franchised bottlers. The bottlers add carbonated water, and perhaps such ingredients as sugar, then bottle and distribute the resulting product to local retailers. The soft-drink company may own a few bottling plants in important markets, but the vast majority of bottlers are franchised. This has proven to be wise because the shipping of prebottled beverages would be economically prohibitive.

Franchising offers any firm interested in rapid expansion some great advantages. For the most part the franchisees will be putting up their own money for their facilities, therefore, the financial resources of the parent company, the franchisor, can be used advantageously in other ways, such as improving production facilities and increasing promotional efforts. The franchisees, being independent entrepreneurs, can be expected to take far more interest in their end of the operation than the hired manager. The franchising idea initiated by Coca-Cola is now used by almost all soft drink manufacturers and by many other types of retail, manufacturing, and service organizations as well.

WHAT CAN BE LEARNED?

When Coca-Cola was getting its start the market was unsophisticated and competition was opportunistic but with little of today's marketing savvy. Also, in the very early days of Coca-Cola, the South was still getting over the Civil War and Reconstruction and took to its heart a product that was born in the South and became its proud accomplishment.

The four developmental and growth decades of roughly from 1890 to 1930—by which time Coca-Cola was firmly established as one of the most successful single products of the world—give us these lessons:

- When a product can be readily identified as the pride of a city, a state, or a region, it can engender almost fanatic support. Around the turn of the century, the need of the South was to find something to rejuvenate its lost pride. But the possibility exists for other products in other times to develop a strong regional loyalty, support, and pride. Present examples that come to mind are the brands of beer associated with particular communities, such as Milwaukee and St. Louis, as well as other major firms with strong community identification, such as Eastman Kodak of Rochester, New York, Boeing of Seattle, and 3M of St. Paul, Minnesota. Community pride in such firms can be a great source of dedicated personnel as well as financial backing, and can provide the solid foundation that a firm needs.
- At first view, the success of Coca-Cola might be credited to the power of advertising. And certainly Coke advertised heavily for that day. However, the really heavy promotional efforts occurred after it had become rather well established. In 1901, advertising expenditures reached $100,000; not until 1911 did they come to $1,000,000. But mass media advertising was

only one of the tools used; its effectiveness is muted if the other aspects of the marketing mix are deficient. Furthermore, the theme and the image developed through the advertising is vastly more important than sheer expenditures. We saw how the company groped for the best slogan or theme, and did not stumble onto a great one until 1929 with "The pause that refreshes." The right theme, one that will foster an attractive image in the minds of the customers of the day, will have a powerful impact. The wrong theme or image, or one that is merely uninspiring and mediocre, will waste advertising dollars. Sheer advertising expenditures do not guarantee success.

- The importance of channel and dealer relations in the early success of Coca-Cola is inescapable. Great efforts were made to win dealer support, to arouse their "push" of the product. Coca-Cola was one of the very first firms to view its dealers, and bottlers, as part of a team in which all should share the rewards. Today, many decades later, some firms still have not fully realized the importance of strong and positive dealer relations.
- Candler may have stumbled onto the idea of franchising independent bottlers. But this was certainly a powerful strategy to foster growth. Asa Candler is quoted by his grandson, Charles Howard Candler, in his biography, as saying that "the system which evolved of allowing Coca-Cola to be bottled in hundreds of communities by persons native to and respected in those communities, who themselves profited greatly by the energy and initiative which they put into the promotion of Coca-Cola, is probably largely responsible for much of the success which the company has enjoyed."[7] A further benefit gained from this franchise arrangement that manifested itself in later years concerned unionization. Unions had great difficulty in organizing Coca-Cola because they had to deal with each plant individually, and a good many were able to escape unionization altogether.
- Finally, and perhaps most important, we can learn from these early decades of the success of Coca-Cola the very real importance of uniqueness or product differentiation. This produce could be easily imitated. The major tangible difference was supposedly a better taste. But the subtleties of taste are ephemeral and one might think hardly the tangible substance from which a lasting and unassailable uniqueness could be wrought. However, Candler achieved this and Woodruff perpetuated it. Here we have psychological differentiation exerted to its fullest. (In the next case, we will see that some cigarette manufacturers were also able to develop powerful psychological differentiation.) At this early stage of marketing history, we can see clearly the effective use of differentiation, not physical but psychological. The name, the image-building advertising, the distinctive bottle—

[7]As quoted in Pat Watters, *Coca-Cola* (Garden City, N.Y.: Doubleday, 1978), p. 66.

these enhanced the differentiation and allowed it to prosper and endure. The power of psychological differentiation is not always recognized as fully as it should be by marketers of today, despite our much stronger promotional and research tools and techniques. The lessons of the old masters are worth studying.

Questions

1. Can advertising buy market share? Discuss.
2. Evaluate the pros and cons of Coca-Cola owning its own bottling facilities rather than franchising them.

Invitation to Role Play

Place yourself in the position of a competitor of Coca-Cola in the early years of this century. Coca-Cola has already gained market dominance, but you believe your cola drink is just as good. How would you attempt to compete with the rapidly growing Coca-Cola? Be as specific as you can.

CHAPTER 4

The Battle for Cigarette Supremacy, 1920s and 1930s

Although Coca-Cola was an early user of mass media advertising, tobacco products have been perhaps the most intensively advertised of all products. Just after the Civil War, Bull Durham smoking tobacco was widely promoted, and its trademark became one of the best known at that time. In the 1880s and 1890s, J. B. Duke spent up to $800,000 a year to advertise individual brands, a huge sum for those days. By the 1920s, cigarette advertising reached a peak in the battle for market share and efforts to tap new customer segments, particularly youth and women. The competitive battle clearly demonstrates this marketing tool's power—made all the stronger by the new media, notably radio, emerging on the scene. It was a power to sway millions, and not always in the most desirable way.

The personality who stood above all his contemporary competitors was George Washington Hill.

GEORGE WASHINGTON HILL

George Washington Hill was born to the tobacco business. His father was president of American Tobacco Company, and George had been exposed to all aspects of production and marketing of tobacco. After leaving Williams College in 1904, he worked in a warehouse where tobacco was purchased. Soon he was supervising the production of cigarettes. Then he went on the road selling cigarettes to dealers. By

1907, he was managing a subsidiary of American, one that produced various tobacco products.

He took over American Tobacco in 1925, the year of his father's death. For 41 years he ruled with an iron hand until his death in 1946. He has been described as the single dominant figure in the development of cigarette advertising and the use of the new media, radio. Symbolic of his nonconformity, he was famous for wearing his hat indoors. Before looking at his strategems, let us take an overview of the cigarette industry in 1925 and how it evolved.

THE EARLY YEARS OF THE CIGARETTE INDUSTRY

The use of tobacco is far from new; some say it originated with the ancient Aztecs and Mayas. Certainly in the early days of colonial settlement in this country—even back to the settlement at Jamestown—tobacco growing was an important industry and can claim the title of America's oldest industry. Richmond became the tobacco manufacturing capital of the nation.

By 1880 three tobacco firms in Richmond, Virginia, were making cigarettes. The wholesalers and retailers in the big U.S. cities stumbled on the mystique of the American Indian to sell their cigarettes and even to identify their stores. Wooden Indians began to be stationed outside tobacconists' shops. Turbaned Turks ("the mysterious East") were also used. Cigarette displays at the 1876 Centennial in Philadelphia were so impressive that some visitors thought this Centennial celebration marked the birth of the cigarette as well as the anniversary of the nation.

At this time, all cigarettes were rolled by hand, and skilled rollers were even imported from foreign countries. In 1883, a small tobacco producer, Washington Duke and his sons, leased a cigarette machine invented by James Bonsack. This machine had been rejected by the larger producers who believed that it was unreliable and people would not accept machine-made cigarettes. But soon the Bonsack machine was making cigarettes at a rate *50* times faster than hand rollers. The Dukes cut cigarette prices in half, theirs became the cheapest on the market, and salespeople were sent throughout the world to promote a box of ten cigarettes for 5 cents.

The Dukes proved to be masterful and innovative in promoting their cigarettes. One of the sons, "Buck," after prowling the tobacco shops of New York City, and talking with clerks, customers, and jobbers, developed a promotional scheme using picture cards of actresses, baseball players, boxers, and other celebrities. A folding album of "Sporting Girls" was also distributed. A polo team on roller skates was sent across the country to advertise cigarettes and smoking tobacco. In 1886, the first attempt to tap the feminine market was made with the introduction of the Cameo brand in New York City. By 1889 the Duke firm had spent a staggering amount for advertising in that day, some $800,000. (In the 1880s, however, tobacco advertising was surpassed by sellers of soaps and baking powders.) Premiums, rebates, and bribes characterized the early selling of cigarettes.

"Buck" J. B. Duke began to aquire smaller companies. This was an age in which giant trusts were being formed, and by 1890 the five leading firms combined into the American Tobacco Company, partly to do away with the heavy advertising costs of the individual members when they were competing. Duke was elected president at the age of 30. The new combine controlled about nine tenths of the nation's cigarette manufacturing.

However, in 1890 the Sherman Anti-Trust Act was enacted, which prohibited trusts and monopolies and agreements aimed at restricting competition. Under a 1911 Supreme Court decision, the corporate trust was broken up and four firms emerged from it: American, Reynolds, Liggett & Myers, and Lorillard. With the new competition, selling and advertising expenditures for the industry skyrocketed, going from $18.1 million in 1910 to $32.4 million only three years later.

By 1915, three brands dominated the market. Camel was the first brand to achieve wide success, and it ran with the slogan, "I'd walk a mile for a Camel." It was a somewhat different product, being a domestic blend based on bright leaf tobacco rather than the Turkish blends popular before this. Developed by Reynolds, its market share was 40 percent by 1918. George Hill and his father Percival, who was president of American Tobacco, developed Lucky Strike with a sales campaign using the slogan, "Lucky Strike, it's toasted." Liggett & Myers updated both the ingredients and the advertising of its Chesterfield brand, first introduced in 1912, using the slogan "They Satisfy."

Aggressive marketing strategies seemed to have come of age by the 1920s. Advertising was strident, repetitious, and millions of dollars were spent by competitors. Missionary salesmen (see Information Sidelight) promoted cigarettes in even the smallest retail units by placing display materials in strategic locations, helping dealers rotate their stocks properly, and in general trying to push their brands at the expense of the other brands.

INFORMATION SIDELIGHT

The Use of Missionary Salespeople

Missionary salespeople are used by manufacturers to work with their dealers. They may put up point-of-purchase displays, train dealers' salespeople, provide better communication between distributor and manufacturer, and in general try to have their brands promoted more aggressively by the dealer. In the drug industry such missionary people are known as *detail men;* their specific task is to call on doctors and other professionals, leave samples, and explain research information about new products so as to encourage prescriptions for their brands.

Missionary salespeople generally do not try to secure orders. However, they are widely used to increase dealer push. This function has become increasingly important in recent years in selling to self-service outlets—supermarkets, discount stores, and drugstores. Because such outlets have no retail clerks involved in selling to customers, everything depends on the amount of shelf space given to a particular brand and its location. Missionary salespeople can be influential in this situation and may even be involved in stocking and merchandise arrangement.

Advertising campaigns began increasingly to be aimed at two customer groups: women and youth. Youth, of course, was a natural target as millions of young people reached adolescence and smoking age every year. Cigarette smoking was promoted as the socially accepted thing to do, and it was associated with health, good looks, and celebrity emulation. Testimonials were widely used, with doctors, athletes, and movie stars signing for large fees to extoll the merits of a particular brand.

ADVERTISING TO WOMEN

Tobacco had been used sporadically by women for many decades by a few iconoclastic individuals. Some daring women tried the Cameo brand introduced by Duke back in 1886. But in those days and earlier, women who smoked were considered loose; they were warned by opponents of smoking that they would become sterile, that they would grow a mustache, or would come down with tuberculosis.[1]

In the 1920s social mores began to change. The "flapper" became an object of emulation by many young women, representing a disdain for conventional dress and behavior. But opposition to such young women was also strong and emotional. Expulsions from colleges were not uncommon for those who smoked. One, however, sued the president of Michigan State Normal College in 1922 on the grounds that her personal freedom had been violated.

Although the potential market of tens of millions of women was profoundly attractive to cigarette makers, the long-standing taboo against smoking by women beset them. The cigarette moguls hesitated to use any direct appeal to women or to picture women smoking in their advertisements. In the early 1920s, the most daring venture was to hesitatingly depict a woman saying, "Blow some my way."

By the late 1920s, American women began turning to smoking in large numbers. Persuasive and intensive advertising, notably by George Washington Hill, was yielding results. But the age was one of women becoming more emancipated as they were given the right to vote and hold office. Furthermore, the widespread violation

[1]Susan Wagner, *Cigarette Country* (New York: Praeger, 1971), p. 41.

of the Prohibition law had turned attitudes in favor of smoking and away from traditional conformity.

THE MAXIMIZING OF PROMOTIONAL STRATEGIES, 1925–1940

Hill vigorously attempted to crack the feminine market with Lucky Strikes as the vehicle. He used testimonials from Madame Schumann-Heink, a noted opera singer—probably the first woman to provide a public testimonial for a cigarette. Her subsequent experiences, however, caused her to have second thoughts. After a number of engagements were canceled on her tour of women's colleges, she changed her mind and even denounced the use of tobacco. But her testimonial proved to be the start of the breaking down of prejudices. Romance was increasingly used in advertisements with testimonials by women and showing women smoking cigarettes in romantic situations. In a social revolution, advertising helped in breaking down taboos and in spreading cigarette usage to tens of millions of women.

Mass advertising slogans—on which millions of dollars were to be commited—were shifting as each firm sought somehow to get an edge on competition. Hill changed his slogan, and advertising agency, from "It's toasted," to "No throat irritation—no cough"; but this was surpassed by the Old Gold's slogan, "Not a cough in a carload."

Hill finally came up with a slogan that is credited with making smoking fully acceptable to women. He had tried to tell them, through advertising, that smoking was good for them. And his search ended with the slogan, "Reach for a Lucky instead of a sweet." The appeal to figure-conscious women was immediate, and the image of health could easily be incorporated. Even Helen Hayes was induced in one ad to assert that she believed Luckies accounted for the trim figures of modern women.

The denigration of sweets, of course, aroused the ire of the National Confectioners' Association, and other organizations. An appeal was made to the Federal Radio Commission, predecessor to the Federal Communications Commission, to stop the "unfair propaganda." The candy–tobacco fight finally involved the Federal Trade Commission, and the issue was resolved with the FTC banning American from selling cigarettes as a reducing device, even by implication.

By 1931, Lucky Strikes led all cigarettes in sales, and for the next two decades, up to 1950, Luckies alternated with Camels for number one spot in brand preference. In gaining this market dominance, Hill pushed heavily into radio advertising. He sponsored such programs as the Metropolitan Opera, the Hit Parade, Ben Bernie, Kay Kyser, Eddy Duchin, Jack Benny, Wayne King, and others—all the top programs and names of the time. Hill paid two tobacco auctioneers $25,000 a year each to sound their almost incomprehensible chants that culminated in the trumpeting of "So-o-old American!" A decade later, Hill dreamed up the "L.S./

M.F.T.'' slogan (''Lucky Strike means fine tobacco'') that was recited ad nauseum for years, yet appeared to be effective.

For a time in the 1920s and 1930s it seemed that achieving sales volume in the industry totally depended on sheer volume of advertising expenditures. And the leaders, the Big Three (Lucky Strike, Camel, and Chesterfield) were spending at a rate of $7,500,000 to $8,500,000 a year from the late 1920s through the 1930s, these sums equaling or greatly exceeding those of all other brands combined. But still they could not maintain their market share. In 1930–1931, the Big Three accounted for 90 percent of total consumption. By 1939 their share had fallen to 67.3 percent.[2]

Low-priced (10 cent) cigarettes increased their share of the market from less than 6 percent in 1933 to over 17 percent by 1939, despite the fact that such lower priced brands spent less than one fifth as much on advertising per unit as the leading brands. The opportunity for the lower priced brands had come in the Depression. The major cigarette manufacturers in the depth of the Depression in 1931 actually raised their prices from 14 cents to 15 cents a pack. More and more people were rolling their own cigarettes during these hard economic times, often with not very satisfactory results. Wings, Avalon, and several other brands in one year's time captured over 20 percent of the market. The leading brands were forced to reduce their prices and the smaller price differential helped them regain some of their lost market share over the lower priced, somewhat lower quality brands.

While this was going on, Philip Morris launched a new blend of cigarettes in 1933 that were priced higher than the market, by as much as 5 cents a package, when the leading brands were trying to counter the inroads of the 10-cent brands and had reduced their own prices to retail around 11 cents. Philip Morris was able to induce dealers to maintain its suggested prices, which brought them trade margins greater than those of the leading brands. An advertising budget of around $1,500,000 conveyed the quality image sought. The hiring of Johnny, a diminutive page boy from the Hotel New Yorker, led to one of the most familiar sounds on radio, with his high-pitched ''Call for Philip Morris!'' This was further enhanced by the name, which had been used for a brand of Turkish-blend cigarettes dating back to a London tobacconist of the 1850s and had sold at one time for 35 cents a package. By 1940, Philip Morris had secured fourth place in the industry.

SOCIAL PRESSURES AGAINST CIGARETTES

Almost from its beginning, tobacco had faced social disfavor from certain sectors of the population, notably medical and religious groups as well as others who espoused certain moral beliefs. The term *coffin nails,* for example, was affixed even before the Civil War. A group of educators, clergymen, doctors, and the late P. T. Barnum

[2]Neil Borden, *Advertising in Our Economy* (Chicago: Irwin, 1945), pp. 60–61.

formed an alliance to fight the tobacco habit. Later, Horace Greeley, publisher of the New York *Tribune*, decried the habit. School children were exhorted to join the Anti-Cigarette League with a pledge to abstain. Some businesses refused to hire men and boys who smoked.

Antismoking legislation was also passed, some of which banned the use of cigarettes by any person under 16 years of age; some of this legislation prohibited the use of coupons in cigarette packages; some even went to the extreme of declaring it illegal to make or sell any form of cigarettes (a 1901 New Hampshire law). In New York, women were absolutely forbidden to smoke in public. By 1910, only in the states of Wyoming and Louisiana had no antismoking legislation been passed by either state or local bodies.

World War I brought a major change in attitudes toward smoking. The cigarette fitted perfectly the needs of fighting men for an easy-to-carry and easy-to-use short reprieve from the rigors of military life. The public was encouraged, by no less than John J. Pershing, commanding general of the armies, to send cigarettes to soldiers, most of whom were ardent cigarette smokers when they returned home.

The increased tempo of life coming with the congestion and strains of urban life favored the short smoke of cigarettes over the more leisurely smokes of cigars and pipes. This trend was further accentuated by the shift of population from rural to urban areas. The voices of the social reformers were drowned out by the stampede to cigarette smoking in the late 1920s by all sectors of society. Table 4.1 shows the growth in cigarette production from the late 1800s up to 1940. Notice in particular the great increase during the years of World War I and also during the 1920s. Table

Table 4.1 Cigarette Production 1870–1940

Year	*Cigarettes Produced (Millions of Units)*
1870	16
1880	533
1890	2,505
1900	3,870
1910	9,782
1914	17,944
1916	26,203
1918	47,528
1920	48,091
1930	124,198
1940	189,508

Source: U.S. Department of Commerce, Bureau of the Census, Historical Statistics of the United States Colonial Times to 1957, pp. 414–415.

Table 4.2 Growth in Radio Advertising, 1935–1943

Year	*Dollars Spent in Advertising*
1935	$112,600,000
1937	164,600,000
1940	215,600,000
1943	313,600,000

Source: U.S. Department of Commerce, Bureau of the Census, Historical Statistics of the United States Colonial Times to 1957, p. 526.

4.2 shows the increase in total radio advertising—a major new media for cigarette advertising—that occurred in the short period from 1935 to 1943.

INGREDIENTS OF SUCCESS

Is the secret of the successful cigarette incursion into the social fabric of our culture simply due to massive advertising expenditures? Can we conclude that the firm—or the industry—willing to spend vast sums on mass media advertising is virtually assured of great and growing success? In the previous case, Coca-Cola, we concluded that advertising is only one tool and that it needs other sound marketing strategies to be most effective. Here we come to a similar conclusion, fortunately, that advertising is not all that simple—fortunately, because otherwise we could be victims of advertising and not necessarily the beneficiaries. Furthermore, not many would like to see an unassailable competitive advantage given to those firms who have the mightiest financial resources to pour into advertising.

In perhaps the most profound analysis ever made of advertising in our economy, Neil Borden identified four conditions necessary beyond having the money to spend, for advertising to be effective or, as he put it, for "advertising opportunity" to occur:

1. The primary demand is favorable.
2. A large opportunity exists for product differentiation.
3. The product has hidden qualities that can be played up in the advertising.
4. The possibility exists to develop strong emotional appeals for the product.[3]

Where all of these conditions do not exist in the particular product or situation, heavy advertising may not produce very good results. But we must also recognize

[3]Ibid., pp. 116–120.

that advertising effectiveness depends on the inspired creativity of the ad or the campaign, the theme, the message, the media used, and the various attributes of the advertising. Furthermore, as we approach ever closer to the $100 billion-a-year expenditure for advertising, the sheer impact of advertising expenditures on a satiated population tends to be less than when total annual expenditures were $2 billion, as in most of the 1920s and 1930s.

We can identify particular elements of the tobacco industry's efforts—and particularly, the strategies of Hill—as engendering the most effective use of advertising expenditures:

First, the use of testimonial ads inaugurated a new and most effective use of advertising, that is, having well-known and admired people promote products. For two major segments of the population, the youth segment and the female segment, such testimonials proved highly effective in the 1920s. Both of these consumer groups were key targets of the cigarette makers. These two groups were particularly swayed by attractive peer advocates. Although testimonial advertising may never achieve the same rate of success it did in the 1920s when advertising was in its infancy, we should not minimize its power today in other circumstances.

The use of athletes had a powerful influence on the youth of our country, regardless of any ethical considerations in espousing what decades later were found not to be a healthy product, but the opposite. Women, led by the testimonial advertising of a few admired indivduals, also took up the concept with as much enthusiasm as the youth. The power of advertising to sway was never better exemplified than in the 1920s and 1930s in its promotion of the smoking among youth and women.

Second, related to testimonial advertising, is image-building advertising. If the product can be imbued, through advertising, with a certain desirable image, then success is likely. With cigarettes, an image of health and fitness was subtly conveyed, especially by Hill. His theme, "Reach for a Lucky instead of a Sweet," graphically expressed this. And picturing cigarettes being smoked by successful people in nice surroundings was a further powerful psychic appeal.

Despite the daring expenditures for advertising and the inspired slogans and themes, it is doubtful that cigarette smoking could have been so stimulated without fortuity: the time was right, the elements were in place, or in the words of Borden, "the primary demand was favorable." Table 4.1 shows the tremendous spurt of demand for cigarettes during World War I, with production almost tripling between 1914 and 1920 and almost tripling again during the 1920s. Wartime seemed an absolute natural for a product like this, a palliative that was convenient to carry and use. And by the 1920s, women, or at least a growing segment of women, were finding the real need to assert their independence and disavowal of traditional customs and restraints. Turning to cigarettes was the most natural way to express this. The compatibility of Hill's advertising efforts with the wave of women's aspirations of freedom could not have been better timed.

WHAT CAN BE LEARNED?

The success of cigarettes in the early decades of this century shows clearly the power of mass media advertising to accentuate and accelerate ongoing social trends. Such trends usually represent rather powerful forces that are shaping society in new and not always well-understood ways. Advertising can help influence and shape such trends when they can be identified and when they are more than mere fad and transitory moods. But we must not be so impressed with the power of mass media advertising that we conclude it can necessarily start new trends or reverse strong existing ones, which it is sometimes given credit for doing—for example, inducing women to take up smoking. But let us remember that the time was ripe for this: advertising did not have the power to reverse the tide of custom and attitudes.

One of Borden's criteria for effective advertising is the ability to promote selective demand, that is, demand for a particular brand. The successful cigarette advertising of this period showed the potency of such selective demand promotion, even when real differences among competing products were practically nil. It was found that psychologically perceived brand differences could be promoted effectively. By creating different images, promoting the subtleties of slightly different flavors or barely detectable ingredients, a product could achieve mastery over competitors—only through effective advertising.

The success of Lucky Strikes in particular during this period shows the challenge and opportunity for creativity in advertising: the right slogan or theme can be worth millions of advertising dollars. For example, during much of this period, the Big Three cigarette manufacturers were advertising about equally; yet one, Lucky Strikes, had stumbled on a theme that brought it market dominance.

The power of repetition, ad nauseum, unfortunately also became evident from cigarette advertising, especially in the 1930s. The constant repetition of a theme or message, far from alienating listeners seemed to be an insidiously persuasive influence. The idea of the power of repetition reached its apogee with the L.S./M.F.T. slogan that taxed the patience of many radio and TV listeners in the 1930s and into the 1950s. Yet, it seemed to be effective in gaining and maintaining market share.

Finally, we can learn from these cigarette battles a comforting notion for most marketers and most consumers, too. Advertising is not the sine qua non. It is not the whole answer to success of marketing strategies. Other aspects of the marketing mix may substitute for advertising, and win certain sectors of the total market. We saw the considerable success of the low-price brands during the 1930s, despite their meager advertising budgets compared to the Big Three. We also saw that other brands can successfully tap the higher quality market—as did Philip Morris—without indulging in the frenzy of sheer advertising expenditures that the Big Three deemed necessary.

Marketers could finally realize that the total market was big and complex. Many different strategies could be used to successfully tap its diversity. This recognition was somewhat of a revelation in earlier days, but today we are more cognizant of it. Though many firms are still intimidated by the marketing resources and advertising prowess of industry leaders, opportunities usually exist in all markets for creative and innovative marketing strategies to tap diverse and unsatisfied customer segments.

Questions

1. How do you explain the phenomenon that repetitious advertising (even ad nauseum, as was the case of the "L.S./M.F.T." slogan) still seems to be effective?
2. Social pressures against cigarette smoking have had little effect. Now even medical warnings have by no means brought the industry to its knees. Can the durable commitment of many people to smoking be explained entirely by the addictive nature of tobacco?
3. How can strong emotional appeals be developed for cigarettes? Does this suggest that all types of products can be given strong emotional appeals?

Invitation to Role Play

You have reason to believe that society is moving to more acceptance of women smoking small cigars. How would you as a tobacco company executive plan an advertising campaign directed to women?

PART TWO

THE DEPRESSION YEARS: STRATEGIES HONED IN HARD ECONOMIC TIMES

The Great Depression lasted through the 1930s, practically to the start of World War II. Despite the hard economic times—or really, because of them—certain adaptations of marketing strategy and institutions developed that had practically a revolutionary impact. (In periods of more economic stability, these developments might have been more evolutionary.) In particular, the supermarket concept was introduced early in the decade of the 1930s and spread so rapidly, devouring the typical full-service, higher priced grocery stores of the day, that by the end of the decade profound changes were almost universal in grocery retailing. Michael Cullen is generally credited with introducing this innovative and disruptive concept. His King Kullen stores rapidly gained customer acceptance. However, the concept was easily imitated, and a host of big and small firms changed their operations or started new ones with the supermarket idea of low prices supported by high volume, self-service, big assortments, and free parking.

In the decade of the 1930s marketing research advanced profoundly. Before this, most research had involved simply assessing governmental census statistics; more sophisticated researchers used correlation analysis, which proponents thought could solve all problems of knowledge simply by measuring the relative variation between series of numbers. But correlation produced no miraculous discoveries.

Marketing research for several decades had been influenced by political polling, in which qualified voters expressed their preferences for political candidates. The transference of political polling to marketing-preference surveys, of course, was obvious. The infatuation with such surveys of intentions reached its apogee with the *Literary Digest* disaster of 1936 in which the biggest survey ever conducted before or since yielded erroneous data. (See the Information Sidelight for specifics on this monumental research disaster.)

INFORMATION SIDELIGHT

The *Literary Digest* Fiasco

The *Literary Digest* was a weekly magazine that had been conducting an extensive mail poll of its readers before national elections for many years. For over a quarter century it had never failed to reflect the distribution of actual votes in its preelection polls. In 1936 it conducted probably the largest sampling ever undertaken. More than 10 million ballots were mailed to its readers and to names drawn from auto registrations and telephone directories. Some 2,350,000 persons responded to the poll. Of the ballots returned, 55 percent favored Landon and 41 percent were for Roosevelt. On this basis, the *Digest* confidently predicted a Landon landslide. Actual results: Roosevelt polled 60 percent of the votes cast and his was the landslide.

That same year Gallup used a sample of only a few thousand interviews with voters, yet accurately predicted that Roosevelt would be elected and the *Literary Digest* would be in error.

The groundwork was laid for researchers versed in careful sampling techniques, most notably Roper and Gallup. However, in 1933 A. C. Nielsen started a service to provide manufacturers with data about the consumer sales of their products and competing products, which led to imitators; that is, other syndicated services. By the latter part of the 1930s marketing information was both more valid and available in greater scope than ever before. And it became a tool for many marketing successes to come.

A classic example of sound and aggressive marketing planning and strategy, a good part of it based on using the newly available marketing research techniques against a powerful entrenched competitor, is Spry's successful market entry against Procter & Gamble's Crisco. Just four years after introducing Spry shortening, Lever had captured 45 percent of the U.S. shortening market, while P & G's share dropped from complete dominance to 55 percent. A wide range of sophisticated marketing techniques were used in this confrontation. The strategic implications of such major confrontations as that between Spry and Crisco were not fully grasped by most marketers until later, but eventually such campaigns were to be likened to military strategies. Indeed, some books compared offensive and defensive marketing strategies to offensive and defensive military strategies:

> By offensive strategies the market of a competitor is attacked; by defensive strategy a company guards against attack from a competitor . . . basis of any marketing strategy is an uninterrupted flow of communication and marketing intelligence.[1]

Sources such as the following were referred to:

Brodie, B. *A guide to Naval Strategy,* 4th ed., Naval War College Ed. (Princeton: Princeton University Press, 1953).

Clausewitz, K. *Principles of War* (Harrisburg, Pa.: The Military Service Publishing Company, 1942).

Miksche, F. O. *Attack, A Study of Blitzkrieg Tactics* (New York: Random House, 1942).

[1]Myron S. Heidingsfield, *Changing Patterns in Marketing: A Study in Strategy,* (Boston: Allyn & Bacon, 1968), pp. 21–22.

CHAPTER 5

King Kullen and the Emergence of the Supermarket

The year was 1930, and the nation was in the throes of the worst economic depression it had ever experienced. Many say that the supermarket was a Depression product, honed to meet directly the needs of consumers wracked with diminished income and already conditioned to expect major changes in life-style. And yet, this was not exactly true, as we will see later.

Of course, we are familiar with supermarkets, but let us define the characteristics of this new breed that emerged primarily in the 1930s:

> A departmentalized retail food store, operated on a self-service basis, and having four basic food departments—groceries, meat, produce, and dairy—and perhaps other departments as well.

Up to the 1920s, the retail food industry was composed of many single- or limited-line retailers, such as dairy stores, grocery stores without meat, meat markets, confectioners, and delicatessens. Although the 1920s brought some movement toward multiline operations, usually these were small, were located within walking distance of their customers, and offered such services as credit and delivery. Some huge chains had evolved in this industry and had brought cost savings because of their quantity purchasing over what smaller independent stores could achieve. The major chain was the Great Atlantic & Pacific Tea Company. This organization, which had actually started in 1859, had changed to a cash-and-carry operation in

1912, and this had permitted great cost savings that were passed on to consumers in the form of lower prices. By 1929, A & P had 15,150 stores, mostly small neighborhood units, and sales had passed the billion dollar mark.

Several embryonic supermarkets had emerged before 1930. Large public or farmers' markets had come onto the scene in major cities, as early as 1658 in Boston, and by the 1800s in other cities. Essentially, these were a hodge-podge of stalls or booths leased by individual farmers or proprietors, all under one roof. The most notable of these were Faneuil Hall in Boston, the Lexington Market of Baltimore, and the Catherine Market of New York City.

In 1916 in Memphis, Tennessee, Clarence Saunders started perhaps the first self-service grocery. This was the beginning of the Piggly Wiggly chain that went through several ownership changes before being acquired by Safeway Stores and the Kroger Company. Some of the Piggly Wiggly stores approached the supermarket in size; however, most were much smaller but had a lower expense ratio than conventional clerk-service stores because of self-service.

Several prototypes of the supermarket developed in the Los Angeles area and in parts of the Southwest before 1930. These took two forms: (1) a large, self-service food store under centralized management, and (2) an open-front, drive-in market, which consisted of a group of independent units in a single building, reminiscent of the earlier farmers' markets of the East, but adapted to the auto-oriented California and Western environment. These were rather upscale food outlets that apparently did not offer low prices as their primary appeal; they were considered to be uniquely suitable for the Western life-style, hardly an institution of wider appeal.[1]

Back East, however, Michael Cullen was the change maker with a form of supermarket that was to be quickly followed by others and spread far and wide. The product of his imagination was to transform food retailing in less than a decade.

MICHAEL CULLEN

In 1930 Michael Cullen worked for the Kroger Grocery Company in Cincinnati, Ohio. He had come up with a wild idea on how to operate a grocery store much more profitably. So he sent a letter to Kroger's vice-president. Here are some excerpts:

> This is the kind of cut-rate chain of wholesale direct-to-the-public that I want to operate: I want to sell 300 items at cost, 300 at 5 percent above cost, 300 at 15 percent above cost, and 300 at 20 percent above cost. I want to gross 9 percent . . . and make a net profit of 2½ percent . . . when I come out with a two-page ad and advertise 300 items at cost and 200 items at practically cost . . . the public . . . would break my front door down to get in. It would be a riot. . . . I would convince the public that I could save them from one to three dollars on their grocery bill. . . . when the great crowd . . .

[1]Frank J. Charvat, *Supermarketing* (New York: Macmillan, 1961), p. 17.

came to buy those low priced items, I would have them surrounded with 15 percent, 20 percent and, in some cases, 25 percent items.[2]

Kroger turned him down. But Cullen was able to obtain other financing, and on August 30, 1930, he opened his first store in Jamaica, New York. By 1932, he had eight such markets in the Long Island area, which he called King Kullen Stores, and was doing an annual sales volume of $6 million in the grocery departments alone. By 1935 he had 15 large units and was doing more business than could be done by a hundred neighborhood stores.

The stores were located in abandoned factories and warehouses, in low-rent locations on the fringe of thickly populated areas. Furnishings and facilities were crude. Counters were made of rough pine boards. Service was minimal, with customers gathering their own goods. At first baskets were used, but shopping carts were soon added to accommodate much larger purchases. The objective of the operation was sales volume never dreamed of before in a grocery store operation.

The great price advantage, the cavernous interiors with goods stocked high, and the no-frills bargain atmosphere had mass customer appeal, especially during hard economic times. Cullen sought to entice customers from miles around with heavy advertising of brand name goods. Always providing adequate parking adjacent to the premises, Cullen wanted to appeal to auto rather than walk-in trade, because the car allowed customers to carry home large quantity purchases. Typical of his promotional approach was this ad in 1931:

Come in your Lincoln, Come in your Ford, Come with the Baby Carriage. Come with any Old Thing, but Come, Come, Come![3]

The price advantages that Cullen offered were significant for 1930, and would still be today, as the following comparison of Cullen prices with those of other stores shows:

	Elsewhere	*King Kullen*
All 10-cent drug items	$0.10	$0.09
Campbell's tomato soup	0.07	0.04
U.S. rubber tires for Fords	5.50	3.78
G.E. vacuum cleaners	35.00	11.94

Source: "The Cheapie Thrives," Business Week, Feb. 8, 1933, p. 11.

Notice that in addition to food products, Cullen and his King Kullen stores were stocking such nonfood items as vacuum cleaners and tires.

[2]Robert Drew-Bear, *Mass Merchandising* (New York: Fairchild Publications, 1970), pp. 24–25.
[3]Drew-Bear, *Mass Merchandising,* p. 25.

Such diversity of goods, or "scrambled merchandising," was an innovation of major consequence for the food stores of the time. Although the greater portion of space in King Kullen stores was allocated to the grocery, meat, bakery, and dairy departments, considerable space was leased to utensil, produce, paint, hardware, and auto accessory concessionaires. Cullen's operating principles regarding this were that (1) the other departments must all sell merchandise at reduced prices and (2) the income from the concessions should pay the rent of the entire establishment.[4]

The concept of scrambled merchandising has carried over to the modern supermarket—and indeed to many other types of stores—today, although generally not to quite the degree of Cullen's store. For example, few supermarkets today carry tires and vacuum cleaners. However, leased departments or concessionaires are not used much today. The incentives for scrambled merchandising are discussed in the following Information Sidelight.

INFORMATION SIDELIGHT

Scrambled Merchandising

Scrambled merchandising is the practice of adding nontraditional lines of merchandise (usually with a higher markup and profit) to the regular assortments. Thus, in the supermarket a wide assortment of nonfood items may be carried, ranging from toys, housewares, and health and beauty aids, to pantyhose—or to tires and vacuum cleaners, as King Kullen and its imitators did. Many drugstores today stock cameras, hardware, auto accessories, jewelry, even camping equipment and lawn furniture. Oil companies have added convenience food stores to their stations. Many stores today are taking on the characteristics of the old general store, stocking all sorts of unrelated merchandise under one roof.

The incentive for scrambled merchandising is increasing total sales and profits. Consequently, the practice today is to select products that will permit a higher profit margin than regular merchandise and also yield satisfactory sales volume. This poses some interesting problems, however, because many different types of stores seek the best sellers of diverse product lines. As a result it is difficult for a store to maintain its individuality and a loyal group of customers. For example, a hardware store, the traditional source for lawn supplies such as grass seed and fertilizer, now faces competition from variety stores, supermarkets, discount stores, drugstores, and even convenience food stores and gasoline stations.

---

[4]M. M. Zimmerman, *The Super Market: Spectacular Exponent of Mass Distribution* (New York: Super Market Publishing Co., 1937), p. 10.

King Kullen and its imitators were referred to at the time as "Cheapy" stores. And the word certainly described the price structure and the appearance of these stores. Although the name was coined as a slur, it quickly caught on. Customers loved this major change in grocery retailing.

By 1932, other entrepreneurs were following the cheapy format. Big Bear stores opened in 1932, and whereas King Kullen called itself the Price Wrecker, Big Bear became the Price Crusher. Other supers followed with such descriptive names as The Whale, Giant Tiger, Big Chief, and Little Bear. A revolution was in the making, sweeping all before it in just a few years. However, by 1935 the supermarkets were beginning to change, with the "cheapy" being replaced by more attractive stores. Increasingly, new outlets began to be located in better neighborhoods, began to incorporate larger investments in equipment and buildings, and started to assume the appearance of supermarkets as we know them today.

By the mid-1930s, King Kullen and most of the newcomers to the retail grocery field had lost their momentum as the better financed chains began converting their outlets to supermarkets. King Kullen, however, is still in existence today, although its importance in the industry is relatively minor. In 1980 it was the forty-first largest supermarket chain with sales of $318 million.

THE CHAINS FIGHT THE NEW COMPETITION

By 1936, such chains as A&P, Kroger, First National Stores, and American Stores were realizing that the supermarket was no passing fad but a phenomenon that could destroy them. They began opening experimental units to test operating problems and to gather first-hand statistics on expenses and profit margins. By 1937, the

Table 5.1 Number of A&P Supermarkets and Small Economy Stores for the Years 1936 to 1943

Year	*Number of Supers*	*Number of Small Economy Stores*
1936	20	14,426
1937	282	12,776
1938	771	9,900
1939	1,119	7,902
1940	1,398	5,677
1941	1,552	4,490
1942	1,633	4,188
1943	1,646	4,105

Source: United States v The Great A&P Tea Company, U.S. Circuit Court of Appeals, 7th District, Docket 9221, Records and Briefs, Vol. 1, p. 323.

Table 5.2 Number of Supermarkets in the United States, and Percentage of Total Food Store Sales, 1935–1941

Year	*Number of Supermarkets*	*Supermarket Sales as a Percentage of Food Store Sales*
1935	300	1.7
1936	1200	5.6
1937	3066	8.2
1938	3700	10.5
1939	4982	14.7
1940	6175	18.3
1941	8175	19.8

Source: Frank J. Charvat, Supermarketing (New York: Macmillan, 1961), p. 3.

industry leader, A&P, was already convinced and made the major decision to switch its resources to the supermarket. This represented a tremendous turnabout decision for a chain of over 14,000 small units, many of which would have to be closed within a few years. Table 5.1 shows the change in the number of supermarkets and small economy stores for A&P over the years from 1936 to 1943. As an example of the rapidity of the changeover, in one month in 1937 A&P closed 28 neighborhood stores in and around Detroit, and replaced them with two large self-service supermarkets.

Some of the first chain supermarkets opened under different names, the rationale being not to obviously show price differences with their conventional stores. For example, Kroger's early supers were called "Pay'n Takit," and Safeway's, "Sunny Jim Markets." Table 5.2 shows the growth in total number of supermarkets from 1935 to the start of World War II in 1941. Of course, during the war years growth slowed down, but outlets rapidly increased again after the war. Also shown are supermarket sales as a percentage of total grocery store sales. The rapid inroads of supermarkets onto the retail grocery environment is remarkable. Much of this represents the belated but wholehearted commitment of chains to making the transition to supermarkets, a recognition that there was no way to counter this competition except to join it.

FACTORS BEHIND THE VULNERABILITY OF CONVENTIONAL GROCERY STORES

In 1933, when King Kullen and Big Bear Stores were pioneering the new movement, Roy Dawson, founder of Big Bear said that

Table 5.3 Motor Vehicle Registrations, 1915–1935

Year	*Number of Registrations*
1915	2,491,000
1920	9,239,000
1925	19,941,000
1930	26,532,000
1935	32,035,000

Source: U.S. Bureau of Census, Statistical Abstract of the U.S. (Washington, D.C.: U.S. Government Printing Office, 1959), p. 559.

> Some day, supermarkets will do nearly all of the business all over the country. It's inevitable because it's cheaper, because people have automobiles, and because they like to shop. It's the method of retailing.[5]

This was at variance with the opinions of many people that the supermarket was the poor man's store:

> It was confidently said for a long time that self-service would be all right for poor people but that the middle class would never go for it.[6]

Although most experts at the time were crediting cost economies that permitted lower prices as the fundamental and only reason behind the success of supermarkets, Dawson correctly noted that certain social factors also contributed to the success. The automobile made it unnecessary to shop in the neighborhood food store. People could now take longer trips, visit new shopping centers, certainly make larger purchases, and easily transport them home—in short, make grocery shopping both more exciting and more convenient by shopping less frequently and making it more of an adventure. Table 5.3 shows the growth of auto ownership from 1915 to 1935, a social phenomenon of major import.

Undeniably, grocery retailing had been backward. Product specialization had been carried to a high degree up to the 1920s, with numerous small shops, each specializing in a certain type of food, such as meat, baked goods, dry groceries, and so on. Such product specialization brought with it inefficiencies in both costs and other operating aspects as well as in shopping time and effort. In the 1920s,

[5]"The Supermarket: Revolution in Retailing," *Business Week,* June 28, 1952, pp. 40–41.

[6]A quote of Professor Malcolm McNair, noted retailing expert at Harvard, as cited in "The Supermarket: Revolution in Retailing," pp. 41–42.

however, some improvements evolved with more combination-type grocery stores that provided one-stop food shopping. But such neighborhood stores still necessitated hand-to-mouth purchases of foodstuffs—the quantity that could be easily carried home in sacks or shopping bags. The need for more efficiency was clamoring to be heard.

Life-styles were changing, not only because of the popularization of the car, but also because major population shifts were occurring between farm and city. This meant less dependence on home-grown and home-canned foodstuffs and more reliance on the retail food store. And as the United States became more industrialized, new tastes were developing, convenience of shopping was becoming more important, and the old traditional ways of food retailing became vulnerable.

In addition to the auto, another technological development spurred the popularity of supermarkets: refrigeration. Table 5.4 shows sales of refrigerators from 1926 to 1937. Refrigeration reduced the need for frequent buying trips; it made buying in quantity more feasible and more desirable. It also paved the way for frozen food sales that required the capital only large retailers could provide.

Of course, the operating economies and the lower prices possible because of the self-service supermarket operations was a powerful consumer incentive. Table 5.5 shows the profit and loss statements for typical conventional food markets and supermarkets in the 1930s. The much lower gross margin percentage that would cover the expenses and profit margin for a supermarket was of major significance. This was of particular interest to chains in the 1930s because of federal and some

Table 5.4 Manufacturers' Sales by Units of Refrigerators, 1926–1937

Year	*Number of Units*
1926	205,000
1927	375,000
1928	535,000
1929	778,000
1930	791,000
1931	906,000
1932	798,000
1933	1,016,000
1934	1,283,000
1935	1,568,000
1936	1,997,000
1937	2,310,000

Source: Frank J. Charvat, Supermarketing (New York: Macmillan, 1961), p. 39.

Table 5.5 Operating Statements for Average Grocery Store and Supermarket Expressed as a Percentage of Sales

		Average Grocery Store		*Supermarket*
Sales		100.00		100.00
Cost of sales		74.19		87.99
Gross margin[a]		25.81		12.01
Expenses				
Rent[b]	0.98		0.71	
Utilities[b]	1.23		0.35	
Payroll[c]	10.32		5.40	
Advertising	0.31		1.32	
Delivery	2.77			
Insurance	0.15		0.16	
Miscellaneous	2.53		0.40	
		18.29		8.34
Net profit[d]		7.52		3.67

[a]The much lower gross margin of the supermarket accommodates much lower prices than regular stores.
[b]Note the substantially lower occupancy costs for the supermarket expressed as a percentage of sales. These reflect the high volume produced on supermarket premises.
[c]Payroll costs are much lower for supermarkets because of both high sales volume and the need for fewer employees with self-service.
[d]The lower percentage of net profit really translates into much higher dollar profits because of the high sales volume for supermarkets compared with conventional outlets.
Sources: Charvat, Supermarketing, pp. 22 and 24.

state laws aimed at protecting smaller competitors. State chain store taxes penalized chains with a large number of units within the state, thus creating an incentive to change to fewer but bigger units. And the Robinson-Patman Act, enacted in 1936, prohibited a manufacturer from selling similar goods to different buyers at different prices, with certain remote exceptions. This federal law made it difficult for chains to obtain lower merchandise costs than their smaller competitors, despite their larger volume purchases. Therefore, any lower prices chains could offer would have to come from operating economies. And these the supermarket could provide.

The major cost advantage of supers over conventional grocers of the day came from the self-service operations in which the customers performed some of the marketing function, namely, gathering the goods they desired rather than having store personnel do it. But there were other economies as well:

- Low ratio of rent to sales because of big volume.
- Avoidance of such service costs as delivery and credit.
- Division of labor (stock boys, checkers, packers, etc.), which made for greater operating efficiencies.

- Large average orders, which increased sales volume, but also greatly increased transaction efficiency (i.e., fewer large orders could be more efficiently handled than many small ones).

WHAT CAN BE LEARNED?

In examining the great inroads of the early supermarkets into the existing retail competitive environment, we see that the innovators in all instances were not the established firms, the major chains such as A&P, Kroger, and Safeway, but rank newcomers, interlopers, outsiders to the establishment. When we examine the inroads of discount stores some two decades later, we will see the same phenomenon, which has occurred elsewhere with other major innovations as well, such as the following:

> The air-brake, automatic coupling, the refrigerator car, and the streamlined train—none of these important railroad innovations were invented by a railroad man.
>
> The motel was not originated by traditional hotel keepers; the success of motels forced hotels to enter the field.
>
> Drive-in movies were not pioneered by the great movie chains.
>
> Paperback books were not initiated by the big publishers, who entered the field only later when it was already thriving.[7]

We are led to conclude that major firms, despite their resources and often heavy commitments to marketing research and research and development, lag behind the major changes and innovations in their industries, which come from the small, hungry individuals who have no ties with the status quo, no entrenched positions to protect, and are free to be flexible and audacious enough to try the untried.

We see in the supermarket grand entry a confirmation of the "wheel of retailing" theory of retail institutional change proposed by Professor Malcolm McNair, the eminent retailing expert from Harvard. This theory is briefly described in the Information Sidelight.

INFORMATION SIDELIGHT

The Wheel of Retailing Theory

The wheel of retailing theory is offered as an explanation and a prediction of major institutional changes in retailing. New types of retail firms may enter the

[7]These examples are taken from Leo Burnett, "Marketing Snags and Fallacies," *Journal of Marketing*, July 1966, p. 2.

marketplace as low-status, low-markup, low-price operations. However, as they become successful they open more elaborate stores and offer more services. As a result, their costs grow and they have to charge higher prices. In turn, they also become vulnerable to new low-status, low-markup, low-price retailers, and the wheel turns and the cycle begins again.

The theory accounts for the coming of supermarkets in the 1930s and for the entry of discount stores in the late 1950s and 1960s. Further back, in the late 1800s and early 1900s, the development of department stores, mail-order houses, and the various kinds of chain stores can be explained by the theory. On the other hand, vending machines, which generally have higher costs and higher selling prices than other retail operations, are not explained by this theory; nor are convenience food stores that afford convenience of place, hours, and quickness of shopping, but charge substantially higher prices than nearby supermarkets.

In 1930 the environment was right for a major institutional change, and the means were available to bring it about. The situation was very similar to the discount revolution of two decades later. In the 1930s, however, the conventional retailers, namely, the chains, reacted rather quickly and joined the rush to supermarkets, even if it meant closing thousands of their conventional stores. In the 1950s, the established retailers were much slower to act. It took most of them at least a decade and a half to act to counter the discount store threats and, in some cases, to join the discount revolution.

We see in the deterioration of the competitive positions of the larger chain operations the importance of rapidly adapting to environmental or competitive changes or facing the danger of being wiped out no matter how old the establishment or how dominant it had been in the past. We have to be impressed with the dynamics of the environment, the uncertainty of the future at least in assuring a continuity of acceptance of traditional successful practices. Figure 5.1 shows behavior responsiveness to environmental change illustrated on a continuum, showing at the one extreme the innovator who initiates change and, at the other, the firm inflexible and unchanging, and consequently highly vulnerable. Most firms fall into the middle area of sooner or later making some adaptations to the change.

Not all firms are willing to accept the rewards and risks of being outright innovators—large established firms least of all. But a firm must at least be adaptive or it will be severely wounded by the changing environment.

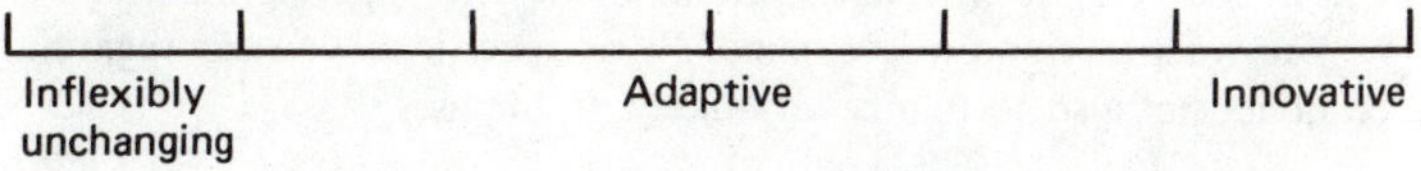

Figure 5.1. Degree of responsiveness to environmental change.

The supermarkets made a major appeal to price, offering consumers considerably lower prices than they had previously been able to obtain even in chain outlets. This raises some questions:

What can a firm do to defend its market position?

Is becoming another supermarket the only reasonable option?

Does a firm have any recourse but to compete head-to-head on a low-price basis?

We know the answers to these questions better today than marketers did five decades ago. No, a firm does not have to match the pricing efforts of competitors to be successful. *But it must find for itself a niche, or some basis of operation that is relatively unique and appealing to a sufficient number of customers.* This could be gained by offering better services, better quality, larger assortments, or some other characteristic that is rather different from the offerings of competitors.

Finally, from this example of five decades ago, we are left with the realization of how quickly success can draw imitators. The significant success of King Kullen and shortly after of Big Bear spawned a host of imitators in barely months. The supermarket revolution swept along, and the initiators soon found themselves only part of many. The chains with their much greater resources quickly capitalized on the opportunity and achieved market dominance, despite the trauma of shutting down thousands of obsolescent units.

Therefore, we are forced to conclude that a successful innovator has only gained a short-lived advantage. The opportunity must be grasped strongly and aggressively, or the field will be left to those who came on the scene later but with more resources.

Questions

1. The early history of the supermarket industry suggests that the successful innovator has only a short-lived advantage over aggressive imitators. How can the innovator fight off such imitators? Evaluate the likely effectiveness of such efforts.
2. How do you account for the fact that the major grocery chains themselves were not first to introduce the supermarket concept? Do you think your generalizations are also valid for other industries and other times?

Invitation to Role Play

Place yourself in the role of Michael Cullen. Your first supermarket is an outstanding success. Now you want to vigorously expand. Be as specific as you can regarding how this might best be done, but also recognize any likely problems.

CHAPTER 6

Lever's Massive Attack on Crisco with Spry, 1936

One of the most successful massive introductory marketing strategies ever conceived was that of Lever Bros. against the strongly entrenched Crisco of Procter & Gamble. It was fifty years ago when this took place, but its lessons are timeless. Coming in the depths of the Depression, the strategic planning and execution were precursors of marketing tools and techniques that could hardly have been improved decades later. Few firms have so successfully, and so quickly, invaded a market against perhaps the most feared competitor in consumer packaged goods, Procter & Gamble. Two marketing techniques in particular need to be singled out as proving their effectiveness: marketing research, and mass sampling. Until then, these had never been used to such powerful effect.

PROCTER & GAMBLE'S CRISCO

As the year 1936 was beginning, the nation was still mired in the greatest economic depression it had ever experienced. But Procter & Gamble's Crisco shortening was virtually depression-proof. It was enjoying a large and profitable sales volume. Crisco stood practically alone as the only nationally advertised product of its kind. No threat to its leadership was in sight. A national survey of housewives had just revealed that Crisco was the brand of shortening used by 58 percent, with no other brand named by as many as 8 percent of the women surveyed.[1]

[1]Richard D. Crisp, *Marketing Research* (New York: McGraw-Hill, 1957), p. 285.

Shortenings are fats and oils of animal or vegetable origin that are used in doughs to give crispness to baked products. They include butter, lard, processed shortenings, and margarine. Processed shortenings, such as Crisco and Spry, are usually vegetable oils, which are 100 percent fat, treated to produce an odorless, white shortening with solid, smooth consistency, and good plasticity. Hydrogenated shortenings are made by adding hydrogen gas to the heated oil to produce a firm substance. All-vegetable shortenings have advantages over lard, which comes from the rendering of the fatty tissue of hogs, in that they are less likely to become rancid, can be made with more uniformity, and are more workable for cakes and pastries. And they cost less than lard.

Crisco was introduced in 1912 as an all-vegetable, hydrogenized shortening with clear advantages over the lard and vegetable oil compounds of the day. It made marketing history at the time of its introduction with a long and sensational advertising campaign that cost $3 million over a five-year period. Before long, Procter & Gamble became the world's largest user of cottonseed oil, a major component of Crisco.

LEVER BROS.

Lever Bros., headquartered in Cambridge, Massachusetts, was a wholly owned subsidiary of Unilever of London, a world colossus that was widely diversified. In 1930, Lever Bros., the U.S. subsidiary, was one of the three major soap producers, following Procter & Gamble in domestic sales, and ahead of Colgate-Palmolive-Peet.

Unilever itself was founded in England by William Lever, a grocer's son, who in 1870 was a traveling salesman. Fifteen years later, he entered the soap business with a yellow soap that he named "Sunlight." Partly because the soap was good and lathered well, and perhaps partly because of its appealing name, sales of Sunlight skyrocketed in only three years and William began his heady thoughts of world conquest. In 1888, only three years after introducing the soap, he visited the United States and Canada to study merchandising and advertising techniques and established sales offices in both countries. In 1897 he acquired a controlling interest in the Curtis Davis Company of Cambridge, Massachusetts, a small soap company. He promptly started it making Sunlight soap and Lifebuoy for the American market.

By 1900, Unilever had factories in Cambridge and Philadelphia, Germany, Canada, Switzerland, Australia, the Netherlands, Belgium, France, and South Africa. Coconut plantations and other sources of raw materials were quickly added. William Lever's greatest expansion, however, came during World War I, when he entered the margarine business. After his death in 1925, several competing firms merged, and by 1930 Lever became Unilever Ltd.

The success of Lever Bros. U.S.A. can be attributed largely to one man,

Francis A. Countway. He became president of Lever in the United States in 1913. At that time, domestic sales were less than $1 million a year. By 1920 sales had risen to $12 million, then $45 million by 1930, and $90 million by 1939. As a result, Francis Countway received the highest compensation paid to any industrial executive in the United States, some $469,700 in 1939.

FRANCIS A. COUNTWAY

Countway's dedication to the work ethic and his hustle helped propel him to the highest-salaried rank. He started his business career at 18, as a bookkeeper for a wholesale molasses business. The owner of this business later bought an interest in Curtis Davis Co., and invited Countway to switch from molasses to soap. The young man was agreeable to this on the condition that he be permitted to go into sales. When Lever acquired the company a short time later, Countway came to Lever's attention because he was making three times as many sales calls as anyone else in the organization. It is said that when asked for an explanation, Countway replied that all he did was to start each day by calling on the grocer who he knew would be the first to open his store in the morning and to end it by visiting the last grocer to close his store at night.[2]

Lever naturally was impressed with this young man who evinced some of the same qualities that he himself had. He instructed his executives to keep their eyes on Countway and to begin grooming him for positions of greater responsibility. Part of the grooming consisted of giving him all the most difficult jobs that could be found, and such challenges Countway welcomed and he acquitted himself well with these.

The move to president of the small soap manufacturer was not surprising. And now Countway could really flex his creativity, his flair for selling, and a firm yet morale-stimulating organizational flair that brought him the admiration and respect of his subordinates. He engineered the attack on Crisco in the 1930s. But his effectiveness had built the fortunes of Lever in the years before, with such products as Rinso, Lux Toilet Soap, Lux Flakes, and Lifebuoy Health Soap.

One of his more memorable flashes of inspiration occurred with Lifebuoy in 1926. Lifebuoy had made slow progress for almost 30 years with its targeting as a health soap: "More than Soap, a Health Habit." But in 1926 after a round of golf on a hot afternoon, Countway noticed that he smelled from sweating, and he reasoned that if he could smell himself, he could be offensive to others. He conceived the idea of promoting Lifebuoy as a means of eliminating the chief obstacle to the general public's ambitions and happiness, "Body Odor"—soon shortened to "BO."[3] The odor approach was so stimulating to Lifebuoy sales that it was also

[2]"Mr. Countway Takes the Job," *Fortune*, November 1940, p. 114.

[3]This story is recounted in "Mr. Countway Takes the Job," pp. 95–96.

used to promote Lux flakes as a means of overcoming something called ''Undie Odor.''

THE SPRY ONSLAUGHT

By the late 1920s, Countway was looking for another product to launch. Shortening seemed the natural route to go. Lever was familiar with handling vegetable oils from which shortening was made because these were also used in soap products. A potential problem admittedly would be how to make one that was superior to competing products, particularly Crisco. But a great deal of technical information had been developed in Europe about the hydrogenation process and this was available to Unilever. Countway constructed a $4 million plant in 1931 for the new venture. The product could have been introduced at that time, but in a courageous decision, Countway delayed its introduction to consumers until the time seemed ripe, although a lard substitute was cautiously marketed to bakeries.

In 1931 the country was in the worst stage of the Depression, and low prices prevailed for butter and lard. Such a situation hardly augured well for a substitute that would cost more. Not until 1936 did Countway think conditions were satisfactory. Although such a wait was frustrating, it did allow time for careful planning and product adjustments to more fully meet consumer preferences. In 1936, bad harvests and government policies had cut down agricultural overproduction, and the United States was faced with a shortage of real lard, which led to higher prices.

There are few examples in the annals of business history in which a product introduction was purposefully delayed for so long or the planning was more carefully and minutely done.

Marketing Research Efforts

As an important early step in attacking the entrenched Crisco, one of the most comprehensive marketing research efforts that any firm had engineered up to that time was commissioned. This research covered a period of years and was a major influence on the marketing strategy that followed.

Lever wanted to enter the shortening market, deeming this as most compatible with its worldwide technical know-how and resources, however, the product attributes needed to be much more specifically determined. Panel research, using the new Nielsen Food Index facilities, revealed the size and characteristics of the shortening market and the market shares of the various competitors. (See the Information Sidelight for more specifics about Nielsen and other syndicated services.) Facts on the size and growth of shortening volume confirmed the initial interest in introducing a new shortening. Of course, Crisco was quickly identified as the leading brand. But further research was needed on the dimensions of its dominant position, such as the geographical distribution of the volume and any variations by city sizes, different types of stores, and the like.

INFORMATION SIDELIGHT

A. C. Nielsen Company and the Syndicated Research Services

Since 1933 the A. C. Nielsen Company had been operating a marketing research service to provide manufacturers with data about the consumer sales of their products and competing products. Today, Nielsen still conducts store audits in grocery, drugs, and certain other fields. The Market Research Corporation of America (MRCA) also gathers information on expenditures based on a panel of consumers who maintain a record of their purchases in diaries. Burgoyne Index, Ehrhard-Rabic Associates, and Store Audits also provide store audit services. Many companies are now provided consumer samples from National Family Opinion, the best known after MRCA. Speedata provides an intermediate step in measuring product flow by recording shipments of grocery products through 100 major warehouses.

Figure 6.1 compares the type of invaluable information provided by the two major syndicated services, Nielsen and MRCA.

Offered by Both

Total U.S. consumer sales by brand
Consumer sales by regions or districts
Sales by type of grocery and drug outlet
Sales by size of package

Offered by Nielsen	*Offered by MRCA*
Dealer markup	Characteristics of families buying products and specific brands
Average order size by dealers	Repeat buying
Local advertising	Rate of addition of new customers
Shelf price.	Source of new customers
Stock condition and inventory	Lost customers
Store displays	Frequency of purchase
	Volume moving at various price levels
	Volume accounted for by coupon redemptions

Figure 6.1. Information furnished by Nielsen and MRCA services.

Lever conducted consumer research targeted especially at Crisco users. Housewives all over the nation were interviewed during a two-year investigation in 1931–1933, probing for any weaknesses and identifying the major strengths. The strength of Crisco was clearly evident in its high acceptance, the brand awareness developed through decades of aggressive advertising and display, and the solid entrenchment in practically every grocery outlet in the country. There was no doubt that it was a good product. However, the probing consumer interviews revealed several weaknesses. The color was not always uniform, nor was the flavor and consistency. It had a tendency to turn rancid if kept unrefrigerated. Yet when cold it became stiffer and was difficult to mix in doughs. It was not as white as some housewives would have liked, and there were complaints about it not always being evenly packed in the can. Some complaints were even registered that the outside paper wrapper was torn or dirty by the time it reached the housewife. These were not serious weaknesses, due more to careless quality control than anything intrinsic. Yet they represented areas to be capitalized on by an aggressive competitor.

This consumer research guided the technical research people in their product development. They sought to develop a new product free from the limitations of Crisco. No magic formula proved to be needed, no new ingredients. In fact, Spry and Crisco were made from the same raw materials. Only a few minor changes in the manufacturing process were devised, and a more careful quality control established. Various formulations were then matched against Crisco in comparative product tests. Finally, when the formulation was deemed to be ready for production, additional comparative product tests were conducted with housewives to confirm the product advantages of Spry. The resulting product was uniform in every respect. It never turned rancid in the can. It could be left open on the kitchen shelf. It was snow white and had no flavor at all. And it was neatly packed.

Tests, closely monitored by marketing research people, were also conducted to determine the most effective promotional emphasis. Nielsen data was again relied on to develop specific marketing plans for the new product. Since the company had no experience of its own in this product category, it needed information as to what size the initial orders should be and how large retail inventories should be in outlets of different types and sizes to minimize lost sales and match Crisco inventory levels.

By the end of 1935, plans for Spry had been perfected, a further $3 million plant addition was completed, and the attack could begin.

Strategy Implementation

The decision was made to start the offensive in January 1936, and to do so with a burst of efforts rather than waiting for advertising to gradually build demand as was most commonly done at that time. Some $4 million was allocated for promotion and for the most ambitious sampling campaign ever contemplated up to that time. Hundreds of Lever representatives fanned out across the continent, going door-to-door and giving a sales pitch, distributing one-pound sample cans of Spry and a 52-page cookbook with Spry recipes, and in some parts of the country also giving a coupon good for 10 cents toward the purchase of another can of Spry.

By summer, some 10 million pounds of Spry had been placed in one third of all the homes in the United States. In February 1936, a supporting ad campaign was started in small-town newspapers. As the sampling tapered off, a secondary merchandising campaign was developed. Later, Lever maintained contact with consumers through a mobile cooking school and lecture service that operated nationally and was staffed by company home economists. The school moved around the country offering daily two-hour demonstrations and talks on how to use Spry. Cooking classes were promoted, and in model kitchens at Lever's headquarters in Cambridge, Massachusetts, new recipes were tested and competing products were continually analyzed. Lecturers coached by Spry's research department also spoke before cooking classes sponsored by newspapers around the country.

The impact of Spry was phenomenal. In one year, it had already reached half the market share of Crisco, with sales of $12 million. Procter & Gamble reacted vigorously and quickly made improvements in Crisco, particularly increasing its creaminess. The market shares of the two competitors continued to narrow, however, although Crisco's sales began to improve also as the promotional efforts of the two firms expanded the total market by making the general public more shortening conscious.

INGREDIENTS OF SUCCESS

The factors behind the success of Lever's massive attack seem rather obvious. They point to extensive and bold planning, based on careful research, as the answer. This seems almost worth formularizing, but not quite. The factors or ingredients of a successful marketing strategy still must be properly executed. Also, a major environmental condition needs to be present: planning must correctly assess the competitive and consumer-preference environment; furthermore, this environment must not change significantly between the planning of the strategy and its execution. This was the downfall of the ill-fated Edsel venture of two decades later (described in *Marketing Mistakes*)[4] in which extensive planning was used and carried to the extreme of specificity, only to find too late that consumer preferences had shifted dramatically between the research and planning and the final execution.

[4]The Edsel case is described in Robert F. Hartley, *Marketing Mistakes,* 2nd ed. (Columbus, Ohio: Grid, 1981), pp. 115–128.

We can identify these specific elements of Spry's successful planning and implementation:

- Strategic Use of Marketing Research. Such research was perhaps used more thoroughly and at a higher level than ever before by any firm. It enabled Lever to carefully assess competitive weaknesses and develop a product and strategy to capitalize on these weaknesses.
- Mass Sampling. Lever introduced the distribution of free samples on a wider scale than ever before attempted. Previously, most big marketing campaigns had stressed mass media advertising, sometimes accompanied by dealer push efforts, as the key to market entry and dominance. Although Lever did not repudiate advertising, it based its major thrust on the samples distributed door to door. The effectiveness of this mass sampling was enhanced by giving a sample of sufficient size—a one-pound can—a 52-page cookbook crammed with Spry recipes, and a coupon good for a discount on the purchase of another can of Spry. Merely sampling a small container with none of the supplementary items would probably not have had nearly the impact.
- Mass Onslaught. Rather than slowly building up demand, Lever opted for the mass attack, a storming of the citadel. Risks may be increased by such a strategy in that no field testing or experimentation can be carried out and the stakes are high on "one roll of the dice." However, in retrospect we can see, not only the appropriateness but even the necessity of this strategy. It did not give Crisco time to react and improve their product, which could readily have been done, before Spry had gained a major foothold in the market.
- Proper Timing. Lever could have attempted to enter the consumer shortening market at least five years before they did. The temptation was resisted, a restraint that few executives have—to wait for better environmental conditions when there is no assurance that conditions will improve and to devote not only months but years to carefully assessing the market and planning the eventual conquest. But lard and butter prices did rise by the mid-1930s, and this enabled vegetable shortening to be more attractively priced, and increased the chances for success during the lean and price-conscious Depression years. Decades later we can marvel at the tightness of the security regarding Lever's intentions: no word leaked to Procter & Gamble. Or did P&G get such information but refuse to believe that any firm could be audacious enough to attack them?

WHAT CAN BE LEARNED?

The need to move fast before powerful competitors can retaliate or adjust is classically illustrated in this case. Crisco's product was not hard to improve, and certainly Procter & Gamble had the resources and willingness to exert any promotional efforts needed to counter an interloper. Any initial product advantage of Spry could have been dulled very quickly and the market entry of Spry blunted or even denied in some markets had the introductory efforts been slower. A firm sometimes cannot afford the luxury of test markets and extensive trials before going national. Although the risks of product failures may be somewhat increased without such testing, the actions of competitors must be considered. A new product is often not difficult to match by competitors and long introductions invite this.

We have seen that sampling can be a powerful strategy. But let us recognize that it is not a panacea. In the later case of Lestoil, we will see that sampling did not prove to be effective in gaining market entry. We can generalize that sampling is most useful when accompanied by ancillary materials, such as cookbooks or tips for improving cleaning or whatever, coupons, premiums, contests, and the like.

Obviously, the effectiveness of marketing research is suggested by the case. But let us not delude ourselves here either. Just as sampling per se does not guarantee success, neither does the use of marketing research. Numerous examples of marketing mistakes that occurred despite the use of marketing research can be cited (such as the Edsel and DuPont's Corfam, cases described in *Marketing Mistakes*). Although marketing research can improve the batting average of decisions, it does not guarantee the correct decision. Also, it must be timely and carefully done or it may give the illusion of success for a venture that is far from assured and rouse false expectations and overoptimistic commitment.

We see in the invasion of the domain of Crisco what should be a sobering realization by all frontrunners: any entrenched position can be successfully assailed; nothing is invincible and forever. The executives of a dominant firm might well shudder at how quickly Crisco's market share was lost. But could this happen today, 50 years later? Why not? Competition and the environment are not too much different today. Hungry and aggressive competitors are still around and even more numerous in many industries. Marketing tools and techniques have been more sharply honed. Research techniques are more sophisticated, and we certainly have more powerful advertising media available today than in 1936.

Finally, this case shows the danger of complacency for the long-dominant firm. In such a situation, the temptation is to scorn the smaller competitors as representing no threat now or in the future. A firm can lull itself into not keeping attuned to customer dissatisfactions and slacken its efforts to maintain rigid quality control and performance standards. It may permit its service to slip. Thirty years ago, Richard Crisp noted that a product that has shortcomings of which its users are aware is inherently and inescapably vulnerable to a competitive challenge.[5]

Many firms today, whether market leaders or not, fail to keep attuned to

[5]Crisp, *Marketing Research,* p. 562.

customers' satisfactions and dissatisfactions. They equate sales and market-share results with customer satisfaction. Yet these lack sensitivity because many other determinants, such as environmental elements, quality of competition, and economic factors, affect sales and market share. Such data give no indication of the degree of satisfaction: Are customers strongly pleased, or merely tolerant of the product and buy it because of the effort involved in switching or because no good alternatives are available? Also, sales results tend to lag behind changes in customer satisfaction.

Most direct feedback from customers that reaches the ears of responsible executives comes from occasional letters of complaint. Such feedback is fragmentary at best; it is seldom representative of most customer attitudes because it comes from a vocal minority of customers most difficult to satisfy (or most desperate to have a product or service deficiency corrected). Other dissatisfied customers simply take future business elsewhere. For most firms new customers offset the loss of old customers, and this can disguise the full seriousness of business erosion.

What is the answer to obtaining better feedback on customer satisfaction and any vulnerability in this area? The answer would seem to lie in systematic research—on dealers and sales representatives and on customers. Customer attitude surveys, in particular, ought to be done periodically, to detect any emerging problem areas, and also to foster customer goodwill. Simply to assume, as Crisco did, that because sales and profits are steady customer satisfaction is at a high level may be complacent in the extreme.

Questions

1. Discuss and evaluate other alternatives Lever might have used in introducing Spry.
2. Could Spry's marketing research have been successful without the use of such newly offered syndicated services as Nielsen? Why or why not?

Invitation to Role Play

You are a staff assistant to the general manager of P&G's Crisco operation. It has come to your attention that Lever is planning to enter the shortening market against Crisco. As persuasively as you can, present a specific proposal for protecting the position of Crisco and thwarting Lever's imminent attack.

PART Three

POST-WORLD WAR II: MARKETING STRATEGIES SHAPED TO A BOOMING ECONOMY AND A HIGHLY COMPETITIVE ENVIRONMENT

After World War II, with its drastic restraints on consumer goods and on expansion of business facilities (because these were nonessential to the war effort), a pent-up demand and a rush by business firms to tap this demand was hardly unexpected. However, the demand exceeded expectations, with much higher family incomes than in previous decades and burgeoning consumer needs and wants. The market had suddenly become much bigger and competitors more numerous. But we find the same competitive struggles as in other decades. As we would expect, marketing tools have become more sophisticated and a major new media, television, has developed and become a dominant force in mass-media advertising.

Marketing research has made further substantial progress since its major advances in the 1930s. Now we find operations research and similar quantitative techniques, some of which were developed during the war for the military, coming into commercial use. Such mathematical techniques, despite their early promise, were not very practical for typical marketing problems except for inventory control, routing and scheduling of salespeople, and warehouse locations. But another side of marketing research—a qualitative perspective—also gained ascendancy during this period. This was motivation research in which consumer motives and attitudes were probed by various psychological techniques, such as depth interviewing, to shed light on hidden feelings, drives, and preferences that might be exploited by those marketers who could understand such inputs for their decision making. But motivation research was also found lacking, despite wild enthusiasm for it in the late 1950s, except for exploratory studies, and some advertising and packaging appeals research.

Research and the entire discipline of marketing were enriched by two developments during this period: (1) emergence of consumer behavior as a fertile field of interest and study, and relevant to this, (2) the recognition that marketing could draw on other disciplines, such as psychology, sociology, and even anthropology, to better understand the marketplace and its consumers. The interdisciplinary perspective of marketing and the unraveling of the mysteries of buyer behavior continue to this day. Yet, the success factors during this time are not much different from in earlier years. Marketing, for all its more sophisticated tools, most of which afford more promise than actuality, still resists being set to a formula and becoming a science instead of an art.

We examine three cases during this period of roughly 1945 to 1960. One is the Pepsi-Cola Company, which at the beginning of this period was a desperately ailing concern, hardly worthy to stand in the shadow of the mighty Coca-Cola. But in the space of just a few years, with an aggressive and integrated marketing strategy, the company was completely turned around, until even Coca-Cola had cause to fear it. The second case involves a gnat of a company trying to gain a small toehold on supermarket shelves, alongside the likes of Procter & Gamble and Lever Bros., with its unknown but superior detergent. Lestoil's struggle to gain market entry continued for decades. Eventually, television enabled it to not only gain market entry but be a considerable success.

The last case involves another revolutionary retail institutional change reminiscent of the supermarket ''revolution'' of two decades earlier—the discount store. One of the very earliest discounters, and one who in just a few years became the mightiest of them all, was Eugene Ferkauf and his Korvette. But success proved ephemeral for him, not because his ideas or strategy were deficient, but because his execution as the organization grew larger was sadly lacking.

CHAPTER 7

Pepsi-Cola in the 1950s: A Competitive Resurgence

The marketing savvy and dominance of Coca-Cola left precious little room for a struggling competitor. It seemed audacious to expect any other firm to be able to wrest market share from the industry leader who had not only an unparalleled name and international acceptance, but the massive resources that had accumulated from success over the decades. By the 1950s, however, after some fits and starts, Pepsi was able to obtain a beachhead and expand on it. Interestingly, the man who was instrumental in this was a former Coca-Cola executive, Alfred N. Steele.

THE EARLY YEARS OF PEPSI

The start of the Pepsi-Cola Company was not greatly different from that of Coca-Cola. It also was a product of the new South arising after the Civil War. Caleb Bradham, a North Carolina pharmacist, developed a soft drink that became popular with his customers. The taste was derived from sugar, vanilla, oils, spices, and the kola nut. It was called ''Brad's Drink,'' and was intended to relieve dyspepsia (upset stomach) and peptic ulcers. But in 1893 Bradham changed its name to Pepsi-Cola, and in 1902 incorporated the Pepsi-Cola Company with the backroom of his drugstore as its headquarters. By 1904 Bradham had moved to larger quarters and was now using a franchise system similar to that of Coca-Cola to market Pepsi in bottles as well as in syrup form.

The fledgling Pepsi-Cola Company had a checkered existence. Bradham's sales continued to climb until World War I, when rationing of sugar caused severe production cutbacks. Then after the war Bradham speculated unwisely with sugar, having stockpiled in order to hedge against rising costs, only to see the cost of sugar plummet. By 1923 Pepsi-Cola was bankrupt and its assets were sold to a North Carolina holding company.

A few years later the Pepsi name, formula, and goodwill were purchased by Wall Street interests. But with the Depression of the 1930s, Pepsi went bankrupt again. Once more the company was salvaged by outside investors, but sales languished until the decision to offer Pepsi in a 12-ounce bottle (versus 6½ oz for Coca-Cola) and still sell it for a nickel. During these hard times, the theme, "twice as much for a nickel," caught on quickly and sales quadrupled in the next few years. Pepsi's appeal was primarily to the poor, and this appeal was strengthened not only by the greater value offered but also by a plain bottle with a "cheap" paper label. The image conveyed was low-quality bargain, but with mass unemployment such an image appealed to many.

By the beginning of World War II the deficiencies of Pepsi's second-class image were apparent to top management. In an effort to impart more of a quality image without sacrificing the greater value connotation, a new theme was widely trumpeted: "More bounce to the ounce." The War spurred sales of both Coca-Cola and Pepsi as the soft drinks followed the troops around the world. During the war, Pepsi passed Royal Crown Cola, Dr. Pepper, and the rest of the industry to become second in sales only to Coca-Cola. Its bottle sales were about one third those of Coke, although it was badly beaten in fountain sales. Further domestic growth could be expected through population increases, and Pepsi executives were optimistic that Pepsi would continue to gain market share against Coke. The international arena also looked promising, although Coca-Cola admittedly was making strong inroads there.

Alas, Pepsi had problems in dissociating itself from the "poor man's drink." The slogan, "More bounce to the ounce," and its successors did not quite convey the image of quality that Pepsi needed. And Coca-Cola remained unassailable in the soda fountain business. Furthermore, after the war Pepsi was badly hit by inflation—the rising costs of sugar, labor, and other expenses—which made it unprofitable to sell the 12-ounce bottle for a nickel. The price was raised to six cents, and then to seven cents, and the promotional efforts of Pepsi lost their punch. From 1946 to 1949, sales leveled off at $45 million, while earnings dropped 70 percent. Now Coke outsold Pepsi by five to one. Table 7.1 shows the sales and profits of Pepsi and Coca-Cola and their relative market shares from 1941 to 1950.

Along with market share, the morale of the company and its bottlers sank at the end of the 1940s. Confronted with the heady success and market dominance of Coca-Cola, the very viability of Pepsi was in danger. But a savior came on the scene, a man destined to rejuvenate Pepsi not only to hold its own but even to outfight the market leader.

Table 7.1 Sales and Profits and Relative Market Shares, Pepsi and Coca-Cola 1941–1950

	1941	*1945*	*1950*
Coca-Cola			
Net sales (thousands of dollars)	128,158	148,621	215,248
Operating profit (thousands of dollars)	57,076	41,724	55,673
Relative market share versus Pepsi (%)	77.6	77.5	84.3
Pepsi-Cola			
Net sales (thousands of dollars)	37,527	43,141	40,173
Operating profit (thousands of dollars)	15,004	10,858	2,948
Relative market share versus Coca-Cola (%)	22.4	22.7	15.7

Source: Compiled from company annual reports and Moody's.

ALFRED N. STEELE

Al Steele came to Pepsi in 1949 as first vice-president in charge of U.S. sales and operations. A better man to lead the faltering company could hardly have been found. Latent problems by now had surfaced with a vengeance: poor image, a taste too sweet for many, uninspired packaging, uncertain quality control, and a defeatist attitude among both company executives and bottlers. Steele had years of experience in the soft-drink industry, including an important stint with mighty Coca-Cola itself. He was tough-talking, flamboyant, a showman. Indeed, he began his career by running a circus, and the flair for hoopla led him naturally into advertising. He joined D'Arcy, the ad agency that for more than 40 years had serviced the Coca-Cola account. With his expertise in marketing and advertising, he jumped to vice-president at Coke. ''Steele could talk the horns off a brass bull,'' said one Coke executive.[1]

Steele's abrasive personality proved incompatible with the staid and conservative style of Coca-Cola headquarters, and particularly irritated Robert Woodruff, the long-time head of Coke. Steele soon found his career at Coke in limbo. At this point, Walter Mack, the top man at Pepsi who had engineered its temporary successes in the 1930s and early 1940s, enticed Steele to come to Pepsi for $85,000 a year, plus stock options. As an added attraction, Steele brought with him some 15 of Coke's key management people, including several from the marketing research department.

By 1950, as can be seen from Table 7.1, conditions at Pepsi had worsened, and Steele demanded and got complete control. The directors moved Mack to board chairman and elected Steele president over Mack's objections. Mack resigned a few

[1] J. C. Louis and Harvey Z. Yazijian, *The Cola Wars* (New York: Everest House, 1980), p. 80.

months later, unable to get along with the new leadership and with the man he had only recently hired. Now Steele was free to mold the Pepsi Company as he saw fit and seek revenge on Coca-Cola and Robert Woodruff.

THE REBIRTH OF PEPSI

In his nine years as president of Pepsi, Steele accomplished a complete facelifting. An inefficient and lackluster operation was revamped and rejuvenated in a multi-faceted marketing strategy. As a first step, in order to improve the weak cash position and to obtain seed money for the aggressive moves he envisioned, Steele shut down or sold the old money-draining operations. A packaging experiment with cans was stopped. The bottle-cap manufacturing operation was liquidated. A Cuban sugar plantation had been acquired during the war to supply this essential commodity that was becoming scarce at that time. But conditions were different by 1950, and its sale for $6 million contributed greatly to Pepsi's liquidity and increased its line of credit.

Distributor Relations

In his first message to shareholders in 1950, Steele focused attention on dealer relations. He reaffirmed the company's intent to establish a better relationship and emphasized the importance of this to the profitability of both parties. He followed such words with positive actions. Previously, Pepsi's management had been concentrated in New York City, and communication often suffered in other areas of the country. Steele decentralized leadership into eight districts so as to foster closer contact with local bottlers. Training programs for bottlers and their sales personnel were conducted in each region, and assistance for any bottler problems was quickly available.

Steele also moved to centralize Pepsi's promotional program, rather than continue the loosely coordinated efforts of the past in which dealers independently promoted Pepsi in their own areas. He standardized Pepsi trucks, logo, and signs, as well as the bottles. Bottlers were urged to upgrade their bottling and distribution facilities and were promised the aid of the parent company if needed. Some of the bottling plants were company-owned, and these Steele used to set an example with some $38 million invested in new plants and equipment during his first five years as president. "You can conserve yourself into bankruptcy," he told the dealers, "or you can spend your way to prosperity."[2]

The Product

In the past, the taste of Pepsi had been marginal; perhaps even worse, it was inconsistent from bottler to bottler, who added varying levels of carbonation to the

[2]Ibid., p. 82.

syrup. The result was that customers could never be sure just what taste a Pepsi would have. Steele ordered the formula changed by reducing the sugar content, to give more appealing flavor. To ensure that the drink was bottled consistently, mobile laboratories were established to roam the country sampling the quality of product put out by the local bottlers. The home office lab was also upgraded. Training and refresher courses were conducted at the regional offices on the blending and quality control of the product. In search of better quality control techniques, a joint venture with RCA resulted in the development of an automated bottle inspector capable of processing 150 bottles per minute.

The old bottle of the 1930s and 1940s had rugged straight sides and big block lettering on a glue-on paper label. This was changed. Steele's new bottle was sleeker, had a distinctive swirl pattern and a baked-on label with subdued lettering in place of the glue-on label.

Promotional Efforts to Change the Image

The old image of Pepsi had been that of a low-quality product, at least in comparison with Coca-Cola. This image was appealing enough during the stark Depression days, but times had changed; employment and income were up for vast sectors of the American market. Steele determined to upgrade the image through advertising. Very quickly the "Twice as much . . ." theme was dropped. Now advertising featured Pepsi being consumed by well-dressed people in affluent surroundings. Initially a theme, "More bounce to the ounce," was tried, but Steele was not satisfied with this. Then in 1952 a new theme was introduced: "The light refreshment," "Satisfying without filling." Young, slim men and women were pictured. The objective was to lend class to Pepsi, but there was also the indirect suggestion that the competitor, Coke, was "heavy."

Promotional Efforts to Gain Dealer Push

If the aggressive strategy of Steele was to achieve maximum effectiveness, cooperation and strong push actions by bottlers were necessary. The first moves to improve dealer relations had already been made. Now Steele wanted to spur his bottlers and salespeople to greater efforts. He chose 25 cities for special promotion to win market share. Company funds were added to those of local bottlers in order to provide more advertising resources. To win new retailers, he instituted a "Guaranteed Profit Concept," whereby Pepsi would be offered to dealers on a 30-day trial basis. All stock would be bought back if a dealer was not satisfied.[3] (See the following Information Sidelight for a perspective on the ultimate incentives to dealers to stock a particular product.)

Success with these selected markets helped convince other bottlers of what

[3] "Guaranteed Profits for Retailers," *Printers' Ink,* July 4, 1951, pp. 26ff.

could be achieved with more aggressive efforts. In 1955, Pepsi's annual ad budget, including the bottlers' share, was $14 million out of total soft-drink industry expenditures of $80 million.

INFORMATION SIDELIGHT

The Ultimate Incentives to Dealers to Stock a Particular Product

A new firm, or an established firm such as Pepsi, in attempting to market its particular brand, frequently faces problems in getting dealers to handle its goods. The more aggressive dealers already have strong relationships with established producers and are naturally reluctant to take on distribution for a competitive brand, and one not as well known and salable. The manufacturer in such a dilemma may be forced to offer dealers such inducements as consignment or guaranteed sales:

Consignment means that the manufacturer keeps title of the goods until they are sold by the dealer, thereby bearing all the risks and inventory costs.

Guaranteed sales is similar to consignment in that anything unsold or selling too slowly in the opinion of the dealer can be returned to the vendor. The difference is that the dealers take title or ownership when the goods are placed in their stock, thereby committing funds for inventory and assuming such risks as fire and flood damage.

The Market

Demand for soft drinks is primarily concentrated in two markets: the ''on-premise'' market, and the ''take-home'' market. The on-premise market was composed of soda fountain, vending machine, and refrigerated sales such as take place at sporting events. Coca-Cola was particularly strong in the on-premise market. But Steele saw a trend toward at-home consumption. He sought to get Pepsi into America's living rooms. The old 12-ounce bottle was ideal for this, although it was often too filling for the on-premise trade of popcorn, peanut, and hot dog vendors. Steele therefore initially sought to expand Pepsi's foothold in grocery retail sales; he introduced still larger bottles, as well as ''family sizes'' and achieved reasonable success with this.

By 1955 Steele mounted an offensive against Coke in the ''on-premise'' market. He introduced other sizes of Pepsi, particularly an eight-ounce bottle. He also offered to finance bottlers who were willing to buy and install Pepsi vending machines, and this part of the business expanded nicely. The only market that Steele left unassailed was the soda fountain business, which he saw as declining, with Coke possibly too strongly entrenched to be uprooted.

REACTION OF COCA-COLA

As Pepsi began increasing its strength and aggressiveness, Coca-Cola did virtually nothing different. Not until 1955, five years after Steele had begun his transformation, did Coca-Cola finally recognize Pepsi as a competitor. The evidence was becoming indisputable. In 1954, Coke's sales had fallen by $8 million from the previous year and profits had also shrunk 8 percent. Meanwhile, Pepsi's sales rose 12 percent, while profits jumped almost 25 percent.

The conservatism of Coca-Cola over the years was evident even in its packaging. Since 1916, the only way a customer could buy a coke, outside of a soda fountain, was in the small 6½-ounce bottle. Meanwhile the larger bottles of Pepsi were becoming more and more appealing to the take-home market. Yet, more than 6 billion of the 6½-ounce bottles had been used through the years, and the Coke bottle could almost stand with the flag, the baseball, and the hot dog as a symbol of the American way of life.

With such a tradition and symbolism, both bottlers and corporate executives resisted any change in the bottle. Finally, in 1955 the decision was made to introduce 10- and 12-ounce bottles, as well as a 26-ouncer aimed directly at the take-home market. When Coke finally introduced its larger bottles, Pepsi gloated in an ad: "Now another well-known Cola is bringing out a big bottle. This is gratifying to us . . . It's fun to be followed—to be recognized as the leader."

Coke's advertising themes in the 1950s left something to be desired. The 1953 themes were "The refreshment of friends," and "Drive safely—drive refreshed." In 1954 Coke tried the slogan "Have a Coke and be happy." "America's preferred taste," and "almost everyone appreciates the best," were used in 1955, now openly admitting that there was more than one cola. In 1955, after decades of collaboration with the D'Arcy agency, the account was shifted to McCann-Erickson, a worldwide firm that had been doing some advertising for Coke's international division.

In 1957 the so-called Taj Mahal campaign was instituted. Since Coke was consumed all over the world, a dramatic campaign showed Coke consumed in various exotic places—by Indians, by Turks, by Africans, all in their native settings, such as the Taj Mahal, the Great Pyramids, and Constantinople. But the expensive campaign seemed to miss the mark; Pepsi enjoyed its biggest sales increase in over a decade and the campaign was abandoned.

Among the subsequent campaigns were "Be really refreshed," and "No wonder Coke refreshes best," again, themes subtly admitting to competition. While Coca-Cola attempted to regain its composure, Pepsi had seen its sales tripling from 1950 to 1958, during which the industry as a whole increased only 30 percent. Coca-Cola management had referred to Pepsi only as the "imitator" in the 1940s; now it was forced to view Pepsi as the "competitor," or (under its breath) as the "enemy." Table 7.2 shows the change in sales, profits, and relative market share of Coca-Cola and Pepsi for the years 1951 to 1959.

Table 7.2 Sales and Profits and Relative Market Shares for Pepsi and Coca-Cola, 1951–1959

	1951	*1952*	*1953*	*1954*	*1955*	*1957*	*1959*
Coca-Cola							
Sales (thousands of dollars)	225,655	245,639	251,238	243,265	252,883	296,796	342,257
Profits (thousands of dollars)	58,298	60,281	60,181	55,374	59,264	66,316	79,107
Relative market share versus Pepsi (%)	83.0	82.2	79.2	76.7	74.1	71.2	68.4
Pepsi-Cola							
Sales (thousands of dollars)	46,759	53,298	66,107	74,200	88,971	120,331	157,769
Profits (thousands of dollars)	3,970	7,770	11,142	12,992	18,361	19,308	30,857
Relative market share versus Coca-Cola (%)	17.0	17.8	21.8	23.3	25.9	28.8	31.6

Sources: Compiled from company annual reports and Moody's.

STEELE, AGAIN

Steele was elected chairman of the board in 1955. Since 1950 he had continually urged his bottlers to expand their advertising efforts and this was notably successful. By 1959 they were contributing two thirds of Pepsi's $30 million advertising budget. The advertising continued to stress quality, and emphasized modernity in contrast to the more nostalgic themes of Coca-Cola. From Table 7.2 you can see the market gains of Pepsi compared to Coca-Cola. By 1959, Pepsi had almost 30 percent of the total domestic soft-drink market.

Steele's efforts to tap the on-premises market, particularly the vending machine sector of it, was paying off handsomely. He had persuaded the bottlers to invest $15 million annually in vending machines, and by 1959 sales through vending machines had doubled and now accounted for 11 percent of total business.

Competition was also intense in overseas markets. Previously, Coca-Cola had been content to develop foreign markets at a slow and deliberate pace. Now with Pepsi chomping just behind, a frenzied effort commenced to build bottling plants all over the world. By 1959 Coke had 647 foreign bottling plants; Pepsi had 237 foreign plants, whereas a decade earlier it had had only 67. Foreign sales now accounted for half of Pepsi's total revenue.

In 1955, Steele married film idol, Joan Crawford. She relished the idea of being the company's first lady, and complemented Steele's showy style and promotional hoopla. Perhaps nowhere was this better exhibited than with bottler relations. The opening of a new plant would trigger a promotional extravaganza, with Crawford drawing bottlers from all over the region for the event. Robert Windt, a Pepsi public relations man, describes Steele's approach:

> Every time a Pepsi bottler did anything in terms of an expansion, it became a "plant opening." . . . the local bottler would be king for a day. By the time the week was over, there was nobody in that market area who didn't know that there was a spanking-new, clean Pepsi-Cola plant that was putting money into the community and getting jobs. Even for the blessing of the plant there would be a rabbi or a priest. We pulled out all the stops.[4]

And when Joan Crawford came on the scene, she dazzled the bottlers and their wives by calling them by their first names and conveying the glamor that only the leading lady of Hollywood could convey. The enthusiasm was contagious, and many a visiting bottler, swept up by the events, would make plans himself for new facilities and thus have his own prestigious reopening.

On April 17, 1959, Steele was inaugurated as the new national chairman of the multiple sclerosis campaign. The outgoing chairman was Senator John F. Kennedy. The last photos of Steele alive were taken with the young senator from Mas-

[4]As reported in Louis and Yazijian, *The Cola Wars*, p. 91.

sachusetts. For on that same day, Steele passed away, at the age of 48, from a heart attack. He had not only saved the Pepsi Company, but he had made it into a dynamic and aggressive enterprise, that now could seriously challenge Coca-Cola. The gains achieved by Steele in his nine years were solid, and his successors were able to continue them.

INGREDIENTS OF SUCCESS

The successful Pepsi offensive against Coca-Cola illustrates the impact of an integrated and comprehensive marketing strategy involving almost all aspects of the marketing mix.

- The product was improved in taste, consistency, and not the least, packaging (i.e., the bottle).
- The target market of the 1930s and 1940s—the poor—was shifted to cater to the growing and affluent middle class. The improved package and a different theme and advertising conveyed the new target. A relatively untapped target market that had great growth potential, the take-home market, was recognized and efforts were made to tap it well before Coca-Cola did. Also, the vending machine market segment was quickly catered to, again beating Coca-Cola to the punch.
- The image of the product was changed to be compatible with the new target market sought. The staid, second-class, bargain image was completely spurned in the advertising and in the more quality-connoting bottle.
- Distribution was greatly improved as bottler and dealer relations were given priority attention. Steele recognized the need for a mutuality of goals of bottlers and the parent corporation. He was extremely successful in gaining dealer cooperation in maintaining quality control, obtaining additional investment in facilities, and assuming a strong role in the advertising of Pepsi. With a blend of hoopla, strong recognition of dealer contributions, and a ready commitment of company funds in support of dealer activities, relations with other members of the channel were exemplary.
- Although much of the success of Pepsi must be attributed to shrewd promotion, this really merely reinforced the strong efforts with the other aspects of the marketing mix. The advertising was successful in changing the image and the theme, "the light refreshment," certainly conveyed the desired image—one that was in harmony with the sentiments of the general public in the 1950s. The inability of Coca-Cola to match the modernity of Pepsi advertising appeals helped.

All these elements of the strategy were harmonious with each other. It is doubtful that the use of one or two of these efforts, in the absence of the others, would have been effective.

WHAT CAN BE LEARNED?

A large and powerful firm which has maintained this position over some decades, creates an awesome sense of invincibility among its competitors. Yet, we have seen in this, as in other, cases that even at the height of its power, a firm can be bearded by the aggressive, shrewd, and undismayed competitor. Specifically, this is what we can learn from this confrontation of three decades ago:

- No firm is invulnerable to competition, no matter how well entrenched, the duration of the dominance, the extent of the resources, or the completeness of the market share. Complaceny tends to develop, conservatism to hold sway, and the strong inclination is to stay wedded to the traditional, the "way we have always done it." In this case, as Pepsi began making its aggressive moves, for some years Coca-Cola did virtually nothing different. This is the typical reaction of such dominant firms when confronted with a small interloper: they tend to write them off, to be unconcerned and assured of their own invincibility. Both the company founders and the bottlers had grown rich and complacent. Actually by now, second- and third-generation sons were mostly in control, and their interests were diluted by commitments to civic activities, art collecting, and other nonbusiness activities. But this helps create the pervasive flaw and vulnerability of dominant and successful enterprises.
- This is another case showing the power of mass media advertising—and its limitations. Here advertising gained worldwide acceptance for both Coke and Pepsi. It convinced generations throughout the world that the product was useful—and even essential—for their well-being. Yet, it afforded only a pleasant taste and a slight caffeine buzz. Image sold these products. It identified these brownish colored drinks with cherished values and institutions and coveted life-styles. We have seen how the right slogan or theme can have a powerful appeal. But a wrong or a mediocre theme or slogan may be impotent, despite millions spent for its promotion. The Taj Mahal and some of the other themes of Coca-Cola during its struggle in the 1950s exemplifies this.
- The importance of dealer/bottler relations is epitomized in Pepsi's efforts with its bottlers. Its dealers were motivated to contribute heavily to advertising, expansion of vending machines, geographical expansion through new plants, maintaining strict quality control, and so on. This is an example of a symbiotic relationship, in which parties work together for mutual advantage, carried to the ideal.
- Finally, we have to be impressed by the speed with which a faltering operation can be turned around. In only two years, from 1950 to 1952, Steele more than doubled profits; in five years he increased profits sixfold; in nine years, tenfold. We are brought to the realization that an aggressive

shift of marketing strategy can accomplish wonders. Of course, we cannot always be sure that a drastic shift is the right move, or which drastic shift is best to make. But sometimes the deficiencies of the present operation are so obvious, and the untapped opportunities in the marketplace so evident, that success seems almost ensured if a firm is willing to make a major change, with all the organizational trauma this involves.

Questions

1. List as many ways as you can that Pepsi (or any consumer-goods manufacturer) might gain more dealer push. Which of these are more desirable for the newer or weaker manufacturer? Which would you recommend for the more strongly entrenched firm?
2. Do you think Steele was wise to leave the soda fountain business of Coca-Cola unchallenged? Why or why not?

Invitation to Role Play

You are the bottler relations manager for the Midwest Region. Steele has ordered strenuous efforts to persuade bottlers to invest in the vending machine market. To date, vending machine operations in the Midwest are lagging behind those of the rest of the United States. How would you improve this situation?

CHAPTER 8

Lestoil: Battling the Giants to Gain Market Entry

We are all rather intrigued by confrontations that pit the lowliest underdog against powerful competitors. Almost without exception we root for the underdog and feel a great sense of satisfaction on those occasions—usually few—when the nose of the high and mighty can be tweaked. In this case we have one of the finest examples in history of such an underdog success. This did not come easy, however, despite the underdog's superior product. But such perseverance and overcoming of adversity and great odds makes Lestoil's success all the more satisfying.

JACOB BAROWSKY

Jacob Barowsky was born in Russia but came to the United States at an early age. He was raised in Holyoke, Massachusetts, and went to Harvard where he majored in philosophy. He worked at paper jobbing, metal goods manufacturing, and real estate before going into the dry cleaning business in Holyoke. It was then that he encountered first-hand some of the deficiencies of the available cleaning agents. For years, Barowsky and chemist John Tulenko experimented trying to come up with a formula to overcome some of the tougher cleaning problems. Finally, they found a way to make oil miscible in water. Barowsky mixed the first batch of what was to be called Lestoil in a baby's bathtub. It was the first liquid synthetic detergent. The name itself, Lestoil, was derived in part from the names of his three children: *L*enore, *E*dith, and *S*eymour.

In 1933 Jacob began this little family business, which he named the Adell

Chemical Company, after his wife, Adeline. With one assistant to help with the mixing, he went out to sell the new concoction, first to commercial laundries and dry cleaners, and then to paper and textile mills, the lithographic and automotive trades, and for maintenance cleaning in such places as factories, stores, and a variety of other buildings. Although these industrial sales were steady, they were certainly far from spectacular: for the first two decades of the company, sales did not exceed $250,000 a year.

World War II caused Barowsky to change his perspective. Severe shortages of soap materials because of the war effort suggested an opportunity to tap the consumer market. But this was not easily done, despite Barowsky's realization that heavy promotional efforts would be necessary to gain entry into this market. It took eight years of expensive and frustrating trial and error against the powerful competitors who dominated grocery store shelf space.

For 13-week periods in Holyoke (with long lapses between) Barowsky tried the following tactics:

1. Many small newspaper ads to dominate the paper, and large newspaper ads to dominate the page, including full-page ads.
2. Several radio spots per week on the best stations.
3. A 15-minute radio newscast each Sunday.
4. A daily offer of $5 to the first housewife in whose home Lestoil was found.
5. Couponing and house-to-house sampling (housewives often refused to take the samples).
6. A few TV station identification commercials per week and for a relatively short period.[1]

By 1953 industrial sales had crept up to $450,000 a year, but there were few sales to consumers, and for these Barowsky was spending $3 in merchandise samples and advertising for every $1 in sales. He decided to give one last, expensive push before giving up the effort and recognizing the invincibility of the goliath competitors, Procter & Gamble and Lever Bros., and their control over grocer shelf space.

SUCCESS, AT LAST

As his last effort, Barowsky decided to try a TV blitz, in one market area only, in the home town of Holyoke, Massachusetts, and use spot TV on one station, WHYN-TV. He contracted for 30 one-minute commercials a week to run for a year at $200 a week, thus gaining a volume discount. The spot commercials ran at

[1]Lawrence M. Hughes, "Spot TV in Four Years Sends Lestoil Soaring 56,000%," *Sales Management*, Feb. 21, 1958, pp. 48–52.

nonprime times so as to keep costs within the firm's limited resources. A Holyoke bank was persuaded to back up this year's contract with the station if it became necessary. Four years later, Boston and New York City banks were eager to offer Barowsky unlimited credit.

The saturation and the continuity of the commercials began to pay off. The last roll of the dice at long last just might produce a winner, Jacob must have thought. And wonderfully, within three months revenue had risen sufficiently that Jacob felt encouraged to add three more TV stations and markets: in the Springfield area, in New Britain, Connecticut, and in New Haven, Connecticut. The same strategy was used, and the results were similar, as Jacob could soon elatedly realize. Within a year, the market-by-market conquest of New England had begun.

Barowsky and his employees wrote the commercials, which told about Lestoil in jingle form. The early filmed commercials cost only about $500 each, plus $1000 for animation. Barowsky was more concerned about quantity of commercials than quality, although he did want to convey the truth about the product with no exaggerations—credibility he saw as essential. Therefore, in commercials showing a housewife using Lestoil to remove crayon marks from a wall, he used actual crayon marks and showed that one swipe of the cloth was not sufficient, but several wipes were necessary, and eventually the crayon marks were removed. He continued to make annual contracts with stations, thereby obtaining the maximum quantity discounts.

By the second year of the TV blitz, Barowsky was spending $3847 a week for between 9 and 30 spots on each of 12 New England TV stations, plus $1243 a week for 25 to 50 spots on each of 15 radio stations in those areas.[2] Providence, Rhode Island, was the biggest expenditure to that time, with $75,000, and Boston was attacked with a $150,000 budget that started in March 1956. Capturing the Boston market was Barowsky's ultimate aim. But his goals were rising, and New York City was tempting. His advisers warned against it, however, because of the costs involved.

Barowsky yielded to temptation when one station, WRCA-TV, offered him two spots for the price of one. In June 1956 commercials started on that station at $2800 a week. By October Lestoil was being heavily promoted on six of New York's seven TV stations at a rate of $16,000 a week, or $832,000 a year.

New markets were gained from New England to the Midwest to the South, and even to Puerto Rico. With each new market area Barowsky used the same strategy:

1. He required a representative of the station to come to Holyoke to negotiate the contract. He wanted the station to know the firm and its business philosophy so that there would be a more knowledgeable mutuality of interest.

[2]As reported in "TV in 10 Years Transforms America," *Sales Management*, Nov. 20, 1955, pp. 63–64.

2. Advertising time was purchased from each station in the new area.
3. Advertising was commenced some months before Lestoil was to be introduced to the stores in order to develop strong pull demand by the consumers in each area.

Barowsky lured grocers into purchasing Lestoil. As soon as the television advertising began, one of the company salespeople visited the store and left samples with the proprietor. No pressure was used at all, but a card was left in case the grocer should decide to buy at a later date. With the impact of the television commercials, customers were clamoring for Lestoil, and the grocers themselves would seek the product. To make carrying Lestoil more attractive to these dealers, they were offered a 26 percent profit margin, and fair-traded (nondiscounted) prices were insisted on.

The results of these market-by-market campaigns were phenomenal. By 1958 production had increased to 2.3 million bottles per week—66 times the production of only two years before. Over 50 percent of all detergent business had been captured. Table 8.1 shows the sales figures during those glorious years.

Barowsky plowed practically everything back into the business. He automated the production in order to provide for the increased demand. In 1959 the product line was expanded to include Lestare, a dry bleach, and plans were in the making for a hand cleaner.

Advertising themes ranged from heavy-duty laundering to cleaning white sidewall tires and paint brushes; from making spring cleaning easier for mother to easing outside spring chores for the "man of the house."

By the late 1950s, the smallish Adell Chemical Company was spending more for advertising its single product than such firms as Philip Morris, American Tobacco, Coca-Cola, Pepsi-Cola, Anheuser-Busch, Schlitz, National Biscuit, Kellogg, Ford Motor, Shell, Esso, Bristol-Myers, and Gillette were spending for any one of their products.

Table 8.1 Sales of Lestoil, 1955–1959

Year	*Sales (in dollars)*
1955	500,000
1956	1,650,000
1957	7,220,000
1958	20,000,000
1959	24,500,000

Source: As reported in "Lestoil: The Road Back," Business Week, June 15, 1963, pp. 118–119.

Barowsky did not believe in "forcing" distribution. By 1959 his product was being promoted by 7000 commercials a week on 230 TV stations. The consumer demand thus generated was practically irresistible to dealers. But Barowsky also included dealer incentives of rapid turnover and high profit margins. He provided examples of dealers who were able to turn over their stock every week, which meant that a very small investment in Lestoil could produce big sales. Furthermore, the per-unit profit margin on Lestoil made it one of the higher profit items in supermarkets, and in some stores it could be demonstrated that Lestoil was providing one third of the profit of the entire soap department.[3]

INTENSIFIED COMPETITION AND THE DECLINE OF LESTOIL

In 1958 the giants of the cleaning industry finally began to react to Lestoil. Each came out with its own liquid detergent:

Procter & Gamble's Mr. Clean
Colgate's Genie
Lever Bros.' Handy Andy
S. C. Johnson's Bravo
Texize Chemical's Texize

Each used a television strategy similar to that of Lestoil. Fringe television time was bought at lowest rates, 52-week contracts were signed for volume discounts, and 10 to 30 spots per week were used to ensure saturation. In 1958 this advertising was minimal compared to Lestoil, but the competitors were rapidly catching up, as shown in Table 8.2.

About this time Barowsky was deviating somewhat from his initially successful strategy. Television advertising rates had been jacked up and now he felt he could no longer enjoy the exposure he once had. He cut back some on the TV spot advertising and shifted more of his expenditures to radio and newspaper advertising. However, this did not prove to be as effective as the extensive television commercials.

At first, Barowsky was not overly concerned about the entry of competitors into his market. It even seemed that primary demand had been stimulated and that people had become more cleaning-conscious and were cleaning more than ever before, so that total market sales were increasing nicely to the benefit of all competitors. However, by the end of 1959, market share for Lestoil began to slip, as shown in Table 8.3. In particular, the tremendous resources of Procter & Gamble began to tell.

[3]"Lestoil Keeps on Growing Among 'Ganged-up Goliaths,'" *Sales Management,* Dec. 18, 1959, pp. 57–59.

Table 8.2 Television Advertising of Lestoil and Competitors, 1958–1959

Company and Product	*Advertising Expenditures* 1958	1959
Adell—Lestoil	$12,300,000	$17,627,120
Lever Bros.—Handy Andy	740,730	—
Colgate—Genie	319,840	—
Procter & Gamble—Mr. Clean	421,300	5,796,130
Texize Chem.—Texize	—	4,611,480

Source: "Lestoil Sales Ends Epoch in Marketing History," Advertising Age, April 4, 1960, pp. 99–100. Reprinted with permission, copyright © 1960 by Crain Communications, Inc.

On May 31, 1960, Jacob Barowsky sold Adell Chemical Company to Standard International Corporation for $10 million. Barowsky and his family were to remain as operators of the business and their policies on product promotion were to be maintained. Standard, however, did make some changes. The equipment was modernized, fair-trading was dropped so that the price could be discounted, and the advertising budget was slashed to $6 million. Now a concerted effort was made to seek the last untapped market in the United States, the West. The container was changed to a light-weight, easy-to-grip polyvinyl chloride bottle, and this was the first nonglass container in the cleaning-products industry.

A promotion was inaugurated in which Lestoil teamed up with *Look* magazine for a personally addressed coupon offer for both Lestoil and Lestare. A national television strategy was also instituted in hopes of regaining lost ground. But none of these promotional efforts was able to blunt the inroads of the more powerful competitors. In the end, Standard cut back on its promotions and conceded national ranking to the giants, while settling on a reasonably profitable regional penetration.

Table 8.3 Market Shares of Liquid Detergents—1959

Company and Product	*Market Share (%)*
Procter & Gamble—Mr. Clean	41
Adell—Lestoil	25
Lever Bros.—Handy Andy	21
Colgate—Genie	2

Source: "Mr. Clean Muscles Past Lestoil," Printers' Ink, Nov. 27, 1959, p. 16.

Table 8.4 TV Households

Year	*Number of Households with TV (in Thousands)*
1948	172
1949	940
1950	3,875
1951	10,320
1952	15,300
1953	20,400
1954	26,000
1955	30,700
1956	34,900
1957	38,900
1958	41,924
1959	43,959
1960	45,750

Source: U.S. Department of Commerce, Bureau of Census, Historical Statistics of U.S., Part II, Colonial Times to 1970, p. 796.

INGREDIENTS OF SUCCESS

Obviously, the vital ingredient in the belated success of Lestoil was concentrated and prolonged TV exposure. In the 1950s, TV was a relatively new advertising media. Table 8.4 shows the growth in the number of TV households before and during this period. The ability of TV to permit both a product to be seen and the message heard was a powerful extra dimension for advertising, and it particularly benefited products that could be demonstrated, as Lestoil could. Rather interestingly, Barowsky only found advertising success when he had a much greater concentration of commercial messages—30 a week or more—and when he carried this on for a long period of time—at least a year in most markets.

But although the TV commitment is widely claimed to be the major factor leading to the success of Lestoil, another strategic factor was also important in getting wide coverage. Barowsky made the product attractive for grocers to carry. Even though the typical grocery and supermarket had only limited shelf space, much of which was tied up with products of the major consumer brands, Lestoil offered a better profit margin for the grocer than competing brands. This, combined with the consumer advertising that was generating demand, opened the market for Lestoil.

Somewhat overlooked in most of the publicity about Lestoil at the time was the fact that Barowsky had really developed a superior product. Still, no matter how good a product is, it must be promoted to gain market acceptance, and even to gain market entry, if it comes from a small and unknown manufacturer.

WHAT CAN BE LEARNED?

The Lestoil case graphically illustrates the plight of the small unknown firm with a superior product attempting to gain market entry against large entrenched competitors. This is very difficult, especially with packaged consumer products such as are found on supermarket shelves. But entry *can be* achieved.

Specifically, we can learn the following from this example:

- Having a superior product gives no assurance of marketing success. The old adage "Build a better mousetrap and the world will beat a path to your door" just does not recognize the real-life marketing environment. Smart and aggressive efforts are needed to gain market entry for even the significantly superior product (and most are not that much superior) and to persuade both dealers and customers to try it.
- Although the Lestoil example suggests that only TV has enough promotional impact to spur market entry, perhaps this notion should be tempered. Certainly, promotional efforts should be both concentrated and intense, and also conducted over a sufficient period of time. But with the diverse advertising media available today, it can be disputed that TV is the only viable choice, especially now that its novelty and the great growth in ownership has ended.
- The need for and the potency of the combination of push and pull efforts is evidenced. Such efforts give far more assurance of widespread market entry than either used alone. Although some market entry can be achieved without the combination, the impact may not be sufficient to open up enough of the market to give needed customer trial and acceptance.
- An objective of promotional efforts should be to impress dealers as to the manufacturer's commitment to back up the product and promote it. Dealer support, especially for the not-well-known brand or firm, is more likely to be gained if there is some assurance of strong pull efforts.
- Dealer push is also important in gaining market entry. This suggests that some salesperson contacts need to be made and the product be made as attractive as possible for dealers to try. Such attractive aspects may be the pull-type promotions mentioned above; but they also ought to include some profit incentives over competing brands. In the case of Lestoil, a better markup per unit than that given by the large established manufacturers was also offered to dealers. Other inducements might be display allowances, free goods, and even return-good privileges whereby the dealer can return any goods for full credit if sufficient sales are not realized.
- The market-by-market additive approach used by Lestoil represents a potent strategy for the small and medium-size firm to gain market entry and expand. Resources can thus be concentrated in such a way that the great advantage of larger competitors can not only be neutralized but even out-

maneuvered. This strategy is very much like the army that can concentrate a mighty force on a narrow sector of the enemy lines and thereby crush the opposition. Only when entry has been achieved in a particular market are efforts directed to adjacent and then additional markets. Although entry is slower than with an immediate commitment to national distribution, the risks are less and the whole strategy is more practical for smaller firms.

- Any product superiority in today's competitive environment tends to be short-lived. The product superiority of Lestoil was not lasting. The giant firms were quick to bring out their own versions of a liquid synthetic detergent, once they recognized the growing popularity of Lestoil. The firm with a superior product must capitalize on this very quickly, for the competitive advantage tends to be short indeed for most consumer products. This militates against a slow and cautious market entry, but company resources have to play a major role in initial market entry and expansion and may dictate against a nationwide "Spry-type" onslaught.

Questions

1. What other methods might Barowsky have used to gain market entry? Evaulate their likelihood of success.
2. Discuss the pros and cons of the market-by-market approach of Barowsky.

Invitation to Role Play

Assume the role of Jacob Barowsky. Your last-ditch effort to tap the consumer market through spot TV commercials on one Holyoke station has proven successful—so successful, in fact, that a major detergent maker has offered to buy you out for $250,000. "Otherwise, we'll blow you out of the water." Evaluate the pros and cons of accepting this offer (without benefit of hindsight).

CHAPTER 9

Korvette: Inaugurating the Discount Revolution

It is March 1962, a momentous month for Eugene Ferkauf, founder and head of the nation's most successful discount store chain, E. J. Korvette, Inc. He and his ideas had shaken up retailers and forced into submission some of the biggest manufacturers who had attempted to have their dealers maintain high "fair-trade" list prices. Starting from a small second-floor walkup loft on an off-street of Manhattan in 1948, his enterprise had grown to 15 large discount store centers by the end of 1961, with another one just opened in February 1962, and seven more planned.

The capstone of his career to date, however, had just opened in the heart of New York City's Fifth Avenue, only a few blocks from some of the most fashionable and prestigious stores in the world, such as Bonwit Teller and Lord & Taylor. A massive chandelier was placed in the lobby, indicative of the disavowal with the "sordid discount" image. "We have Cadillacs that pull up to the store, and women get out and enjoy, as everybody enjoys, being able to buy something a little bit cheaper than they normally would. We have some of the most famous people coming into our store."[1]

EUGENE FERKAUF AND THE BEGINNINGS OF KORVETTE

Gene Ferkauf began his retail career in his father's luggage store in New York City. He went there directly from high school at the age of 16. But he was no ordinary

[1]As reported in Robert Drew-Bear, *Mass Merchandising* (New York: Fairchild Publications, 1970), p. 124.

high school graduate, but visionary and eager to grasp opportunities as he saw them. He disagreed with his father's traditional philosophy of merchandising, which was to sell goods at list or manufacturers' suggested prices or fair-trade prices and reap the rewards of good profit per unit sold. Ferkauf wondered if only a small profit per unit sale might yield the greater total profit, *if sales volume could be greatly increased by doing so.*

So Ferkauf struck out on his own, to prove an idea he had been grappling with, and just perhaps to grab firm hold of a great opportunity. With $4000 capital, he opened a luggage shop with discount-priced luggage in a second-floor loft on an off-street of Manhattan. The year was 1948, a great postwar boom for appliances was about to begin, and Ferkauf was ready to ride with it.

He chose the name of the business rather arbitrarily: E. J. Korvette. (The E stands for Eugene, his first name; the J for Joseph Blumenthal, his friend who became treasurer of the company; and "Korvette" came from the name of a Canadian subchaser in the First World War, Corvette. Although the basic stock was luggage, as an accommodation to his customers, Ferkauf began selling appliances at close to cost. Soon he branched out into fountain pens and photography equipment. In the early days, Ferkauf sold all appliances for $10 over the wholesale price. "If a guy came in to buy stereo equipment that cost the firm $1,000, we would just mark it up ten bucks and he took it home."[2]

People began lining up on the sidewalk outside and down the block to get into the store to purchase such bargains. Ferkauf found he was making money with the appliances and was operating at a million-dollar-a-year rate. By the end of 1951 he had moved his store to street level and opened a branch in Westchester. Sales climbed to $9,700,000 in 1953.

Gene Ferkauf was a quiet man; he shunned the public limelight. At stockholder meetings he liked to sit mute. He even stayed away from a reception celebrating the new quarters for Yeshiva University's Ferkauf School of Social Work. He believed in casual clothes, had a contempt for formality, and spurned an office and other executive amenities. But he believed in friends.

In the early 1950s, a group of 38 men, almost all Brooklyn high school pals of Ferkauf, ran the company. They were called the "open-shirt crowd" or "the boys." Korvette's management operated from a dingy old building with Ferkauf presiding at a beat-up desk in one corner. And the company grew, incredibly, from $55 million to $750 million in sales within ten years, thereby becoming one of the fastest growing companies in the history of retailing. In the early 1960s, the company was opening huge new stores on the average of one every seven weeks.

In the 1950s and early 1960s, Korvette led the discount revolution that was sweeping the country. The American consumer relished the idea of low prices—items priced up to 40 percent less than department store prices. Korvette profits and

[2] "Korvettes Tries for a Little Chic," *Business Week,* May 12, 1973, p. 124.

stock seemed headed for the stratosphere. And the business philosophy was simple: if you have sales volume, you will make a profit even with a low markup. To do so, however, Korvette and the other discounters operated in austere surroundings. Stores and fixtures were simple—pipe racks were even used for hanging garments; no services such as credit or delivery were offered at first; and self-service was the rule in order to cut down on salary expense. Just as important as paring costs, lean stocks of merchandise were offered—a narrow selection of best selling sizes and styles—to maximize merchandise turnover and thereby increase the return on investment. (See the following Information Sidelight for an example of the effect of turnover on profitability.)

Originally, Korvette had sold only luggage and small appliances, but gradually it had taken on other hard goods lines such as photographic equipment, records, toys, sporting goods, and major appliances. Then in 1953, Korvette made its first entry into the soft goods field by stocking some apparel and other dry goods at one store in Manhattan. With new store openings, it expanded soft goods operations, so that by 1955 it was stocking complete selections of low- and medium-priced apparel and accessories for men, women, and children. By the middle 1950s, about the only department store merchandise not sold was furniture and floor coverings. Now Ferkauf began introducing a one-stop shopping concept in the new stores, with furniture and floor coverings offered by franchises given to experienced operators of furniture and floorcovering stores and with the institution of complete food supermarkets. By 1957, 56 percent of the company's total sales were in hard goods, 30 percent in soft goods, and 14 percent in food.[3] By 1965, soft goods were to account for 45 percent of the merchandise mix, and the company was becoming less of a

INFORMATION SIDELIGHT

Importance of Turnover in Profitability

Consider the following comparison of a department store operation and a similar size discount store for an example of the effect of higher turnover on profitability:

Department Store	
Sales	$12,000,000
Net profit percent	5
Net profit dollars	$600,000
Stock turnover	4
Average stock (12,000,000 ÷ 4)*	$3,000,000
Return on investment (without considering investment in store and fixtures)	$\frac{600,000}{3,000,000} = 20\%$

[3]Malcolm P. McNair, Elizabeth A. Burnham, and Anita C. Hersum, *Cases in Retail Management* (New York: McGraw-Hill, 1957), p. 169.

*To simplify this example, inventory investment is figured at retail price, rather than cost, which would technically be more correct. However, the significance of increasing turnover is more easily seen here.
A similar size discount store might have a turnover of 8, whereas net profit percentage might be only 3%:

Discount Store	
Sales	\$12,000,000
Net profit percent	3
Net profit dollars	\$360,000
Stock turnover	8
Average stock (12,000,000 ÷ 8)	\$1,500,000
Return on investment	$\frac{360{,}000}{1{,}500{,}000} = 24\%$

Thus, the discount store can be more profitable than the comparable department store (as measured by the true measure of profitability, the return on investment), even though the net profit is less. Furthermore, the discount store not only has a lower investment in inventory to produce the same amount of sales, but also has less invested in store and fixtures.

discounter and more of a promotional department store with higher markups and more promotional prices and special sales. Table 9.1 shows the great growth in sales and profits of Korvette during its initial growth spurt from 1950 to 1956.

As the company persisted in its discounting policies, it came up against state fair-trade laws, which permitted manufacturers to set the minimum prices for which

Table 9.1 Sales and Profits, 1950–1956

Year	*Sales (\$)*	*Profits (\$)*
1950	2,005,235	27,296
1951	2,779,713	39,952
1952	4,653,438	40,330
1953	9,706,199	163,263
1954	17,810,809	353,604
1955	36,292,393	1,175,740
1956	54,847,140	1,558,876

Source: Korvette annual reports.

their goods could be sold by retailers. Some of the major manufacturers, including General Electric, wanted to maintain an image of quality and protect their regular dealers from price cutting. Korvette, by selling below the fair-traded prices, was vulnerable to lawsuits by such manufacturers. At the time the company went public in 1955, 34 fair-trade lawsuits were pending against it. This was not as bad as it might seem, however. Enforcement of fair trade rested with the manufacturers who wanted it for their products. And in 1956, Korvette received a legal boost when a New York court threw out a suit brought by the Parker Pen Company on the grounds that Parker was not sufficiently enforcing its fair-trade program. Many manufacturers were finding enforcement difficult amid the spate of discount stores. In addition, the lack of severe penalties prescribed by the courts for violating fair trade (in many cases, only court costs were levied against the offending discounter) further limited its effectiveness as a deterrent to price cutting by Korvette and others. Actually, fair-trade and list prices aided discount stores because customers could readily see the base price from which the item was discounted.

By 1962, 14 years after his humble beginning, Ferkauf had parlayed an investment of $4000 into an operation with sales of more than $180 million. And the one-third block of Korvette's stock that he controlled was worth, at 1962 market prices, around $57 million. With his simple strategy of undercutting department stores 10 to 40 percent, his corporation grew to $750 million in sales by 1965. In the process, he revolutionized merchandising and profoundly altered the policies of conventional retailers. Malcolm McNair, Harvard's famous professor of retailing, rated Ferkauf as one of the six greatest merchants in the United States, alongside men like Frank Woolworth, John Wanamaker, and J. C. Penney.

Ferkauf's theory of growth was that it was better to open a cluster of stores in a metropolitan area, to saturate an area, than to spread out more thinly nationwide. With three or four or more stores located in one metropolitan area, advertising costs could be shared, as could warehousing, servicing, and certain other expenses. Customer acceptance could be gained more quickly from the massive presentation of stores and promotional efforts. Following this strategy, by 1966 Korvette had ten stores in the New York metropolitan area, five in Philadelphia, and four in Baltimore–Washington. Between 1963 and 1965, five large stores had been opened in metropolitan Chicago, three in Detroit, and two in St. Louis.

Still, his success did not reduce Ferkauf's 12-hour working day. He continued to shun his office and prowl through his stores, observing and making decisions along the way. On weekends, after this frenetic pace, he would slip home to his 14-room suburban residence to watch TV with his wife and children and walk his dogs.

In the early and middle 1960s, Gene Ferkauf could see no limit to his growth probabilities. Asked of his expectations for ten years later, he could say, "a lovely, nationwide retailer, with a permanent place in the American home."[4]

[4]"Discount House Puts on Airs," *Business Week*, February 10, 1962, p. 73.

INGREDIENTS OF SUCCESS OF KORVETTE AND OTHER DISCOUNTERS

Discounters in General

We can identify a number of factors that contributed to the great retail upheaval brought about by discounters in the 1950s and 1960s, when Korvette was in the vanguard. We will classify these under social, political, and industry factors.

Social. The initial embryonic discount efforts came shortly after World War II. A large and more affluent middle-class market had developed, with millions of families experiencing higher wages, more working wives, and moonlighting. The population was becoming better educated; with more discretionary income, buying power was burgeoning, but so was a diversity of wants. Consumers were becoming more enamored with the idea of one-stop shopping and families shopping together after working hours, in the evening and on Sundays. Many desired more convenience of shopping and some excitement and change from the traditional, whose promotional efforts tended to be staid, conservative, and formal. The supermarket, with its introduction of self-service that allowed the customer to make unsupervised purchase decisions and save money in the process, had had time to become fully accepted and preferred. The transition to the discount store using similar self-service techniques was natural.

Political. The fair trade laws that were enacted in most states disrupted normal competition and maintained artificially inflated prices. Such fixed prices became simply bases for comparing the discount and ''fair-trade price,'' and conclusively reinforced the image of the bargains offered in discount stores over the conventional retailers who stoutly held to their fair-trade prices. Any fines levied against the discount stores for violating fair trade could be easily paid and were modest enough to present no deterrence to price cutting.

Industry. Conventional retailers, despite their intentions, stimulated the inroads of discounters. In the 1950s, many retailers cried out against the ''illegitimate chiselers'' who brought ''unhealthy'' loss leaders and low quality. Their very criticisms made the interloper firms more publicized and more attractive to many consumers. Most retailers still stubbornly persisted in maintaining list prices that assured them a comfortable per-unit profit margin rather than embracing the notion, strongly espoused by Ferkauf and the other discounters, that a lower price and markup could lead to increased sales and more total dollar profits. Furthermore, most retailers persisted until long after the discounter invasion in maintaining a high cost structure and short hours—open perhaps one night a week, and never on Sundays.

Korvette in Particular

Perhaps Ferkauf's greatest strength was his willingness to seize potential opportunities and run with these ideas, expanding as vigorously as possible. Whereas many discounters feared to take on the burdens and risks of great growth, and so remained local enterprises, Ferkauf had no such qualms. Nor did he hesitate to try variations of the discount idea, of modifying and expanding the original concept. For example, in one of his first stores, in 1954, 40 percent of the goods he stocked were soft goods such as linens, domestics, and men's, women's, and children's wear, at a time when other discounters were almost entirely in hard goods such as appliances for which discounts from list prices were more readily perceived by customers. One of Ferkauf's biggest sellers in this store proved to be a $4.60 dress. Every ten days to two weeks, 2500 of these dresses were sold, for a turnover of about 25 times a year.[5] Ferkauf was also a pioneer in expanding the discount store into a one-stop shopping complex, where virtually all kinds of merchandise could be purchased under one roof.

Ferkauf stoutly maintained a lean organization, with no frills, and a tight centralized management. This certainly kept costs down and enabled the organization to have very short channels of communication.

We must note, however, that these factors of a lean, tight organization and a willingness to try new methods of operation are only success factors when used in moderation. Later, as we will describe, the organization of Korvette was unable to cope with increasing size, and the penchant for modification of successful policies was to prove disastrous.

WHAT CAN BE LEARNED FROM THE SUCCESS OF KORVETTE AND DISCOUNTING?

In this case as well as a number of others in this book, one salient success factor stands out: *opportunities for change makers often exist where traditional market structures predominate*. In the 1950s, most retailers—be they small stores or giant chain or department store organizations—were wedded to the traditional idea of high markups (''needed to cover costs of the services expected'') and an unconcern or unawareness of growing consumer desires for lower prices and greater convenience and excitement in shopping. Such a competitive environment created great opportunities for those introducing changes more in keeping with the shopping desires of a large and growing middle class.

The myopia of the majority of retailers at the time and the later severe problems of Korvette bring us to a sobering realization that success does not guarantee continued success. The environment is dynamic and can change subtly or traumatically. To rest on one's laurels is perilous, both for an individual firm and for an

[5] Drew-Bear, *Mass Merchandising*, p. 118.

entire industry. Success may actually promote vulnerability and leave a firm more easy prey to hungry competitors. Part of this problem is complacency. It is difficult for a successful firm or industry not be become smug about its position and disdainful of lesser competitors and new entrants to its market. Success encourages the viewpoint that the future is a mirror of the past. But this is fallacious thinking.

It is insightful to examine the typical reactions of firms confronted with an innovative newcomer. Reactions seem to progress through three stages:

1. Conventional firms initially ignore the interloper as too extreme and radical to deserve more than disdain from the established firms.
2. As the competitive inroads of the innovators become more apparent and more of a threat, then conventional firms turn to publicly condemning, disparaging, and even attempting to restrain by legal methods. Some of the legal attempts to blunt the discount invasion were calling for stricter enforcement of fair-trade laws and unfair practices acts (which forbade selling goods near or below costs) and resurrecting such dusty local ordinances as Blue Laws (which made it unlawful to do business on Sundays). Several decades earlier, similar restrictive measures were used to try to counter the competitive inroads and greater operating efficiencies and lower prices of chains.
3. Finally, and only after considerable time has elapsed and strong inroads have been made by the innovators, conventional firms adapt operations to better combat them, or join the innovators with similar operations or divisions.

Traditional retailers turned to such defenses as (1) stressing their own private brands or manufacturers' brands not offered to discounters, so that direct price comparisons could not be readily made by customers, and (2) reducing services and costs in order to pare markups and be more competitive. Even self-service and central checkout practices of the discounters were adopted by other retailers, at least for some departments.

A number of major retailers joined the discount ranks and some of them became notably successful and in fact, by the 1970s, were able to drive some of the original discounters out of business. K mart (described in a later case), the discount subsidiary of S. S. Kresge Co., was to become the largest discounter of all. So successful was this discount venture that the name of Kresge Company was later changed to K mart. Federated Department Stores developed a successful Gold Circle discount subsidiary, as did Dayton-Hudson Corporation with their Target Stores. Some other major retailers opened discount subsidiaries, but later abandoned them: for example, Woolworth and its Woolco subsidiary, and J. C. Penney Company's Treasury Stores.

We must conclude from the typical reactions to a radical and threatening newcomer that the first two stages should be repudiated. Defensive counter-measures and necessary modifications should be made quickly. A changing competitive environment should trigger adaptive behavior and not a stubborn complacency.

POSTSCRIPT—SUCCESS ABANDONS KORVETTE

Korvette is no longer a factor on the retail scene, and Ferkauf has sunk into obscurity. By the mid-1960s, Professor McNair had retracted his assessment of Ferkauf as one of the great merchants.

In the four years between 1962 and 1966, store space and sales volume more than tripled. When Korvette had no more than a dozen outlets, all concentrated around New York City, Ferkauf could give on-the-scene guidance on ‘‘foot patrol’’. But his organization failed to provide a reasonable substitute for the diminishing face-to-face supervision of Ferkauf and his home-office executives, especially with expansion to Chicago, Detroit, and St. Louis. The constant addition of stores placed enormous pressures on management. There were enough work and problems in running existing operations, much less having to simultaneously bring on the additional stores. Of course, advancement was fast. Section and department managers moved quickly into jobs as store managers and less experienced people took their places. But there was little time either to develop top-notch management people or to be selective in screening for the best.

Further strains were caused by the switch to soft goods and fashion merchandise. While these offered higher profit margins, the risks of markdowns and unsalable inventories due to fashion and seasonal obsolescence were high and the demands on management were more than for staple hard goods. Food merchandising also harassed Ferkauf. There was good rationale for expanding with supermarkets because this was compatible with Ferkauf's one-stop shopping goal; it could also lead to heavier and more constant customer traffic as customers generally stock up with groceries every week.

But these food operations were opened without warehousing, which meant that more goods had to be stocked to minimize out-of-stocks, and a heavy inventory did not permit lean fast-moving stocks, high turnover, and lowest prices. Losses from this operation reached $12 million by 1964, and Ferkauf was forced to turn to the outside for help. Despite a merger of this part of the operation with Hill Supermarkets, profitability was never achieved. Nor was it achieved with the leased furniture and carpet operations, which also seriously drained profit as well as hurt customer relations because of poor service.

At the very time when conventional retailers were fighting back strongly, with some adding their own discount divisions, and other discount firms were aggressively trying to maintain market positions, Korvette was finding its organization incapable of dealing with the size of the operation. It was also lacking in the kind of controls needed—coming from well-defined policies, objectives, and plans for the various aspects of the operation, such as for markups, markdowns, merchandise turnover, and the various categories of expenses. The business was run too informally, with little advance planning and coordination; its size precluded the effectiveness of this type of operation.

Another troublesome factor was Korvette's image. At first, in the golden days of the chain, the discount image (bare-bones prices) had great customer appeal. However, Ferkauf's efforts to upgrade the image from a discount store to a promotional department store, culminating in his Fifth Avenue store, resulted in some of the original customer base being lost. Gradually, Korvette was moving toward the expense structure of traditional retailers, but without the same level of expertise that department and specialty stores possessed in quality and fashion merchandising. Markdowns had risen from less than 8 percent in 1950 to some 33 percent in 1965. Inventory turnover was down by one third from 1961. Sales per square foot had also fallen by one third.

Rather unexpectedly, on September 25, 1966, Korvette was merged with the smaller Spartan Industries. Ferkauf was eased out of active management, and in 1968 he left Spartans and all affiliation with his once booming enterprise. Despite the stronger management that Spartans provided, the Korvette operation could never regain its former strength.[6]

Questions

1. Why did Korvette have such difficulty competing with fashion goods when it was so successful with appliances and other hard goods?
2. One of the serious problems Korvette faced during its rapid growth was a lack of adequate systems and procedures, particularly regarding feedback and controls from the stores. What controls or performance measures would you have established in this situation?

Invitation to Role Play

Place yourself in the role of assistant store manager of one of the Chicago-area Korvette stores. Your particular responsibility is the fashion division of the store: women's dresses, coats, sportswear, and accessories. To date, despite an adequate stock of popular fashions (mostly low-priced copies of expensive styles), this merchandise is just not selling. Develop a recommendation for what you think it would take to make this division more successful. Then, recognizing the constraints of selling fashion merchandise in a discount store, develop modified recommendations that are more likely to be practical and acceptable to higher management.

[6]For more details on the mistakes of Korvette, see Robert F. Hartley, *Marketing Mistakes,* 2nd ed. (Columbus, Ohio: Grid, 1981), pp. 85–98.

PART Four

THE DECADES OF THE 1960s AND 1970s: THE MATURING OF MARKETING

By the 1960s the tools and techniques for marketing strategies seemed complete. The media for advertising, including the newcomer TV, were all in place, well used, and familiar to most marketers, especially the consumer goods firms. The growth in advertising expenditures between 1960 and 1980—$11.9 billion rising to $50 billion—was indicative of the major and growing role that marketing was playing in many firms, as well as in our life-styles. The so-called marketing concept, which essentially represented an upgrading of the role of marketing within the organization, became firmly established in many firms. Perhaps it was triggered by Theodore Levitt's notable "Marketing Myopia," which appeared in the July–August *Harvard Business Review* of 1960. This expanded organizational and philosophical role for marketing became a competitive necessity for firms in many industries (although less so for industrial goods firms and for those primarily involved in defense contracting).

Marketing research was also making rapid strides during these years, not only in refining its tools and techniques but in much greater usage. Although further refinements occurred toward the 1980s, and increasingly sophisticated computers particularly benefited marketing planning, research, and analysis, the arsenal of know-how for effective marketing efforts already existed. Perhaps the biggest change in marketing practices during these maturing decades was the use of sound marketing techniques by many firms and not just a few as in the earlier decades. Marketing truly came of age as manifested in its broadened usage, which was accentuated toward the end of this period (as will be discussed in the last section of the book).

In this section we examine five significant successes during this maturing period. However, the marketing sophistication shown in these examples is not much greater than that of Lever Bros. in its assault on Crisco back in the 1930s. Does this tell us that marketing knowledge and effectiveness has not improved in three or four decades? Not exactly. It does suggest that Lever was far ahead of its time.

First, we have the solid example of Philip Morris transforming Miller beer from an also-ran to one of the great successes in this highly competitive industry—using nothing arcane but simply a solid integrated marketing strategy highlighted by a segmentation approach to target marketing. We see Hanes with its L'eggs tapping a vast new market segment that had been poorly handled before—using marketing research to uncover and define weaknesses and then developing an imaginative marketing strategy to dominate the opportunity. The McDonald's case shows how simply success can be welded by merely doing customer-satisfying things better than anyone else—simplicity, but firm standards and controls and with the franchise format honed to perfection. K mart, coming on the scene with a major shift of its emphasis to discounting—more than ten years after Korvette and other discounters had shown the way and tried to dominate the market—again, achieved success with simplicity; do the basics well, back your convictions to the limit, and less competent competitors will be destroyed. Finally, we come to Perdue chickens, a wonderful success story for a product seemingly impossible to differentiate and create brand awareness for, although we know brand awareness and acceptance are essential for great success. Frank Perdue found the way, and a fortune to boot.

Imaginative marketing, though the discipline is mature, can be a wonderful spur to success, and it is hoped that room for creative efforts will always exist. Up to now, with no end in sight, marketing still reigns as the locus for creativity and imagination to storm the citadel and create outstanding successes.

CHAPTER 10

Miller Beer: Transferring Marketing Muscle to the Brewing Industry

In 1970, Philip Morris Inc. was loaded with excess cash from its very profitable cigarette business, which had produced the nation's leading brand, Marlboro. Aggressive marketing had lifted it to second place in the highly competitive tobacco industry. Now it wanted to acquire a firm in another industry to which its resources and talents might be transferable.

It found such an acquisition in the Miller Brewing Company. However, Miller was only number 7 in the industry, with a modest 4 percent market share. In recent years its sales had been static, while the brewing industry's leaders were growing at a 10 percent annual rate.

Seven years later, by 1978, Philip Morris had brought Miller to number 2 in the industry, behind only Anheuser-Busch.

THE BREWING INDUSTRY

Historically, most breweries were operated by families who had owned their businesses for generations, as was the case with Miller. The processes of brewing, packaging, distributing, and selling were based on tradition. Through the 1800s and into the 1900s brewing operations changed little, except for periodically expanding production facilities. However, in the 1930s there were portents of change.

Conventional wisdom had maintained that beer could not be brewed far from its market without losing its quality. Consequently, it took some 735 local brewers to satisfy all of the markets by the 1930s. Falstaff broke with tradition at that time

Table 10.1 Number of Breweries, 1933–1965

Year	*Number of Breweries*
1933	731
1938	700
1943	491
1948	475
1953	333
1965	184

Source: Brewers' Almanac, 1954, U.S. Brewers Foundation and Brewers' Almanac, 1966, U.S. Brewers Association, Inc., Washington, D.C.

by successfully acquiring breweries away from its St. Louis base. Influenced by the Falstaff success, Schlitz followed in the 1940s and Anheuser-Busch in the 1950s.

The expansion of some brewers beyond their local markets now paved the way for increasing size and concentration in the industry and the weeding out of marginal firms. Table 10.1 shows the change in number of brewers in the three decades from the mid-1930s to the mid-1960s. Mergers and acquisitions partly accounted for this reduced number. However, the larger brewers simply forced many medium and small brewers out of business. More sophisticated marketing methods were also shaking the tradition-ridden industry. In the late 1950s Anheuser-Busch began experimenting with different advertising media and it also pioneered regional price promotions to gain local market share. All major brewers but Anheuser continued to rely on only one beer product through the 1960s.

By 1966 the top ten brewers accounted for 62.9 percent of industry sales. The move toward concentration continued into the mid-1970s. By 1976 the top ten commanded 85.9 percent of the industry. Furthermore, the top five (Anheuser, Schlitz, Miller, Pabst, and Coors) by themselves dominated the industry with a 69 percent market share by 1976. In the ten-year period ending in 1975, the number of brewers had further declined from 184 in 1965 to only 49 by 1976. The major firms during this period had built massive and efficient breweries and thereby gained economies of scale over the small regional and local brewers who were simply wiped out.

Aggressive competition by Miller in the mid-1970s was forcing other changes on the industry. In particular, Miller's methods of market segmentation, special products and packaging, and high advertising expenditures were being followed by most other major firms. Because only a few weak regionals were left from which to take market share, the majors began fighting among themselves for market share.

Price competition during this period was heavy and much-needed price hikes to match rises in costs were delayed, thus further jeopardizing the smaller brewers with their higher breakeven points.

Increasing across-the-board costs, including grains, labor, and advertising costs, coupled with more aggressive competition and restricted price rises, caused industry return on equity to fall from 15 percent in 1970 to 10 percent in 1975. The big brewers moved toward more efficient production facilities in order to blunt this profit squeeze. Anheuser, Schlitz, and Miller in particular opened efficient new plants in the early and mid-1970s, not only to expand capacity but also to replace older less efficient production facilities.

Foreign brands were also affecting the industry. For example, imported beer sales increased 24 percent in 1975 and 23 percent in 1976; during the same time domestic brewers were able to chalk up increases of only 2.2 and 2.5 percent. The greater strength of imports reflected a shift in American consumption toward premium and super-premium beers. Blunting the thrust of foreign brewers, in 1975 Miller acquired the rights to brew Lowenbrau domestically and began test marketing in Texas by late 1976. In 1975 Lowenbrau had accounted for 14 percent of all imports, which was second only to Heineken's 35 percent share of the import market.

Increasing concentration in the brewing industry had a detrimental effect on beer distributors. Many were forced out of business as the brewers they serviced went bankrupt or were acquired by larger firms who already had their own distribution network. Increased competition among the few large firms motivated questionable practices. Schlitz and Falstaff were accused of making payment to an East Coast restaurant chain in order to get exclusive sales privileges for their brands in these outlets. Schlitz fired four top marketing executives in late 1976 because of their alleged involvement with the payoff. Rumors flew that there were other illegal payments such as bribes and kickbacks. Furthermore, predatory pricing was also suspected. Pearl Brewing in Texas filed suit against Schlitz and Anheuser in the summer of 1976 claiming that below-cost regional price promotions of the two giants caused its market share to fall from 23 percent in 1966 to only 6 percent in 1976.

By the late 1970s there was also concern about state legislation banning nonreturnable containers. By 1979, seven states had enacted mandatory beer deposit laws. These hurt not only beer sales but also the major brewers who made many of their own cans. However, the defeats in Ohio and Washington in November 1979 of new environmentalist-sponsored laws were major victories for the industry; Maine voters, on the other hand, overwhelmingly voted to retain their previously enacted deposit laws.

Before the mid-1970s the brewing industry had created few new products. There were, however, two successful new products: Anheuser's Michelob and National's malt liquor, Colt 45. Two significant failures were low-calorie beers introduced in the late 1960s, and fruit-flavored beers brought to market in 1969. The low-calorie beers, of which Heilman's Gablinger was the most notable failure, had two flaws. First, this early formulation of a low-calorie beer did not taste enough like "real" beer. In addition, it was marketed to the diet-conscious beer drinker, and quickly developed an image of a "sissy" beer. Several small regional brewers brought from Europe the concept of fruit-flavored beers. Since "pop" wines such as Boone's Farm had been very successful, these brewers guessed that "pop" beers would also be successful. They guessed wrong. In retrospect, two shortcomings led to the fruit-flavored demise: first, the malt base was not tasteless enough to ensure a good fruity taste, and second, the product needed to be positioned to hit the college market, but with sufficient consumer education to distinguish it from soft drinks and wines.[1]

The beer industry can hardly be categorized as a great growth industry today. The prime beer drinking group, ages 18–34, which in the past consumed 50 percent of all beer, had begun to decline by 1980. The industry hoped, however, that per-capita beer consumption would increase somewhat, mostly because of the premium-priced and low-calorie beers. A declining number of blue-collar workers must be considered bad for the industry. And a growing popularity of wine also has negative overtones for long-term growth of beer consumption.

HISTORY OF MILLER BREWING COMPANY

Frederick A. Miller was 28 years old when he came to Milwaukee from Signaringen, Germany, in 1855. He purchased an idle brewery, the Plank Road Brewery, and became one of the "Milwaukee Brewers." Fred brewed only 300 barrels that first year; by his death, 33 years later, 80,000 barrels were being produced. His sons followed in his footsteps, and by Prohibition in the 1920s they were producing 500,000 barrels a year. The dry years of Prohibition threatened the company, but it was able to survive by making soft drinks, health drinks, and malt syrups.

With the end of Prohibition, Frederick Miller II completely modernized the plant. Miller maintained a high-quality product and when World War II came it was able to assign most of its production to the armed forces. In 1947 a third Fred Miller took over, and the plant was again modernized with capacity expanded to 4 million barrels by the early 1950s. The unbroken lineage of Fred Millers seemed destined to continue with a son, Fred Jr., who was also being groomed to take over at the appointed time. But tragedy struck as both Fred and Fred Jr. were killed in a plane crash in 1952. No one from the family was left to take over, and Fred's counsel, Norman R. Klug, assumed control. In May 1966, Miller Brewing acquired a plant in Azusa, California, the first expansion outside of Milwaukee.

[1] A. J. C. Peill, "Flavored Beer: Will It Succeed in the U.S.?" *Food Engineering*, May 1976, p. 70.

Also in 1966, W. R. Grace Company acquired a 53 percent interest in Miller from the granddaughter of Frederick A. Miller, who sold the brewery because it conflicted with the beliefs of her new religion. Then in June 1969, Philip Morris outbid PepsiCo for the 53 percent of Miller, paying $130 million to W. R. Grace Company (who had paid $36 million for it three years before and added $18 million in expansion and renovations). Philip Morris obtained the remaining 47 percent of Miller in July 1970 for $97 million.

In 1970 at the time of the Philip Morris takeover, Miller marketed one product, Miller High Life. Its advertising slogan was "The Champagne of Beers," and it appealed to two groups, women and upper-income people. Neither of these groups had a high consumption rate. Miller had expertise in brewing, but it lacked a large capacity and an aggressive marketing program.

A CHANGED MILLER

Phillip Morris

In 1961, Philip Morris was the smallest of the six big domestic tobacco companies, with only a 9.4 percent market share. By 1976, Philip Morris commanded over 25.2 percent of the market and was now second only to R. J. Reynolds, which had 33.2 percent. Internationally, Philip Morris was second only to British American Tobacco Company. In these years, Philip Morris had acquired aggressive marketing expertise. Its chairman, Joseph F. Cullman III, attributed the success to "the ability to market and merchandise, using consistent and integrated themes aimed at the growth segments of the market."[2]

What caused so much consternation in the brewing industry when Phillip Morris bought in was not only that it was a highly successful marketer in one of the most competitive consumer-products industries but that it was also making net profits larger than those of the industry leader, Anheuser-Busch (see Table 10.2). It did not take long for the concern of the other brewers to be justified.

Turnaround of Miller

A year after the Miller purchase, Philip Morris brought in John A. Murphy as its president. Murphy had been with Philip Morris for ten years, during which time he had risen to executive vice-president of international operations. Murphy's background was strictly tobacco; he had no experience with beer (except for personal use). As *Business Week* noted: "even his Irish heritage seemed out of place in an

[2]As quoted in, "Philip Morris: The Hot Hand in Cigarettes," *Business Week,* December 6, 1976, pp. 61–62.

Table 10.2 Sales and Profits of Philip Morris and Anheuser-Busch, 1970 (in Thousands of Dollars)

	Sales	*Net Profits*
Philip Morris	1,509,540	77,498
Anheuser-Busch	792,800	62,600

Sources: Company annual reports.

industry still dominated by old-line German families.'' But Murphy joked, ''Every Irishman dreams of going to heaven and running a brewery.''[3]

Murphy employed no esoteric strategy with the Miller operation, but used a classic marketing approach of market segmentation. (See the Information Sidelight for a brief perspective of segmentation and its advantage over the alternatives.) He began catering to different customer segments with specific products, packages, and advertising approaches. The brewers had previously ignored such an approach, relying instead on only one brand of beer on the assumption that the market wanted only one product and one package.

Murphy quickly recognized that Miller's High Life was not only insufficient by itself to sustain the company, but was targeted to the wrong market. It was aimed at consumers who were not the big beer drinkers. No one before Murphy had detected such an obvious deficiency. So Murphy quickly moved to change the image of High Life. This was not difficult to do; it simply required a somewhat different advertising approach. He featured young people in dune buggies, oil drillers relaxing after putting out an oil blowout, surveyors working in difficult

INFORMATION SIDELIGHT

Two Market Targeting Alternatives: Mass Marketing and Segmentation

A sound marketing plan involves identifying and selecting one or more target markets and then designing a strategy to be attractive to such a target market(s). Two different approaches are possible: (1) mass marketing (sometimes called a total market approach or product differentiation) and (2) market segmentation.

In mass marketing, as the brewing industry had traditionally done before the metamorphosis of Miller, all the efforts are geared to the total market rather than a piece of it, usually stressing how the particular brand differs and is better than competing brands.

Market segmentation divides the total market into smaller, homogeneous submarkets (or segments) with marketing efforts then directed to specific groups.

[3]''Turmoil Among the Brewers,'' *Business Week,* November 8, 1976, p. 58.

A segmentation approach is usually more effective and a more powerful competitive weapon because of its specialized tailoring of product and marketing techniques to particular customer needs. The old "one product for everyone" idea is often vulnerable to competitors using an aggressive segmentation approach, as we see in the Miller threat to the brewing industry.

terrain—in other words, people enjoying a Miller's after a hard day of work or play. These were the real beer drinkers.

Murphy then began exploring for new market segments and found a productive one. In 1972 he introduced a smaller 7-ounce pony bottle, which had been spurned by other brewers. Now it became a favorite of women and older people, a segment ignored by the industry until then. The success could be seen in specific terms: in 1976, Miller sold about 2.5 million barrels of beer in 7-ounce bottles. This was about 15 percent of the total year's volume and equal to half of all the beer Miller had sold in 1972. But the real success of Murphy and his Miller project was the introduction of low-calorie Lite beer.

The Lite Phenomenon

Lite was first marketed nationally in early 1975. Miller had bought the unsuccessful Meister Brau Lite from the Peter Hand Brewing Company and reformulated it so that it tasted like the regular beer. The results were amazing. Within one year it had become the most successful new beer introduced in the United States in this century. But it rose from the ashes of other low-calorie beers that had been disasters, namely, the Meister Brau Lite and Rheingold's Gablinger.

What was the difference between failure and outstanding success? It hinged simply on image and market segmentation, perpetrated by the advertising theme. The failures were marketed as diet drinks to diet-conscious consumers who were not big beer drinkers in the first place. Miller's advertising program featured sports and entertainment personalities with the message that Lite, with one third fewer calories, offered the big beer drinker the chance to drink as much beer as before, but without feeling so filled. The following are some of the notable commercials:

> The hefty former Chicago Bear linebacker, Dick Butkus, announces that he drinks Lite, and then sends a bowling ball rocketing into the pins, seemingly turning them into match sticks.
>
> Comedian Rodney Dangerfield is in a beer joint so tough "that the hat check girl is named Dominick."

Women and older people also found the "less filling" beer appealing.

A simple change in image and advertising—but it worked! One year later, in 1976, Miller sold 5 million barrels of Lite. This was equal to its entire beer production only four years before. Competitive brewers who had laughed at Miller's attempt to enter a market they said did not exist were no longer laughing, but were rushing to imitate.

Head-to-Head with Michelob

These first two successes of Murphy were products designed to fill gaps in the market. Now he turned his attention to compete directly with entrenched competition. Michelob was Anheuser's most profitable product. This was a superpremium beer, slightly heavier than Anheuser's Budweiser and sold for about 25¢ more a six-pack. Sales had been growing at more than 30 percent a year, and it was virtually unchallenged in this market. This did not deter Murphy. An agreement was obtained with Lowenbrau of Munich, Germany, and in the spring of 1976 Miller began test marketing a Lowenbrau that it brewed domestically. It was priced 25 percent higher than Michelob. August A. Busch III, chief executive of Anheuser, snarled, "This is Lowenbrau made in the U.S., not the beer imported from Europe, and the consumers are not going to be fooled by that little game."[4] But by 1978, Miller's Lowenbrau had achieved a 20 percent market penetration in the premium area, while charging 50¢ more per six-pack than Michelob.

INFORMATION SIDELIGHT

The Price/Quality Phenomenon

The problem of determining product quality is one of the major dilemmas facing consumers. With today's complex products and ingredients, few persons can appraise the quality of toothpaste or an electric iron, much less the quality of a refrigerator, furniture, or car. More and more, consumers depend on price as the primary measure of quality—the higher the price, the better the quality.

The liquor industry in particular has taken advantage of this perception of better quality for higher prices. The costs of making high-priced versus low-priced whiskey, for example, is 25 to 30¢ a fifth, but prices can vary by dollars. Why are people willing to pay considerably more for some brands? Even though most people cannot distinguish taste differences in beer and liquor when the brand names are hidden, the subtlety of quality and status as evidenced by a higher price still can be a powerful sales inducement for some products with some people.

[4] Ibid., p. 61.

Table 10.3 Advertising Costs per Barrel, 1973 and 1976

	1973	*1976*
Anheuser-Busch	$0.69	$0.98
Miller	1.58	1.58
Schlitz	0.92	1.41
Pabst	0.51	0.61
Coors	0.13	0.15

Sources: Advertising Age, September 26, 1977, p. 112; and Advertising Age, August 29, 1977, p. 24. Reprinted with permission. Copyright © 1977 by Crain Communications, Inc.

Advertising Onslaught

In direct imitation of traditional practices in the cigarette industry, Murphy launched a heavy advertising campaign to promote his old and new brands. For example, in the first year of the introduction of Lite, $6.00 per barrel was spent for advertising, which was enough to nearly wipe out all profits for Lite. The overwhelming sales response by the next year brought advertising costs for Lite in line percentagewise with Miller's other products. But such expenditures were unheard of by the staid and tradition-ridden brewing industry that relied on periodic price discounts to distributors to maintain market share, while keeping advertising to a minimum. Some beers such as Coors did not even advertise, but relied on word of mouth. But this was to change in the industry as the other brewers desperately tried to match marketing tactics and expenditures with the newcomer.

During the 1973 through 1976 period, Miller's advertising expenditures per barrel were almost three times higher than those of Anheuser, its largest competitor, and of course considerably higher than those of the other major brewers. Table 10.3 shows the respective costs per barrel for the major firms during this period. The introduction of massive advertising by Miller had predictable consequences. As can be seen from Table 10.3, the major brewers, except for Miller and Coors, increased their expenditures per barrel significantly by 1976.

Table 10.4 shows the sales and profits of Miller and its major competitors, as well as the market share changes among these major brewers, for the period 1970 through 1978. Note the phenomenal rise in market position for Miller compared to its largest competitors. In terms of barrels of beer, Miller went from 5 million in 1970 to 31.3 million barrels in 1978. This represented an increase in 1978 of 7.1 million barrels for a 29.1 percent rise over 1977. Note also from Table 10.4 that Miller's profits overtook and then substantially passed those of Anheuser-Busch by

Table 10.4 Sales, Profits, and Market Share[a] of Major Brewers, 1970–1978 (in Millions of Dollars)

		Miller	*Anheuser*	*Schlitz*	*Pabst*	*Coors*
1970	Sales ($)	198.5	792.8	462.4	270.2	246.2
	Profits ($)	11.4	62.6	30.2	23.3	31.8
	Market share (%)	10.1	40.2	23.5	13.7	12.5
1972	Sales ($)	211.3	977.5	611.3	335.6	330.4
	Profits ($)	22.8	76.4	45.8	28.5	48.0
	Market share (%)	8.6	39.4	24.7	13.7	13.6
1974	Sales ($)	403.6	1,413.1	814.5	431.3	467.8
	Profits ($)	62.9	64.0	49.0	18.3	41.1
	Market share (%)	11.4	40.0	23.1	12.2	13.3
1976	Sales ($)	982.8	1,645.0	1,000.0	600.5	593.6
	Profits ($)	76.1	87.7	50.0	32.4	76.5
	Market share (%)	20.4	34.1	20.7	12.5	12.3
1978	Sales ($)	1,834.5	2,200.0	880.0	590.0	590.0
	Profits ($)	150.3	113.0	13.0	12.0	45.0
	Market share (%)	30.1	36.1	14.4	9.7	9.7

[a]Market share among the big five.

Sources: Company annual reports and public information.

1978, even though sales had not yet overtaken the industry leader. Note also the decided fading of the other three major brewers by 1978. The battle for market share and industry dominance was clearly developing into a contest between two firms. Miller's growth rate also propelled it from 11 percent of total Philip Morris sales in 1971 to 22 percent by 1976. It was no longer merely a small subsidiary.

INGREDIENTS OF SUCCESS

When an aggressive and marketing-wise firm with virtually unlimited resources for the job at hand invades a conservative industry that had been rather backward in the use of sophisticated marketing techniques, we would expect it to make major waves and virtually shake up the industry. The brewing industry was vulnerable and Philip Morris readily exploited that vulnerability to make major market share gains before its competitors were able to counter effectively.

The ingredients of success are rather obvious and nothing profoundly innovative for most industries. But this is the first case we have examined in which a major factor of the success was bringing a segmentation approach to an industry that had traditionally offered one product for the mass market. As we noted in the Information Sidelight, segmentation is generally the more powerful approach because it better meets the needs of particular groups of consumers rather than trying to satisfy a diverse market with one product for all.

So, new products were brought out, advertising was redirected, and a massive infusion of funds for advertising was committed. The results simply confirmed sound marketing techniques that we have seen developing over decades.

WHAT CAN BE LEARNED?

As we have seen, Philip Morris was highly successful in transfering its marketing expertise from the tobacco industry to the brewing industry. Does this mean that marketing expertise is readily transferable—to other industries, other times, and other situations? Unfortunately, one must recognize that contrary examples can be given of firms whose attempts at transferring resources and expertise either failed or by no means reached the point of success. For example, consider General Foods' invasion of fast-food franchising with the acquisition of Burger Chef, Boise Cascade's venture into recreational land development, or Mobil Oil's acquisition of Montgomery Ward and Container Corporation (Marcor).[5]

So what, if anything, can be learned from this example? The answer lies in identifying those key elements or conditions that contribute to success or failure. Although the presence of these factors may not guarantee similar results in other ventures, they should at least provide such a propensity. Following are conditions that increase the probability of successful transference.

1. Interindustry transferability is immeasurably benefited if the invaded industry is somewhat backward in using aggressive marketing techniques or is composed of small firms of limited resources. As we saw, the brewing industry was tradition-ridden and dominated by family-owned firms of narrow perspectives at the time of the Philip Morris takeover of the lethargic Miller operation.

Besides the vulnerability of the new industry, some similarity of the two industries will help transferability. Specifically, this includes similarity of products, customers, media availability, prices, and distribution.

2. Although at first we might think there is a world of difference between a cigarette and a can of beer, on closer consideration there is product similarity—both are convenience-type items, both are frequently purchased, both are susceptible to strong and durable brand loyalty, and furthermore, both are subject to strong psychological product differentiation rather than physical differentiation. This means that the image of the product and of the people who use it becomes an important factor in the success or failure of any brand. And Philip Morris had proven to be particularly adept at

[5]These particular mistakes are described in *Marketing Mistakes*.

developing widely appealing images, notably with its Marlboro man. It required no great change in thinking to shift the image of Miller High Life and the new Lite beer to identifiable images to appeal to specific and relatively untapped segments of the beer market. Without such similarity of products, an invading firm must start from scratch or grope its way while gaining experience, or be forced to rely on the management of the acquired firm rather than moving in its own people. This latter situation usually results in little policy change, albeit there may be more financial resources to back up the operation.

3. Transference is more likely to be successful if customers are demographically similar such as by age, sex, income, educational level, or family situation. With such a similarity chances are good that advertising appeals and other promotional strategies will have a more predictable impact. On the other hand, with diverse customers an interim period of groping to find the most effective new approach will probably have to be endured. Generally, the tobacco and brewing industry customers met this criterion of similarity: typically the moderate to heavy drinker is also a smoker and, indeed, the two activities often go together.
4. Expediting transference is the availability of similar media to readily reach the customers in the new market or industry. Thus, the firm's experience and expertise can be easily shifted. Philip Morris had the same media available for advertising beer as it had for cigarettes. But the new industry provided an additional media advantage. Now it could use TV and radio, from which cigarette advertising had been banned since January 2, 1971. The complete availability of mass media for the beer industry was a major advantage for a firm already highly successful in the use of mass-media advertising.
5. Similarity of price also helps. If a firm is used to dealing with low-priced items, it may find that its expertise is not very relevant in another industry with high-priced goods. Although cigarettes and beer appeared to differ substantially, in their essentially marketing aspects and prices they were very similar. Both were priced low enough to be convenience goods that could be purchased on impulse, that lent themselves to mass distribution, and that depended on repeat business and thus brand loyalty.
6. A firm's ability to move aggressively into a new industry is also helped if the methods of distribution are similar. It can then use comparable distribution strategies and sometimes even the same sales force. Its position of influence with dealers can carry over to the new products. Beer and cigarettes were not identical in distribution since cigarettes were more widely distributed, but the differences were not appreciable.

With the compatible factors that Philip Morris found as it moved into the brewing industry, it is hardly surprising that it achieved a major impact rather quickly. The resiliency of a threatened and vulnerable industry is worth noting, however. While Philip Morris revolutionized the industry and in half a decade rose to second place in market share, most of the other major firms made efforts to adapt and counter the aggressive interloper, with varying degrees of success. One cannot afford to rest on one's laurels and consider a competitive advantage to be permanent.

Questions

1. At the present time, would you expect a firm such as Procter & Gamble to make a highly successful move into the beer industry? List the factors pro and con for such a move, and weight them as to importance for such a decision.
2. Would you expect the Coca-Cola Company or PepsiCo to be successful in invading the brewing industry? Why or why not?
3. What industries do you think are vulnerable to competitive entry? Why? Recommend some firms as candidates for successful entry into these industries.

Invitation to Role Play

As a top executive of Schlitz you have seen your market share fall from over 23 percent in 1970 to 14.4 percent by 1978. This is largely due to the aggressive efforts of Miller. How do you propose to reverse this most serious competitive challenge?

CHAPTER 11

L'eggs: Innovation in Hosiery Marketing

In the spring of 1976, Robert Elberson, the 47-year-old president of Hanes Corporation, could look back with considerable satisfaction to half a decade of major accomplishment. Under his guidance as the then-president of the hosiery division, Hanes had scored one of the outstanding marketing successes of the decade. Its pantyhose, L'eggs, was introduced in 1971 and in only five years had captured 13 percent of the entire pantyhose market and 41 percent of all pantyhose sold in food and drug outlets. Primarily because of L'eggs, Hanes had doubled its sales and profits from 1970 to 1975. (It was little wonder that Elberson was tapped to be president of the entire corporation.)

Of course, for Elberson and the Hanes Corporation the challenges had not ended. A successful firm does not pause long to savor its successes lest competitors catch up. The total women's hosiery market had shown virtually a flat rate of growth for the previous five years. Elberson pondered: "The only way we can continue to grow in women's hosiery is to continue to take away from somebody else. And that gets progressively tougher and more expensive, and it could create legal problems."[1] Consequently, in 1976 Hanes began testing to see if its L'eggs marketing concept could be transferred to two new product lines: Feet First (socks) and U.S. Male (men's and boy's underwear). The results are another story.

[1] "Hanes Expands L'eggs to the Entire Family," *Business Week*, June 14, 1976, p. 57.

BACKGROUND

Hanes Corporation is a textile producer of both men's and women's clothing. It was formed in 1965 through the merger of two family-owned textile manufacturing firms. At that time the textile industry was suffering from a chronic overcapacity of production resulting in excessive inventories and steadily eroding prices and profits. Mergers of small textile manufacturers were common during this time in the hope that greater size might permit more efficiency.

After the merger the profitability potential of the various product lines was carefully scrutinized. Hanes decided to concentrate most of the production on women's hosiery; this was compatible with the production facilities and experience of both the merging firms.

The decision was a wise one. Although the entire textile industry began to improve by the late 1960s as supply was brought more into line with demand, hosiery consumption in particular began to increase dramatically at about this time. For example, in 1966 the total per capita purchase of pairs of hosiery was 17.3, which was a substantial increase over the previous year. In 1967 per capita purchase rose to 21.0, a 14.7 percent increase. In that year pantyhose sales accounted for 20 percent of total hosiery sales, or some 4.5 million pair. The next year, pantyhose sales were 13.9 million pair. And in 1969, pantyhose volume shot up to 27 percent of all hosiery sales, some 40 million pair.

The basic cause for this phenomenal upsurge in demand was the miniskirt. With short, well-above-the-knee skirts, pantyhose were in wide demand because they covered the entire length of the leg. The miniskirt had been introduced in the United States in early 1967 and had rapidly achieved popularity. However, the success and burgeoning demand for pantyhose was probably not entirely attributable to the mini. Improved wearing material and weaving techniques had recently been introduced in the industry. In particular, new weaving machines developed in Italy produced a weave with less chance of stretching and sagging as well as better resistance to runs.

As a result of pantyhose sales, Hanes had a 25 percent gain in earnings in 1968. It had become a relatively healthy enterprise in three short years. Besides its hosiery products, the company also had been able to expand and hold its own in other lines such as sportswear, sleepwear, and underwear, for both men and women. Still, hosiery accounted for 55 percent of corporate sales.

A concern of Hanes and the other hosiery manufacturers was whether the demand for pantyhose, instigated by the miniskirt, would continue or was entirely dependent on the popularity of this particular style, which all knew would inevitably fade within a few years. Longer skirts were already appearing, though consumers accepted them only reluctantly. But there were some indications that demand for pantyhose might remain relatively high. Many women who had tried pantyhose for the first time found them comfortable and easy to put on. That they covered the entire length of the leg and avoided the unsightly appearance of garters and snaps also induced many women to continue wearing them, even with longer skirts. In particular, younger women were enthusiastic about pantyhose.

Other indicators also suggested that the strong demand for hosiery products would continue, at least for several more years. The United States was beginning to pull out of a slight recession. Total Gross National Product (GNP—a key indicator of the economic health of a country) was expected gradually to pick up through 1970 and continue at least through to election year 1972. Even if these predictions were not fully met, hosiery demand appeared to be somewhat inelastic because the boom in hosiery sales had occurred during a recessionary period. So the industry expected, not unreasonably, that demand would at least hold firm. As for the pantyhose share of the hosiery business, some industry experts thought that this would account for 80 to 90 percent of total hosiery sales by 1972.

In 1968 the hosiery industry was one of the most fragmented of all textile industries. There were virtually hundreds of small- and medium-size firms, but few had been able to achieve any degree of brand recognition with consumers except Hanes. Hanes brand had emerged as the leading seller of women's brand hosiery products in department and specialty stores.

At about this time, Robert Elberson, then president of the hosiery division of Hanes, noticed that a West German pantyhose manufacturer had introduced its line to supermarkets in several metropolitan areas in eastern United States. The brand name was Lady Brevoni.

Up to this time only a small amount of hosiery had been sold in supermarkets and drugstores, mostly private brands sold at very low prices. There was very little brand recognition through these outlets. And with so many competing brands, customers were simply confused.

INFORMATION SIDELIGHT

Private Brands—How Attractive to Customers and Dealers?

Wholesalers and retailers often sell their own brands, called private brands, in place of or in addition to the brand goods of manufacturers. These private or dealer brands usually are lower priced than the nationally advertised brands because of promotional savings and perhaps production economies. The lower prices, of course, can make such private brands attractive to those customers interested in obtaining the best value for their money. Other customers feel that only the nationally advertised brands can give them the assurance of quality and dependability they want.

Dealers are interested in private brands because they frequently permit a higher markup than nationally advertised brands so that the retailer can gain a better profit per unit sold. With many private brands selling for less than the national brands, a retailer is also able to offer his customers an attractive alternative for those seeking the lowest price. And since a dealer's own private brand is not available to competitors, he can thereby escape any direct price competition.

Intrigued with the idea of entering a nontraditional market for hosiery and with the initial efforts of the Lady Brevoni brand already appearing to be effective, Elberson believed that Hanes should attempt to seize as much of the self-service market as it could and as quickly as possible. Hanes had recently developed a one-size, no-sag pantyhose that fitted approximately 90 percent of all women, and this seemed the ideal product to tap this new market. Hanes should enter this market, Elberson maintained, by establishing for itself a relatively strong brand preference here, much as it had been able to do in department stores. But before he could conclusively decide on introducing the new line, he needed more information on how Hanes should best enter this particular market.

Thus, in 1969 the other principal in this case came on the scene. David E. Harrold, 33 years old, a former marketing executive for General Foods Corporation, was hired to plan and direct the efforts to introduce the new line of pantyhose to the food and drugstore consumer market. "Our objective," he said, "is to establish the same brand identity for L'eggs as, for example, Bayer has for aspirin. We are looking for a significant market share in a $1.5 billion market, which now has more than 600 competing brands of varying quality and price in the supermarket area alone."[2]

RESEARCH FOR THE MARKETING STRATEGY DECISION

Using the services of two outside marketing research firms, Mr. Harrold developed a series of objective and projective techniques to determine the extent to which Hanes' one-size pantyhose would appeal to particular target markets over a given length of time. The tests were designed to measure reactions as to comfort, wearability, fit, quality perception, and color and style preference. Group interviews of housewives were used to ascertain the importance of quality and brand image to food and drugstore shoppers. Consumer reactions to various packaging and styles were determined.

In addition to consumer research, trade research was conducted in order to acquire a basic understanding of competitors and their relative market positions and

[2]As reported in "Hanes to Push Sale of L'eggs in Retail Outlets," *Advertising Age*, April 13, 1970, p. 18.

to explore various modes of distribution being employed by the hosiery industry. Research also helped determine food and drugstore outlet preferences (and complaints) pertaining to present marketing approaches.

Altogether, Hanes spent $400,000 for marketing research, an unprecedented figure for the normally staid hosiery industry. Such an expenditure produced a great proliferation of data, much of it irrelevant, whereas other information led to conflicting interpretations. But enough useful information did emerge from the research to help Hanes establish its marketing strategy.

It was found that many women were not particularly impressed by the strong price promotions of hosiery in supermarkets and drugstores, which had resulted in A&P offering private brands for 39¢ a pair and other stores for as low as three for $1. Many customers were disgusted by the lack of uniform quality control: "For a while I always bought medium-tall in the same brand for 79¢ a pair," said one New Jersey consumer. "One week they sagged and bagged, the next week I could hardly sit down they were so tight."[3] A market vacuum appeared to exist in food and drugstore outlets for hosiery items. Although other cosmetic items had reached close to 50 percent of total industry sales in these types of outlets, hosiery sales in supermarkets accounted for only 12 percent of all hosiery sales; this disparity is more significant when it is realized that hosiery and health and beauty aid products were introduced into supermarkets at about the same time: 10 to 12 years before.[4]

A further significant bit of information emerged from the research. Supermarket and drugstore retailers wanted a large profit margin in relation to the "housekeeping" duties attendant to a hosiery display—that is, they liked the potential profits but were decidedly negative about any servicing costs of maintaining sufficient stocks of the various hosiery lines.

Now it remained to translate $400,000 of market information into a successful marketing strategy.

THE L'EGGS MARKETING STRATEGY

Early in the planning of what was to become the L'eggs project Elberson and Harrold determined not to be niggardly in the marketing effort. Such was the planned scope of the operation that a separate subsidiary was created with the major purpose of developing and conducting the marketing functions necessary to capture the food and drugstore market. Therefore, in the spring of 1969, Hanes formally approved and budgeted "Project V-L," the name given to the marketing effort. At this time, of course, the success of the venture was still very much in question, but the data coming in from the research studies and the strategy implications were most encouraging.

[3]As quoted in "Our L'eggs Fit Your Legs," *Business Week*, March 25, 1972, p. 97.
[4]Ibid.

The Product

L'eggs hosiery line consisted primarily of pantyhose of varying shades, but with only a limited number of sizes. What was unique about this pantyhose was its ability to conform to any shape leg. It could stretch and still be comfortable for the wearer. It also had a relatively good resistance to runs, and was thus more durable than most of its competitors. Furthermore, it looked sheer and stylish, qualities desired by most women.

The Name and the Package

Hanes wanted a name that would be distinctive while at the same time convey the company image and the product's use. The name finally chosen, L'eggs, matched the distinctiveness of the package almost to perfection. The sudsidiary was now called L'eggs Products, Inc. And this name would be used to represent all L'eggs hosiery goods and would be prominently displayed to consumers to signify quality, consistency, and uniqueness. Because of the shapelessness of the pantyhose, there was the opportunity to design an entirely different (for hosiery) package. The final result was a four-inch high white plastic "egg"—about the size of an ostrich egg. The "egg" sat in a cardboard collar that varied in color to designate the different styles and shades of the pantyhose.

So Hanes had achieved the perfect marriage of name, product, and package. The name described the use of the product—for legs. And the "eggs" were a clever presentation of the product—distinctive, easily differentiating styles and colors, while maximizing the amount of merchandise that could be stocked in a minimum of space.

The In-Store Display Fixture

In order to tap the supermarket and drugstore market—a largely self-service market in which selling space is at a premium—Hanes deemed it necessary to develop a floor fixture for stocking the L'eggs eggs. Such a fixture would ideally take up a little space but still hold a sufficient quantity of all styles, sizes, and colors of L'eggs to prevent most out-of-stocks and the consequent lost sales. The display finally developed required only a two-foot diameter of floor space. It was constructed of plastic and metal and consisted of a series of plastic tiers arranged vertically along a metal pole. The eggs fit conveniently in holders on the tiers. It was attractive, durable, and amazingly, held 24 dozen L'eggs. The task now remained to convince dealers to permit the display on their premises and stock L'eggs.

INFORMATION SIDELIGHT

What Makes an In-store Display Click?

The trend in retail stores today is self-service. Customers have found this appealing, and retailers are better able to cope with rising labor costs. We know that the actual decision to buy in the store hinges on the customer's attitude toward the brand, with advertising helping to mold attitudes. But often the consumer does not feel strongly about any particular brand, and here is where an attractive and striking package and a good in-store display become important: the product and brand that makes the last impression—at the point of purchase—often makes the sale.

Recognizing this, many manufacturers of consumer goods, and especially those to be sold in self-service outlets, deluge retailers with display materials: signs, banners, easel-back cards; mannequins, merchandise stands or racks; even turntables and expensive mobile displays for in-store demonstrations. The problem the manufacturer faces, however, is enticing the retailer to use the display material even though it is provided free. Much of the material is buried in retailer stockrooms and never used or used ineffectively in poor locations or not for the intended purpose.

Hanes for its L'eggs developed a package and a display that really clicked. It was striking, enticing in its novelty, and performed superbly the function of holding an adequate stock in a minimum of space.

Distribution

With most retail goods, the manufacturer is responsible only for delivering them to a transportation firm, and the retailer then has the job of maintaining adequate, well-filled, neat stocks and displays. This system—especially with self-service outlets that operate with lean work crews—often results in displays that are not well-kept and neat. Some sizes, styles, and colors are often out of stock, resulting in lost sales for both the manufacturer and the retailer.

Hanes made a major deviation from traditional methods of distribution at this point. As an inducement for retailers to take on the L'eggs line and give the display rack adequate and even prime space in the store, and also to ensure that the stock and display would be adequate and neat with minimum out-of-stocks and misplaced goods, L'eggs decided to deliver to stores directly itself, and also to assume responsibility for housekeeping and stock ordering. Accordingly, L'eggs distributed to its dealers through local warehouses on a regular routing basis; the delivery was made through the store's front door to the display itself. And what did the retailer have to do regarding the handling of L'eggs products? Practically nothing: the dealer would incur no maintenance or merchandise handling expense, nor would there be any worry about out-of-stocks, or, conversely, heavy inventories of certain slow selling styles and colors.

From local warehouses a fleet of white vans, driven exclusively by women, delivered the L'eggs products on a regular basis. The vans prominently displayed the L'eggs name on the sides. Some 450 "route girls" wore distinctive red, white, and blue hot pants uniforms and they had tinted glasses and knee-high boots to make them even more distinctive. Besides actually restocking depleted display racks, the route girls recorded sales information for prompt feedback to Hanes. The information was fed into a computer to track product movement on a display-by-display basis, thereby providing balanced product line availability for each van route from warehouse to retail outlet. Such information was also used to organize warehouse distribution, retail inventory, market analysis, and billing into a well-coordinated distribution system.

Perhaps the key factor that sold retailers was "consignment." This meant that the retailer had no investment whatsoever, because the L'eggs products were still owned by the manufacturer until such time as merchandise was actually replaced at the display rack. So all the retailer had to do was provide some two square feet of floor space. And from this the average store made $1300 a year profit. A promotional flyer distributed to potential dealers in 1972 made the following statement:

> Our L'eggs program does everything for you. We start you off with a Boutique and fully consigned inventory. You make no investment—you take no risk. That's why you make *pure profit*. Whenever your Boutique needs restocking or straightening up, our L'eggs girl is there to attend to it. She will also supply you with all in-store promotional material. . . . This year L'eggs is spending over $11,000,000 telling consumers about the benefits of our products to help you sell even more L'eggs than before.

Is it any wonder that hundreds and thousands of retailers jumped on the L'eggs bandwagon?

Price

Hanes determined to maintain a quality image for its L'eggs and it gambled on a program aimed at building brand loyalty and ads emphasizing quality rather than price. Accordingly, it decided to price the pantyhose at $1.39, a price at least 30¢ more than most pantyhose sold in supermarkets and drugstores, and as much as a dollar higher than some of the private brands during special promotions. Furthermore, the L'eggs executives were determined that these prices would be maintained in all outlets and under no circumstances would they permit L'eggs to be discounted from the list price. To do so they felt would be disastrous for the high-quality brand image desired.

Consequently, Hanes decided to fair trade its L'eggs. Fair trade laws supported the manufacturer who wanted dealers to maintain the list price. However, enforcement was left to the manufacturer, and this meant continuous monitoring of prices in all outlets carrying the brand. Competitors scoffed at the idea of fair-trading any hosiery line in supermarkets and drugstores. However, the L'eggs executives were determined to go to any lengths to keep prices stabilized: "In Detroit—the most discount-oriented city in the country—we have to police the retailers in order to maintain a fair-trade position. I have been called arrogant and stupid because we took our display out of one supermarket where the owner insisted on underpricing L'eggs."[5]

INFORMATION SIDELIGHT

Fair Trade

In 1976, after some 40 years of varying use of fair trade, the Congress and President Ford rescinded it. Fair trade laws were enacted by states and they permitted a manufacturer, if it wished, to set the minimum price at which the product could be sold at retail. The original intent of fair trade laws was to protect small retailers from the price-cutting practices of big retailers, especially the chains. But the effectiveness of these laws had been eroding for decades. Most manufacturers found the task of trying to police and bring suit against "discounting" retailers just too onerous and expensive. And the courts often had been more sympathetic with the general public's desire for lower prices than with the manufacturer's desire to maintain a high-quality image and/or assure dealers a high markup. Accordingly, modest court costs were often the only penalty assigned the "lawbreaking" retailer, and the practice of discounting blatantly continued.

A greater deterrent to a price-cutting retailer than toothless fair trade laws has always been for the manufacturer to simply refuse to sell to such a retailer. Although any manufacturer winces at refusing business, if a brand has sufficient consumer demand (usually built up by a good product and heavy advertising), the manufacturer is in more of a "power" position to dictate to the dealers.

Advertising

A major introductory advertising effort was designed for L'eggs at double the amount spent by the total hosiery industry. Some $10 million was spent, using both

[5] Ibid., p. 97.

daytime and prime-time TV, along with full-page ads in magazines and newspapers. A unifying theme was used: "Our L'eggs fit your legs."

In addition to the advertising, $5 million was spent on a national direct mail coupon campaign, offering consumers 25¢ and 35¢ off the $1.39 price of the pantyhose. The coupon effort marked the first time that heavy couponing had been done in the hosiery industry. To gain the brand recognition deemed so important to the self-service market Hanes was aiming for, all promotional materials and advertising showed the L'eggs display. Although the heavy promotional efforts were aimed primarily at increasing consumer demand and brand awareness, another important objective was to convince supermarket and drugstore chains of the desirability of stocking this new brand.

MARKET TESTING

Hanes did not jump into the national market suddenly; rather, despite its heavy marketing research efforts that helped guide strategy, it approached the market carefully, conservatively. In March 1970 it introduced L'eggs in four market areas, selected because they were rather typical of American cities in potential, distribution, and competition; these were Milwaukee, Kansas City, Sacramento, and Portland. L'eggs tested 13 weeks and found that marketing objectives had been doubled in all four cities and L'eggs was a smashing success. Previously, marketing research had found that of more than 600 brands competing in supermarkets and drugstores, no one brand achieved more than a 4 percent market share. Consumer brand awareness was estimated to be no more than 10 to 15 percent for any given brand. But after the test marketing of L'eggs, its brand awareness was 85 percent in these market areas.

These were encouraging results. In November 1970, L'eggs was introduced to the Cleveland, Chicago, Los Angeles, Philadelphia, San Diego, Detroit, Boston, Denver, and Atlanta markets. By now, over 15,000 retailers carried L'eggs and these outlets were servicing close to 65 percent of the U.S. population. For 1970, sales of L'eggs reached over $9 million. For the same year, hosiery sales were estimated at $92 million in supermarkets and drugstores. So, with only limited distribution, L'eggs in its first year had already captured close to 10 percent of its target market.

RESULTS

Over 1971, L'eggs continued to expand its distribution. By the end of the year, it was established in over 75 percent of all urban markets. Sales increased over $48 million from the 1970 figures, to $57 million. Close to 29 percent of supermarket and drugstore sales of hosiery were accounted for by L'eggs.

Finally, by 1972 L'eggs had national distribution. By 1973 it had achieved a

Table 11.1 L'eggs Sales Trend

Year	*Sales (dollars)*
1970	9,000,000
1971	57,000,000
1972	112,000,000
1973	155,000,000
1974	215,000,000

Source: L'eggs flyer to retail outlets, 1975.

market share of almost 10.5 percent of the entire hosiery industry. Its products were accessible to 99 percent of the U.S. population. It was being retailed in over 70,000 supermarket and drugstore outlets. Table 11.1 shows the sales growth of L'eggs in its introductory years: Table 11.2 shows the effect of L'eggs on total Hanes' sales and profits:

In 1973, L'eggs introduced its "Sheer Energy" pantyhose to capture the support hosiery market. By 1974 Sheer Energy had become the largest selling support hose in the United States and accounted for over 20 percent of all support sales.[6]

In 1974 L'eggs introduced its knee high line. By 1975 the Knee High brand had become the largest selling brand of knee high hose in drugstores and supermarkets, accounting for 11 percent of L'eggs sales and commanding 12 percent of the total knee high market.[7]

By 1973 competition began entering the market of L'eggs. The leading com-

Table 11.2 Total Hanes Corporation Sales and Profits

Year	*Net Sales*	*Operating Income*
1970	$177,140,000	$19,800,000
1971	176,080,000	15,760,000
1972	244,650,000	25,050,000
1973	275,880,000	27,520,000
1974	288,770,000	29,480,000
1975	314,790,000	32,780,000

Source: Hanes Corporation Annual Reports for respective years.

[6]Hanes Corporation, 1974 Annual Report.

[7]"L'eggs Steps into Test with Knee High Line," *Advertising Age,* April 15, 1974, p. 1.

petitor was No Nonsense brand, introduced by Kayser-Roth. Also accompanied by heavy advertising, No Nonsense competed on a price advantage by offering a 98¢ retail price. In July 1975 Bic Pen Corporation also entered the pantyhose market, aiming for 5 percent of the supermarket and drugstore market by July 1976 and planning to achieve this through a strong sales force, dealer incentives, and aggressive TV advertising. L'eggs remained dominant, however, and prepared to weather any late competition.

INGREDIENTS OF SUCCESS

The extensive use of marketing research played a substantial role in the L'eggs success. The $400,000 spent for such research was not an inconsiderable sum by any research standards. (We should recognize at this point that expenditures for marketing research do not guarantee correct or optimum marketing decisions. For example, consider the Edsel, for which some $2 million was spent for marketing research. However, it should improve the decision-making batting average.) Although some of the data derived was undoubtedly of little value, the total research efforts outlined the target market, its probable vulnerability to a new competitor, and the particular marketing strategy that might be effective. Such findings did require interpretation and a willingness to act on them, and it might be argued that they could have been achieved for far less cost; however, the fact remains that they provided the foundation for a confident approach to a marketing strategy unique for the industry.

As a result of the marketing research, a good product was developed that met most of the requirements that women had for this product. However, a firm usually needs more than a good product to achieve outstanding success—remember, Lestoil had to struggle for several decades before it gained widespread acceptance, though it was a superior cleaner.

We see in this L'eggs example perhaps the most effective use of point-of-purchase displays and selling tools to be found in marketing annals. The unique, yet highly practical ostrich egg packages combined with an attractive display geared ideally to the needs of retailers (requiring little space and no servicing) were powerful concomitants to the generally superior product.

Strong control of the channel of distribution, enhanced by the unique distribution mode, certainly added to the success. The use of "route girls" to service the displays and stocking goods on consignment, which eliminated risk for the retailer because there was no ownership until the goods were sold, contributed to the success in two ways:

1. The product was very attractive for retailers to carry because no investment was needed and manufacturer service was provided.
2. Hanes was able to maximize its control down the channel because it

> owned the goods until they were sold and took care of all the stocking and servicing. No price cutting was permitted, and the L'eggs image of quality was scrupulously maintained.

The heavy expenditure for marketing research and the over $10 million spent for advertising and other promotions were unheard of in this rather staid industry.

WHAT CAN BE LEARNED?

Hanes was a change maker for the hosiery industry just as Miller was for the beer industry. In both of these cases we have to be impressed by how quickly an innovator can utterly disrupt the status quo in an industry that is complacent and conservative.

We see that innovation can take many forms in the marketing arena. Usually we think of it as pertaining to a product, but here we see the major innovative actions involve (1) packaging (the eggs) and (2) the method of distribution that both maintained stocks and effectively promoted the product because of the showy route girls and the well-signed delivery vehicles.

We also witness a manufacturer's firm policy of maintaining the list price and preventing any price erosion by uncooperative retailers. The relatively high price was deemed necessary to keep customers' perception of quality. Furthermore, not permitting the price of L'eggs to be discounted made the brand more attractive to many retailers who liked the comfortable profit margin provided but could not afford to be undercut by competitors.

Of course, there are trade-offs for the manufacturer who insists on dealers' maintaining a rather high list price. Some customers buy by price and are heavily influenced by the lowest price and price reductions. Some sales volume might be lost because lower prices would generally attract more demand. But Hanes believed the quality image they were able to maintain and the dealer loyalty were worth the dedication to no price erosion. It is difficult to argue with success, but we still should recognize that such a policy is not best for all manufacturers, nor would most be in a position to enforce such a price policy as well as Hanes could.

We can question how test marketing should best be used. Can it be overdone? Can too much time be spent on test marketing before going to wider distribution? L'eggs was test marketed for 13 weeks in four metropolitan areas. Despite the overwhelming success of the tests, the company hesitated to expand nationwide. Instead, L'eggs was entered into nine more metropolitan areas. Not until almost two years after the initial introduction was L'eggs distributed on a national basis. Had the other firms in the industry been more aggressive and alert in realizing the potential (which should have been evident from monitoring the results in the test cities), this slow and conservative expansion might have cost Hanes dearly. As it was, Robert Elberson and David Harrold were heroes.

Questions

1. L'eggs were introduced with a \$1.39 price. Do you think a 98¢ price would have been better? a \$1.79 price? Why or why not? How would you go about determining the optimum price for such a relatively new product and brand?
2. Can you give some arguments for going national without the test marketing that Hanes did? Support your position before a theoretical board of directors.
3. Do you think L'eggs could have gained market entry without resorting to consignment? Do you think consignment was desirable in this case? Why or why not?

Invitation to Role Play

You disagree with the views of some L'eggs top executives that price maintenance must be maintained and no discounting tolerated. How would you defend your position?

CHAPTER 12

McDonald's: Success with Such a Simple Product

Ray Kroc faced a serious dilemma. He was 57 years old and all his life had dreamed of becoming rich. And how he had tried. Ever since he came back from World War I (at 15, he had falsified his age), he had worked hard at getting rich. He played piano with dance bands. Then he turned to selling paper cups for a firm called Lily-Tulip, and moonlighted by working for a Chicago radio station (WGES), playing the piano, arranging the music programs, and accompanying singers. Then he thought perhaps his fortune could be made in a big Florida land boom in the mid-1920s, so he left Chicago and tried selling land. But things did not work out, and he returned to Chicago a year later almost broke. Lily-Tulip gave him his old job back, and he stayed there over ten years. In 1937 he stumbled onto a new gadget, a simple electric appliance that would mix six milkshakes at the same time. So he quit Lily-Tulip again and made a deal with the inventor. He soon became the world's exclusive agent for the Prince Castle Multi-Mixer and, for the next 20 years, traveled all over the country peddling it. He earned a fair living, but by no means was he rich.

Thus far wealth had remained an illusion. Now he had stumbled onto the opportunity of a lifetime. But he needed $1.5 million to make it work. Unfortunately, he had neither money nor credit. His main source of income had dried up when he was forced to sell his mixer business for $100,000 to pay for a divorce. Now his total assets, including his house, were $90,000.

Was this, perhaps the last grand opportunity he could expect in his lifetime, to be ephemeral?

PRELUDE

In 1954 Kroc had received an order for eight of the Multi-Mixers from a small hamburger stand in San Bernardino, California. This was so unusual that he decided to go out himself and get a first-hand look at an operation that needed 48 milkshakes to be made at the same time.

Maurice and Richard McDonald had come to California from New England in 1928, thinking that this was the land of opportunity. They opened their first restaurant in Pasadena in 1940, and then in 1948 opened a self-service hamburger stand in San Bernardino. They had had trouble staffing their restaurant after World War II: unskilled job seekers were primarily drunks and drifters. Dick McDonald recalled thinking "let's get rid of it all. Out went dishes, glasses, and silverware. Out went service, the dishwashers, and the long menu. We decided to serve just hamburgers, drinks, and french fries on paper plates. Everything prepared in advance, everything uniform."[1] These operations proved so successful that they had offers by those who wanted to buy them out or work out franchising deals. But they were conservative and had cautiously sold six other franchises in California while passing up other deals. The brothers lived in a small town, were netting $75,000 a year, and were afraid of getting too big.

When Ray Kroc arrived, he was amazed. He saw crowds of people waiting in line under Golden Arches, and he estimated that the hamburger stand did $250,000 a year. He was even more impressed with the speed of service and the cleanliness. The McDonalds served a standard hamburger for 15¢, and the french fries were always fresh and crispy as they were kept warm under infrared heat lamps. The customers moved in and out quickly so that only a small facility was needed to generate the substantial sales volume.

Ray Kroc badly wanted in on this business. He hounded the McDonald brothers for two days until they finally relented and allowed him to start selling franchises. The agreement was to charge 1.9 percent of revenues for each franchise, of which Kroc got 1.4 percent and the McDonald brothers 0.5 percent.

At the time of the deal, Kroc was most interested in expanding the chain in order to sell more Multi-Mixer machines. By 1960 he had sold some 200 franchises, giving him gross franchise income per year of about $700,000. However, he had substantial travel expenses. And he had taken a partner, Harry Sonneborn, a former vice-president of Tastee Freez, who was drawing $100 a week. Kroc's secretary was taking her wages in stock (when she retired, she had an estimated 1 million shares of McDonald's stock).[2]

Sonneborn had convinced Kroc of the merits of a whole new approach. All new franchisees would also be tenants. Accordingly, the company would select the site, build the store, provide the equipment, and then rent the total package to an

[1] "What McDonald's Had, the Others Didn't," *Forbes,* Jan. 1973, p. 26.
[2] "For Ray Kroc, Life Began at 50. Or Was It 60?" *Forbes,* Jan. 15, 1973, p. 25.

operator. This franchisee would then pay a rental fee, so McDonald's would have a profit from the lease as well as from the franchising fees. A great plan, but it required money—about $1.5 million. And with Kroc's meager $90,000 in assets, bank credit was unattainable.

FRANCHISING

Franchising is a contractual arrangement in which the franchisor extends to independent franchisees the right to conduct a certain kind of business according to a particular format. Although the franchising arrangement may involve a product, a common type of franchise today involves a service rather than a product, with the major contribution of the franchisor being a carefully developed, promoted, and controlled operation, both through external signing and commonality of physical plant to internal standards and procedures.

Franchising dates back to at least the turn of the century. General Motors very early established its first independent dealer to sell and service automobiles. Coca-Cola and the other soft-drink makers granted franchises to their independent bottlers, as we have seen in several previous cases. By 1910, franchising was the principal method of marketing automobiles and petroleum products. By 1920 it was being used by food, drug, variety, hardware, and automotive parts firms. The major growth of franchising began after World War II. Soft ice cream outlets typify this growth: in 1945 there were 100 soft ice cream stands in the United States; by 1960 there were almost 18,000.

Franchise sales of goods and services by 1978 were about $275 billion, almost 30 percent of all retail sales; there were almost half a million franchise establishments in the United States, and employing over 4 million workers.[3]

Advantages of Franchising

A firm has two major advantages in expanding through franchised outlets rather than company-owned units. First, expansion can be very rapid because the franchisees are putting up some or most of the money; almost the only limitations to growth are the need to screen applicants, to find suitable sites for new outlets, and to develop the managerial controls necessary to ensure consistency of performance. The other major advantage is that more conscientious people normally can be obtained to operate the outlets, since franchisees are entrepreneurs with a personal stake rather than hired managers.

A potential franchisee or licensee finds the major advantage over other means

[3]U.S. Department of Commerce, *Franchising in the Economy, 1972–1979* (Washington, D.C.: Superintendent of Documents, U.S. Government Printing Office, 1979), pp. vi, 1.

of self-employment lies in the lower risk of business failure or, to put it positively, greater chance of success. By going with an established franchisor, our entrepreneur will have a business that has a proven consumer acceptance and perhaps wide recognition. The franchisee can also benefit from well-developed managerial and promotional techniques and from the group buying power that is afforded.

Fast-Food Restaurant Franchising

Franchised fast-food restaurants have made a major impact on the food service industry since the Second World War. Employment in fast-food franchising by the 1970s accounted for almost 30 percent of total franchising employment, and over 30 percent of all persons employed in eating and drinking places in the United States.[4]

ONWARD TO SUCCESS

Of course, we know that Ray Kroc got the money he needed, and this propelled McDonald's to a huge success. In only 22 years his firm reached the billion dollar milestone. It took corporations such as Xerox and IBM 63 years and 46 years, respectively, to reach this milestone. And Kroc could boast in his autobiography that the company is responsible for the making of over 1000 millionaires, the franchise holders.[5]

Kroc got the $1.5 million he needed from several insurance companies. As a premium on the loan, they took 20 percent of the company; this they later sold for a $7 million profit. However, had they held on to the stock, it eventually would have been worth $500 million.

A year later, Kroc bought out the McDonald brothers, paying them $2.7 million for everything—trademarks, copyrights, formulas, the Golden Arches, and the name. The brothers took their money and quietly retired to their hometown, Bedford, New Hampshire. Sonneborn also left a few years later. As his health began to fail, Kroc offered him $10 million in cash, and $100,000 a year for life, and Sonneborn retired to Florida.

Figures 12.1 and 12.2 show the tremendous growth of McDonald's in number of outlets and in sales from 1955 to 1975. An investment of $5000 in McDonald's in 1967 was worth $100,000 by 1973.[6] Table 12.1 shows the market dominance of McDonald's against its major fast-food competitors. Notice the steady increase in market share over this four-year period of rapid growth.

[4]Ibid., p. 11.

[5]Ray Kroc and Robert Anderson, *Grinding It Out: The Making of McDonald's* (New York: Berkley Publishing, 1977), p. 200.

[6]"What McDonald's Had, the Others Didn't," p. 26.

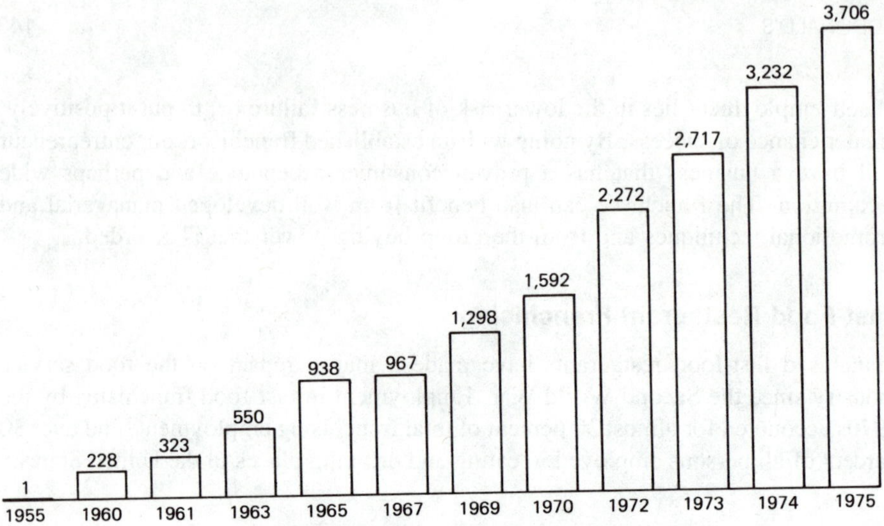

Figure 12.1. McDonald's Corporation, number of outlets 1955–1975.

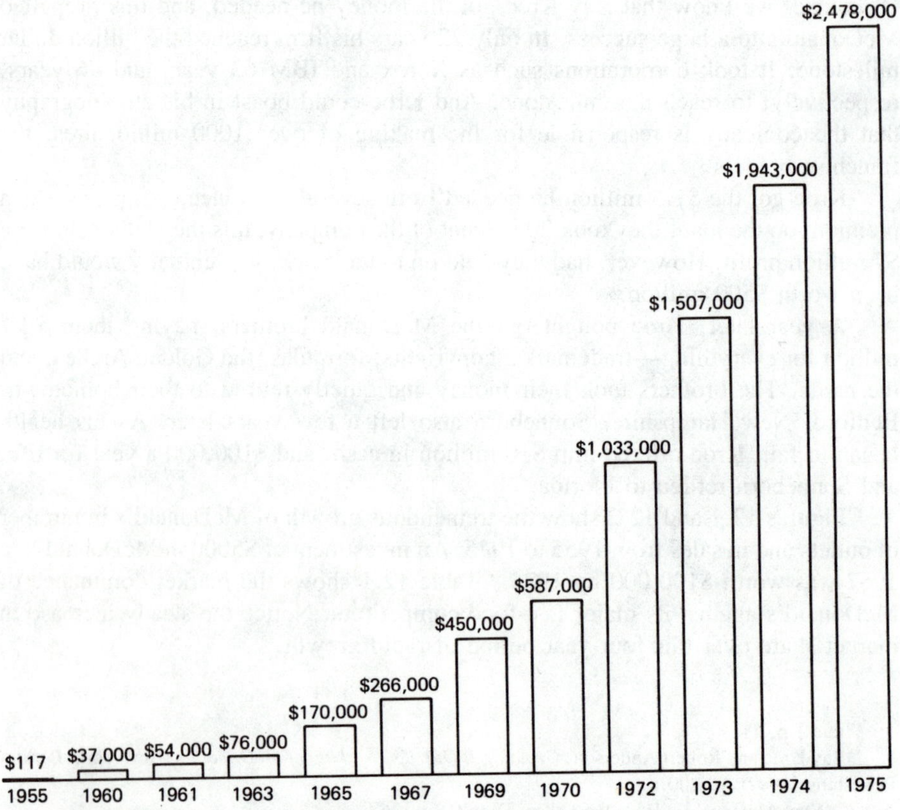

Figure 12.2. McDonald's Corporation, sales growth analysis 1955–1975 (figures in thousands of dollars).

Table 12.1 Top 25 Fast Food Restaurants

	1974		1973		1972		1971	
	A[a]	*B*[b]	*A*	*B*	*A*	*B*	*A*	*B*
McDonald's	1,940,000	19.8	1,507,000	17.7	1,032,000	15.2	784,000	13.4
Kentucky Fried Chicken	1,150,000	11.7	1,000,000	11.8	840,000	12.4	900,000	15.4
International Dairy Queen	590,000	6.0	530,000	6.0	510,000	7.5	424,000	7.3
Burger King	466,500	4.8	388,600	4.0	270,700	4.0	226,000	3.9
Burger Chef	275,000	2.8	225,000	2.6	200,000	2.9	225,000	3.9
A & W International	265,000	2.7	200,000	3.1	241,000	3.5		
Hardee's	259,000	2.6	200,000	2.4	136,000	2.0	107,000	1.8
Denny's	252,964	2.6	204,016	2.4	163,411	2.4	132,332	2.3
Jack-in-the-Box	244,000	2.6	170,000	2.1	132,000	1.9		
Pizza Hut	242,000	2.5	160,000	2.0	115,000	1.7	77,680	1.3
Bonanza	193,000	1.9	140,700	1.7	92,846	1.4	64,000	1.1
Sambo's	190,000	1.9	138,000	1.7	92,152	1.4	61,582	1.1
Gino's	170,521	1.7	170,521	2.1	128,044	1.9	95,300	1.6
Dunkin' Donuts	169,474	1.7	141,757	1.7	126,693	1.8	99,593	1.8
Ponderosa	155,000	1.6	96,552	1.1	96,552	1.4	64,065	1.1
Church's Fried Chicken	126,000	1.3	101,600	1.3	79,354	1.2	51,200	0.9
Shoney's	120,401	1.2	101,349	1.2				
Arby's International	120,175	1.2	100,000	1.2				
Jerrico	98,870	1.0	61,678	0.7				
Frisch's Big Boy	91,000	0.9	88,000	1.0	79,000	1.2	73,000	1.2
Morrison's	90,800	0.9	66,000	0.8	52,250	0.8		
Friendly Ice Cream	90,000	0.9	71,775	0.8	61,249	0.9	49,379	0.8
Shakey's	87,000	0.9	74,500	0.9	63,650	0.9	73,000	1.2
Mr. Steak	85,000	0.9	81,700	1.0	64,000	0.9	49,800	0.9
Sizzler	85,500	0.9	62,200	0.6	43,443	0.7		

[a]A represents total sales (in thousands of dollars).
[b]B represents market share (%).

Sources: Advertising Age, June 3, 1974, p. 52; May 14, 1973, p. 93, and June 30, 1975, p. 49. Permission granted by Becker Paribas Inc., 55 Water St., New York, 10041.

THE MARKETING STRATEGY

Ray Kroc saw a market opportunity in catering to "budget-conscious families on wheels who wanted quick service, clean surroundings, and high-quality food.[7] This was seen as a desirable alternative to the wide variety of drive-ins with car hops, juke boxes, tipping, waiting, and food of inconsistent and rather questionable quality. Kroc defended his approach because "all of those things create unproductive traffic in a store and encourage loitering that can disrupt customers. This would downgrade the family image we wanted to create for McDonald's. Furthermore, in some areas the vending machines were controlled by the crime syndicate, and I wanted no part of that."[8] As the executive vice-president, Fred L. Turner, said, "We want young families in the tricycle and bicycle neighborhoods—the station wagon set, or one car going on two."[9]

During the company's early years, Ray Kroc used the company airplane to spot good locations; he would fly over a community looking for schools and church steeples and then follow with site surveys. In those days, McDonald's favored above-average-income and residential areas, preferably near shopping centers. The rule was that new store sites should contain 50,000 residents within a three-mile radius. This changed by the 1970s when marketing research revealed that three fourths of McDonald's customers stopped by in conjunction with some other activity. As a consequence, stores were located by pattern of customer activity and traffic flows.

Kroc offered the public a clean, family atmosphere in which service was quick and cheerful. Cleanliness of outlets, including the toilets, and friendliness of salespeople became major competitive advantages. Efficient speed, friendly service, and assured cleanliness were not maintained without great pains. At Hamburger University, a special McDonald's training school for managers and owners, heavy emphasis was given customer service. A 350-page operating manual required adherence to strict standards, not only in preparation of food but also in care and maintenance of the facilities. For example, the manual called for door windows to be washed twice daily. Similar tight standards concerned service, food, and cooking procedures. There was even an employee dress code, with men required to keep their hair cropped to military length and their shoes highly polished. Women were to wear dark, low shoes, hair nets, and only very light makeup. All employees wore prescribed uniforms.

The cooking was completely standardized: a pound of meat was to have less than 19 percent fat; buns were to measure 3½ inches wide, no more than one-quarter ounce of onions were permitted per hamburger, and so on. The holding time for

[7]Carol White and Merle Klingman, "'Hamburger,' McDonald's Takes It Seriously," *Advertising Age,* May 22, 1972, p. 117.

[8]Kroc and Anderson, *Grinding It Out,* p. 84.

[9]"McDonald's Makes a Franchise Sizzle," *Business Week,* June 15, 1968, p. 107.

each of the cooked products was set by corporate headquarters: for example, french fries, 7 minutes; burgers, 10 minutes; coffee, 30 minutes—after these time limits the products must be thrown out. Company auditors closely scrutinized this part of the operation to ensure that all food served was of the same quality.

Consistency in adhering to the high standards was another notable aspect of the marketing strategy. Store operation was closely supervised by strong regional offices to prevent the detrimental effect on other stores in the system caused by a weakness in one restaurant. For example, field consultants made two three-day inspections of each outlet every year, grading operators on quality, cleanliness, quick service, and friendliness. This grading system could determine whether an existing operator would be granted desirable additional franchises. On rare occasions, a franchise could be terminated if prescribed standards were not met.

Franchises were granted store by store. This contrasted with most other franchisors who granted area franchises to large investors who promised to put up a given number of outlets within a specified period. Although the rate of growth was rapid, there were few problems with substandard conditions at either company-owned or franchised outlets.

McDonald's rigorously analyzed potential sites to ensure each unit of the maximum chance for success; failures due to poor locations were few. The distinctive buildings and the arches, of course, made a McDonald's unit visible and conspicuous from a distance.

McDonald's was one of the biggest users of mass media advertising of any retailer, budgeting over $50 million each year. Who is not familiar with the jingle "You Deserve a Break Today"? How successful has this mass advertising been? In a survey of school children in the early 1970s, 96 percent identified Ronald McDonald, ranking him second only to Santa Claus.[10]

THE MATURING YEARS

In 1968 Ray Kroc stepped aside and appointed 35-year-old Fred Turner president of the company. Turner had been Kroc's understudy for several years, having started as a cook and worked his way up.

Despite Turner's allegiance and admiration for Kroc, he began instituting a number of changes in established policies. The major changes involved the appearance of the stores. The red-and-white-tile exteriors were replaced by dull-brown brick, more plate glass windows, and a shingled roof. The garish neon Golden Arches gave way to a more sedate logo. The interiors were modified so that people could more comfortably eat on the premises, and the "hamburger stands" were now called "restaurants." Certain outlets were permitted more flexible decor, such as a nautical theme in Boston and a campus theme at UCLA.

[10]"The Burger That Conquered the Country," *Time*, September 17, 1973, pp. 84–92.

As McDonald's gained financial strength, efforts were made to increase the number of company-owned, as opposed to franchised outlets. An aggressive ''buy-back'' policy encouraged old franchise-holders to sell out to McDonald's. And an increasing number of new outlets were company operated. Company stores proved to be more desirable because of their higher profitability and more centralized control. In 1968, McDonald's owned only 15 percent of the outlets, but by 1974 40 percent were company owned.

As choice highway locations became increasingly scarce, McDonald's moved into some downtown locations and shopping malls, zoos, office buildings, hospitals, and even a high school. Central city locations involved some adjustments. Salaries and occupancy costs were higher, and selling hours tended to be much shorter with little business typically done on weekends. But much higher volume—averaging twice the volume of the suburban stores—offset these drawbacks. Along with the central city expansion came the overseas market. By 1980, 1050 stores were located abroad, of which 250 were in Japan and 50 in England; 19 percent of total company sales volume came from this international operation.[11]

McDonald's continued with its traditional Saturday morning television ads promoting Ronald. According to a McDonald's official, ''It only takes one child to influence a meal out.''[12] In addition to advertising directed to children, McDonald's increasingly developed ads aimed at specific segments of the public, such as blue-collar workers, a group that had been hard for McDonald's to draw. Special promotions and giveaways aimed at children have also influenced sales: for example, Kid's Day, featuring free sundaes, premiums in ''Play value'' packages, and in certain cities even a ''Fun Bus'' that takes school children on field trips with, of course, a stop at a McDonald's restaurant for lunch.

The traditional product offering of McDonald's has been simplicity itself. In the early days, the product line was only hamburgers, french fries, milk shakes, and soft drinks. The first successful menu expansion came with the Filet-o-Fish in 1962, which was invented by an operator in Cincinnati, Ohio, who was located in a large Catholic neighborhood and was faced with weak Friday sales. Before the sandwich was introduced chainwide (not until 1965) standards were developed such as how long to cook it, what type of breading to use, how thick to make it, and what kind of tartar sauce to use; it was then test marketed, being offered on Fridays only in a limited number of outlets. Chicken likewise was intensively tested, beginning in 1971, and was not made generally available until 1981. Even the Big Mac was tested for some years before it was made widely available.

The most notable success with product expansion was the breakfast menu. The Egg McMuffin was first tested in 1972, with other breakfast items added shortly after. Initially, breakfast menus were tested in Chicago, Pittsburgh, and Wash-

[11]McDonald's *Annual Report, 1980,* p. 16.

[12]Christy Marshall, ''McDonald's '79' Plan: Beat Back the Competition,'' *Advertising Age,* Feb. 2, 1979, p. 88.

ington, D.C. They proved so successful there that the breakfast menu became available nationwide in 1976 and by 1977 accounted for 10 percent of the company's sales. A major advantage of these breakfast sales was that they brought additional business, during the time when these outlets previously had sat idle. In addition, the breakfast menu lured older customers who the company previously had had trouble attracting. In 1971, only one year after the nationwide rollout of the breakfast menu, patronage from customers over 35 years of age jumped from 18 percent to 22.5 percent of McDonald's sales.[13] Thoroughly testing a few selected menu additions has been a hallmark of the product strategy. The company uses its company-owned stores to test market new product candidates before making them more widely available.

COMPARISON OF MCDONALD'S WITH LOSING FRANCHISE OPERATIONS

Many franchise firms faded in the late 1960s and 1970s because of oversaturation. Competitors had put up more outlets than the market could support, and marginal operations faltered and went under.

Some franchisors failed because of difficulty in obtaining qualified franchisees or licensees. McDonald's believed that a key factor for success was for a licensee initially to work full time in the business. The unsuccessful franchisors failed to attract or insist on licensees who met prescribed qualifications. They tended to be interested primarily in getting the initial franchise fee. Business was viewed as a quick-buck scheme, to be milked dry with the franchisor then exiting.

Poor site selection plagued some operations. In eagerness to secure footholds in major markets they failed to research for satisfactory locations. Too fast an expansion led to indiscriminate site selection, sometimes influenced by opportunistic realtors. Another factor leading to poor locations was lack of capital to purchase the more desirable sites.

When business and the economy in general is going well, ineffective management controls are not always readily apparent. However, when the economy experiences a downturn and, more important, when competition intensifies, lack of effective controls can be fatal to these businesses.

In order to gain quick public attention and recognition, many fast-food franchisors used the name of either an entertainer or a professional sports figure to lure potential licensees. For example, Minnie Pearl's Chicken, Here's Johnny Restaurant (Johnny Carson), Al Hirt Sandwich Saloon, Broadway Joe's (Joe Namath), Jerry Lucas Beef 'n Shake, and Mickey Mantel's Country Cookin' Restaurant. But although the public would pay to see the entertainer or sports figure perform, they would not necessarily frequent a fast-food outlet simply because of the famous

[13] "McDonald's Blends New Products with Savvy Merchandising," *Business Week*, July 11, 1977, p. 59.

name—unless the food and service warranted their patronage, and most of these did not.

The ingredients of success for McDonald's were simple; but few competitors were able to effectively emulate them:

- A brief menu, but of consistent quality over hundreds and thousands of outlets.
- Strictly enforced and rigorous operational standards, as to service, cleanliness, and all aspects of the operation.
- Friendly employees, despite a high turnover of personnel because of the monotony of the automated food handling.
- Heavy mass media advertising, directed mostly to families and children.
- Identifying a fertile target market—the family—and directing the marketing strategy to satisfying it: with the product, price, promotional efforts, and site locations (at least in the earlier years, the suburban locations with high density of families).

WHAT CAN BE LEARNED?

We have to concede that there is nothing exotic about success. It involves simply doing customer-pleasing things better and more consistently than competitors. Even a unique product is not the essential ingredient for success, although it can certainly help. But a hamburger is a hamburger, is a hamburger.

However, franchising presents some significant differences from other types of business operations that present powerful opportunities as well as lurking dangers. Very rapid growth is possible through franchising—far more rapid than a firm can achieve on its own, even if it has substantial resources. Because somebody else is putting up most or all of the capital for an outlet, the major impediment to expansion is finding and wooing sufficient investor-licensees and finding sufficient attractive sites for units to be placed. Both of these requirements can be done carelessly in the quest for wild expansion or, as with McDonald's, carefully for controlled expansion.

A further distinction of franchising is that a few poor operations can be detrimental to the other outlets, because all are operating under the same format and logo. Although this is similar to the situation of any chain operation (a few bad stores can hurt the image of the rest of the chain), a franchise system is composed of independent entrepreneurs who tend to be less controlled than the hired managers of a chain operation.

Illusion of Rapid Growth

The great growth possible through a franchise system can be its downfall. Because growth in number of units can occur easily and quickly, it is tempting to be a slave to it, to rush headlong into opening ever more units to meet the clamoring demand of prospective licensees. Such emphasis on growth often means that existing operations will be largely ignored. As a consequence, they will be undercontrolled and emerging problems will not receive adequate attention. Screening of people and locations tends to become superficial. Eventually the bubble bursts and the firm is forced to recognize that many outlets are marginal at best and will have to be drastically pruned. Although the aggressive and ambitious firm seeks growth, this must be prudent and controlled, even if a slower growth rate must be tolerated in order to achieve adequate assimilation.

Necessity for Tight Controls

All firms need to maintain tight controls over far-flung outlets to be sufficiently informed of emerging problems and opportunities and to maximize their resources and maintain a desired image and standard of performance. In a franchise operation this is all the more essential as we have noted before, because we are dealing with independent entrepreneurs rather than hired managers. Controls should mean not only prescribing standards—for example, the 350-page operating manual of McDonald's—but also monitoring to ensure that the standards are maintained. Regional and/or home office executives should make frequent, unscheduled calls on stores, probably with a checklist in hand, and grade their performance according to the prescribed standards. All aspects of the operation should be checked, ranging from the grease content of french fries to the soap supply in restrooms. Where performance of a particular outlet deviates significantly from that prescribed, remedial action will have to be taken, from warnings to even taking the franchise away in the event of continuing deficiencies.

Other controls are needed for screening and selecting franchisees and for training them. Specifications should also be established for site selection and building standards. Only in this way can uniformity of operation at a desired quality level be achieved and maintained.

Need for a Distinctive Image

All firms need to develop a distinctive image, one that differs from competitors, and is unique and identifiable. This is especially important in a highly competitive environment. Admittedly, uniqueness is not always easy to achieve, especially where many competitors have already adopted more obvious possibilities. But the search should go on. Uniqueness can come from a distinctive design or logo, or roof, or building style; it can come from a different menu, somewhat different services, a different promotional approach; it can even be achieved by appealing to a different customer segment.

Imitation Should Not Be Disdained

A willingness to imitate may seem a contradiction to the need for a distinctive image, but it is not so. We are talking about adopting proven successful business practices, not imitating a sign or a building style, or even a menu without any changes. McDonald's management and operational procedures were not unknown; indeed, they were highly publicized. It required no genius to recognize the merits in what McDonald's was doing, and put these into effect in another operation. But most of the other fast-food operations—such as Burger Chef, and even Burger King in its early years—either failed to fully imitate the successful strategy or did so only belatedly, as Burger King finally began to do in the late 1970s.

When a firm has developed a proven and successful format, why should other firms hesitate to imitate it? Although imitation may be viewed as uncreative, it represents sound and astute learning. Creativity can be reserved for other aspects of the operation. A firm can still maintain its own distinctive image, but based on successful management and control practices.

Questions

1. How do you account for the reluctance of competitors to imitate successful efforts of another firm in their industry? Under what conditions is imitation likely to be embraced?
2. To date, McDonald's has shunned diversification into other related and unrelated food retailing operations. Discuss the desirability of such diversification efforts.

Invitation to Role Play

As a McDonald's executive, you are strongly in favor of significantly expanding the menu offerings. In particular you have been very critical of the slow (four to five years) testing of the breakfast menu before its widespread adoption. Array as many arguments as you can for expanding the menu in specific ways. Be prepared to defend your position against other skeptical executives.

CHAPTER 13

K mart: The Discount Revolution Matures

In an earlier case about the discounter, Korvette, we described a trailblazer. Unfortunately, the early success of Korvette, the great growth that made it for a time the nation's biggest discounter, was ephemeral, and quickly faded.

With K mart we examine a latecomer to the discount scene. But Kresge brought to its K mart operation proven management and marketing techniques and resources, which it was able to convert to the somewhat different operation embodied in a giant discount store rather than a neighborhood variety store. Kresge and K mart achieved the success that might have been Korvette's. In only a few years after opening the first K mart store, the medium-sized variety chain that was Kresge had become the nation's largest discounter, and by 1976 had forged ahead of Penney's to become the second largest retailer, behind only Sears. And one man was the change maker.

HARRY B. CUNNINGHAM

The year is 1957. Harry Cunningham is leaving a meeting with Frank Williams, the president. Harry is in a state of shock, tinged with euphoria. He had just been informed of his appointment as a vice-president of the Kresge Company. This did not completely surprise him, since he had had a feeling that such a promotion was imminent. But his assignment—that was the surprise, and what a wonderful challenge—perhaps.

Harry's thoughts went back to his early years with this firm that had constituted his entire working life. He remembered his beginnings—a stockroom trainee in the Lynchburg, Virginia, store back in 1928, almost 30 years ago. He had been unhappy and frustrated then. After attending Miami University (Ohio) for two years, his money had run out and he could not return to school. And the stockroom job was so uninteresting and unchallenging compared to the intellectual stimulation of college. But he had stuck it out, and had gradually worked up in the ranks of store management. Then the assignment had come four years ago to move to the home office as sales director of the company. There it was only natural that he had gotten to know top management well. They had been impressed with his ideas; he had even been invited to attend some of the board meetings. And now this.

His thoughts swung from his career path to the company and its deteriorating prospects. The S. S. Kresge Company, which had been founded as a five and dime in 1897 by Sebastian Spring Kresge, and which had become second only to Woolworth among variety store chains, was now faced with a reality of greatly worsening prospects. Part of the problem seemed to be social in the sense that the traditional customers' needs and wants were changing. At the same time, discounters such as Korvette had invaded the market with a strong price appeal, and this was particularly threatening to variety stores who also tried to offer low prices but were saddled with a higher expense structure. Part of the problem, as Kresge management was forced to admit, was that Kresge had moved away from the founding philosophy of "quality at the lowest possible price," and been drawn to specialty items with low turnover rates and higher prices. But regardless of these identified factors and any other underlying ones, the situation seemed clear: Kresge was confronted with a serious long-term problem, and the solution was uncertain.

Back in his office, with an effort Harry focused his mind on the present and the promise or disappointments lurking in the future. His assignment as vice-president was completely unstructured; he had no operating responsibilities. Rather he had been told to take two years to study the changing competitive environment, with particular attention to the discount stores that were especially threatening to variety stores. At the end of two years, Frank Williams had told him to come back with his recommendations for the Kresge Company—and what major changes the conservative company needed to preserve its viability and perhaps get on the growth path again! On top of this strange but heady assignment, Harry had stood speechless as Frank Williams told him to prepare himself for the presidency of the company when he returned.

THE TURNING POINT

In those two years, Harry Cunningham logged more than 200,000 air-miles studying competition all over the country. In Garden City, Long Island, he observed in great detail a major unit of Korvette. He concluded that the concept was great, with the key element being the tremendous rate of turnover. But he also recognized shortcomings in the Korvette operation, namely, that Ferkauf was running the business singlehandedly and that it lacked the organizational expertise to handle the growth Cunningham hoped to achieve. He began to believe that Kresge was overstored with variety stores, and was competing with itself in the shopping centers whereas other units were tied to long-term leases in deteriorating neighborhoods. Meanwhile, the discounters were cutting deeper into sales; only a miniscule sales gain was recorded from 1955 to 1960, and profits were slipping.

Cunningham came back convinced that discounting was the way to go. In May 1959 he was made president and chairman of the executive committee. And he began laying the groundwork for the expansion he saw ahead. He was determined that Kresge would not acquire an ongoing concern but build the needed organization within the company. His executives were instructed to intently study the discount industry. He wanted to take Kresge into discounting full scale, with no room for second thoughts, but he had to sell the idea to his organization:

> Discounting at the time had a terrible odor. . . . If I had announced my intentions ahead of time I never would have made president. . . . I had the authority, but if you haven't sold the people in your organization, you'll fall flat on your face. I had to convince them that they were an important part of an exciting venture.[1]

He first had to sell the Board, and this was not easy. His initial presentation was met by reservations such as, "We have been in the variety business for sixty years—we know everything there is to know about it, and we're not doing very well in that; and you want to get us into a business we don't know anything about."[2]

Part of the persuasive argument that Cunningham used to convince the board was that the basic concepts of discounting—low gross margin, high turnover, concentration on return on investment—merely represented a return to the basics of the original variety-store concept, except that the discount format meant much broader merchandise assortments. Looked at this way, the proposed venture into discounting was less daunting, a less extreme diversification than appeared at first glance.

In March 1961, the official decision was made to move into discounting. But Cunningham was finding that some of the older executives at all levels were incapable of making the adjustment and had to be replaced. By the fall of 1961, every operating vice-president, regional manager, assistant regional manager, and regional merchandise manager was fresh on the job. But these new executives were all insiders who had proven themselves in various aspects of Kresge management and who were receptive to new ideas and eager for the challenges Cunningham envisioned.

[1] "K mart Has to Open Some New Doors on the Future," *Fortune*, July 1977, p. 144.

[2] "Kresge Company and the Retail Revolution," *University of Michigan Business Review*, July 1975. p. 2.

A vice-president, C. Lloyd Yohe, was sent out in the field to study exactly how Kresge should enter this market; Yohe was subsequently made general manager of the discount operation. On his return, he set up guidelines for the new operation, including facilities and layout, siting, salaries, operating ratios, and productivity.

In October 1961, Cunningham ordered his real estate department to obtain signed leases for no less than 60 stores, with 40 to be opened in 1963. This was a rental commitment of $30 million—and certainly millions more in fixtures, merchandise, and other needs—before the first prototype store even opened. It was an audacious move, but it was supported by the firm confidence of Cunningham in the viability of the discount concept and the strength of his organization.

To staff the stores, the vice-president of personnel was assigned the job of working out a workforce formula for recruiting, training, and executive development. One of the big questions at that time was whether or not the present Kresge buyers were competent to buy for the new discount operation. The buyers were emphatic in declaring that they were, and the decision was made not to establish a separate buying staff.

Staffing such a vast expansion program was challenging; but it was also highly motivating for the rank and file management personnel who could readily see the vastly expanded promotional opportunities in the months and years ahead. Over 400 new employees were hired after recruiting teams visited more than 100 colleges and universities. Workforce development was considered indispensible to a rapidly growing, far-flung operation.

In the beginning, certain of the new departments were so unfamiliar that it was deemed best to lease them to experienced operators. Accordingly, such departments as cameras, sporting goods, jewelry, men's and boy's furnishings, and food, were leased. Gradually as the organization gained more experience with the diverse lines, these departments were taken over by K mart people. By 1980, of the nonfood departments only footwear was still leased.

ACTION

In the first few years of his presidency, Cunningham was faced with the problem of an increasing number of variety stores in poorer, decaying neighborhoods, but where Kresge had long-term leases. Instead of closing these stores, even though their rent would continue, it was decided to experiment and convert some of them to small discount stores, which were called Jupiter Stores. These were a far cry from the much larger K marts, but they were successful enough that many were again able to turn a profit. The Jupiter Stores sold very basic staple products at low prices in rather austere surroundings. But they met with customer demand and provided the company with an additional taste of discount strategy, and helped as a training ground for future K mart managers.

In March 1962, in Garden City, Michigan, the first K mart was opened. At the

Table 13.1 The Growth of K mart, 1968–1979

Year (as of January 31)	*Number of K marts in Operation*	*Stores Added Each Year*
1968	216	54
1969	273	57
1970	338	65
1971	411	73
1972	486	75
1973	580	94
1974	673	93
1975	803	130
1976	935	132
1977	1206	271
1978	1366	160

Source: S. S. Kresge published reports.

time, the company had 803 variety stores and a few Jupiter stores. The company had just experienced a 34 percent decrease in profits between 1958 and 1962.

This first K mart was an immediate success, as customers thronged to the rather attractive store with the low prices. Cunningham's bold gamble was completely vindicated. Company executives observing the milling crowds and the many busy checkout stands had to believe now that this was the way of the future for Kresge.

Before the end of the decade, S. S. Kresge Company had transformed itself from just another variety store chain into one that also included the nation's largest discount store chain. Table 13.1 shows the great growth of K marts during the 11 years from from 1968 to 1978. The number of new stores added each year is almost incredible. Note in particular the additions for 1976. In that year, Kresge took over 145 former W. T. Grant stores in addition to building 126 new units, for a total growth of 271 new stores. In that year alone, K mart promoted 310 assistant store managers to store manager positions and hired 27,000 additional people to support one of the greatest yearly expansions ever achieved by a retailer, and one that experts believed could never be topped.[3]

The growth of Kresge's sales volume is compared to its major competitors' in Table 13.2. Notice the year-to-year percentage change and how Kresge far surpasses the others. And in 1970, Kresge passed its traditional major competitor, Woolworth, for the first time, by some thirty million dollars. It was now in third place among general merchandise retailers, but this third-place standing was

[3]As reported in *Chain Store Age*, General Merchandise Edition, June 1977, p. 81.

Table 13.2 Sales Volume (Millions of Dollars) and Percentage Change from Year to Year for K mart and Major Competitors, 1959–1976

	Kresge		*Sears*		*Penney*		*Woolworth*	
Year	*Sales Volume*	*Percent Change*	*Sales Volume*	*Percent Change*	*Sales Volume*	*Percent Change*	*Sales Volume*	*Percent Change*
1959	418.1		4036		1437		917	
1960	432.8	4	4134	2	1469	2	1035	13
1961	450.5	4	4267	3	1554	6	1061	3
1962	504.5	12	4603	10	1701	9	1110	5
1963	543.7	8	5116	9	1834	8	1183	7
1964	683.3	26	5740	12	2079	13	1338	13
1965	851.4	25	6390	11	2289	10	1443	8
1966	1090.2	28	6805	6	2549	11	1574	9
1967	1385.7	27	7330	7	2746	8	1669	6
1968	1731.5	25	8198	12	3323	21	1907	14
1969	2185.3	26	8863	8	3756	13	2273	19
1970	2558.7	17	9262	4.5	4151	11	2528	11
1971	3100.2	21	10,006	8	4812	16	2801	11
1972	3836.8	24	10,991	9	5530	15	3148	12
1973	4633.2	21	12,306	12	6244	13	3722	18
1974	5536.3	20	13,101	6.5	6936	11	4177	12
1975	6798.1	23	13,640	4	7679	11	4650	11
1976	8380.5	23	14,900	9	8354	9	5152	11

Source: Moody's Industrial Manuals and company annual reports.

only temporary. In 1976, Kresge became the second largest, passing J. C. Penney Company and trailing only Sears, and by 1976 it was doing almost twice the sales volume of Woolworth.

Table 13.3 shows the five biggest builders in total square footage added during the major growth years of the 1970s. Notice that for most of these years Kresge far exceeded its competitors, some of whom were much larger firms, at least before Kresge overtook them. Notice also W. T. Grant Company and its bold growth efforts during these years. But Grant expanded recklessly, far beyond its resources and on October 2, 1975, entered bankruptcy proceedings that culminated in liquidation on February 11, 1976. Some 1073 Grant stores were closed and 80,000 people put out of work as this 70-year-old company, with sales of $1.8 billion, closed operations never to reopen. Ambitious growth can destroy a company as it did Grant, or it can be the vehicle for superlative success as it was for Kresge. But we may ponder: was Kresge in danger of overcommitment and even bankruptcy with its bold expansion? To shed some light on any financial vulnerability of Kresge, look

Table 13.3 Total Square Footage Added by Biggest Builders, 1971–1976

Store	*1971*	*1972*	*1973*	*1974*	*1975*	*1976*
Kresge	6,532,000	9,602,000	10,528,000	9,500,000	9,500,000	17,400,000
Penney	7,634,000	7,630,000	4,876,000	5,000,000	5,500,000	7,500,000
Grant	7,283,000	7,280,000	5,600,000	3,096,078	750,000	
Woolworth	5,000,000	5,860,000	4,310,000	2,829,129	1,900,000	2,600,000
Sears	5,450,000	5,150,000	4,014,000	3,500,000	3,600,000	3,800,000

Source: Chain Store Age, November 1971–1976. Reprinted by permission from Chain Store Age, November 1971–1976. Copyright Lebhar-Friedman, Inc., 425 Park Avenue, New York, 10022.

to Table 13.4, which shows the long-term debt of Kresge and its major competitors, including Grant. Notice that Kresge was able to finance its expansion for the most part with internally generated funds. Its long-term debt is minimal compared to those of all its competitors. When we examine long-term debt as a percentage of sales, the solid financial footing of Kresge is even more obvious and the problems of Grant all the more clear.

Let us note that during the early and mid-1970s, nearly a dozen discount chains were in bankruptcy, being reorganized, or being put in receivership. In addition to Grant, some of the better known firms that had severe problems were Arlan's (which had acquired the faltering Korvette in 1971; it had initially been taken over by Spartan Industries in 1966, but was still a sick operation), Mammoth Stores, and Spartan. And Penney's Treasure Island stores and Woolworth's Woolco followed a few years later. K mart, however, emerged strong, highly profitable, and dominant in most metropolitan areas. Indeed, up to 1980, only one K mart store had ever been

Table 13.4 Long-term Debt in Dollars (in Millions of Dollars) and Percentage of Sales, 1970–1976 For K mart and Its Major Competitors

	Kresge		*Sears*		*Penney*		*Woolworth*		*Grant*	
Year	*$*	*%*	*$*	*%*	*$*	*%*	*$*	*%*	*$*	*%*
1970	145.9	5.7	630.0	6.8	278.2	6.7	167.3	6.6	35.0	2.9
1971	149.9	4.8	696.0	7.0	210.2	5.1	287.7	10.3	131.5	10.5
1972	23.4	0.6	916.0	8.3	216.9	3.9	278.0	8.8	128.0	9.3
1973	21.1	0.5	980.5	7.5	220.0	3.5	295.4	7.9	126.0	7.6
1974	211.7	3.8	1095.1	8.4	366.4	5.3	413.1	9.9	222.8	12.1
1975	210.3	3.1	1326.3	9.7	368.1	4.8	485.8	10.5		
1976	211.7	2.5	1525.0	10.2	355.0	4.2	480.0	9.3		

Sources: Company records.

closed. This was a converted Kresge's, which was considered to be obsolete and was closed in 1979. However, five new K marts were opened in the same market area at the same time.[4]

On March 17, 1977, shareholders of S. S. Kresge Company voted to change the corporate name to K mart Corporation in recognition of this discount operation, which by 1976 was producing 94 percent of the corporation's annual domestic sales.

INGREDIENTS OF SUCCESS

What made Kresge's venture into discounting such a notable success, while Woolworth's was a failure? They both started at about the same time, had abundant resources, both financial and managerial, and had similar backgrounds of accumulated experience.

A number of factors have been cited by various observers as having major roles in the success of K mart. The following are some of the most commonly mentioned:

- Emphasis on high turnover.
- Emphasis on low markups and low prices, but heavy sales volume.
- Carrying only first-quality goods and national brands, at least at the beginning—no "seconds" or distress goods.
- Across the board discounting, and not just selected "specials."
- One-stop shopping format.
- Clustering.

What these observers have failed to appreciate is that these factors were by no means unique to K mart: almost all discount operations adhered to these same policies and practices.

A strong emphasis on high turnover is the key ingredient of discounting strategy, for all discounters. This is the kingpin that enables such firms to emphasize low prices and yet prosper on the low markups that such prices necessitate. Admittedly, several other factors also were stressed in order to support the low price, low markup format—notably a low-expense structure with self-service and a no-frills decor and emphasis on sales volume. But high turnover is basic because of the lowered inventory and the high return on investment that it involves. (Review the Information Sidelight in the Korvette case, which demonstrates with numbers the impact of turnover on profitability.) The high turnover was achieved by carrying only the most popular sizes and items—there was no room for slow sellers or fringe sizes.

The policy of carrying only first-quality goods with an emphasis on national brands certainly represented no different strategy on the part of K mart. Even the

[4] "K mart to Keep Momentum Growing," *Chain Store Age,* Executive Edition, Sept. 1980, p. 59.

early discounters adhered to this strategy. It was in contrast with the bargain basements of department stores and some promotional-type stores that sought closeouts, distress goods, and seconds that could be sold at low prices and still yield a fairly good markup. The discounters, on the other hand, believed the only way they could gain customer acceptance was to offer regular quality merchandise, preferably well-known national brands—that customers were familiar with and often were already presold by the manufacturers' advertising. Rather than offer loss leaders and other special goods at very low markups to entice people into the store, the discounters usually preferred to build their reputations by offering discounts across the board.

The one-stop shopping format that was approved in the very early planning for K mart was also nothing unique but a practice followed by Korvette and many of the early discounters. A wide range of departments, including food and furniture, was common. Actually, K mart did not go as far with the one-stop format as stores like Korvette, since it did not try to maintain a full furniture and carpeting department.

The idea of clustering—that is, opening a number of stores in a metropolitan area at the same or nearly the same time, rather than ''testing the waters'' with a single store—was also a strategy practiced by Korvette. The advertising impact of a number of stores sharing the expense was more powerful than that of competing firms that had fewer units to share the advertising burden, and the technique also increased the effectiveness of management and control.

Consequently, we have to look further to identify the factors unique to K mart's success at a time when many discount firms were faltering and some areas were becoming over saturated with stores. The following are characterstics we can identify as the unique ingredients of the success of K mart:

- Rapid but controlled growth. The line is thin between overly ambitious expansion and overconservative caution. The first can leave a firm vulnerable to financial overextension, and if things do not quite meet expectations the viability may be jeopardized. The latter, of course, can result in lost opportunity and competitive inroads.

  Kresge may have walked the thin line in its ambitious expansion plans. But it had several trumps. Most of the organizational requirements were already in place. Management personnel and training programs were well established and tested. Store location and planning research and analyses were also well seasoned. Controls for far-flung units had been operational for decades. All of these important factors for a mighty expansion drive already existed. They needed to be enlarged more, more personnel brought into their functional areas, but the foundation was well laid.
- Organizational simplicity. Unlike most of the other established firms, such as Penney and Woolworth, who ventured into discounting with a separate subsidiary, division, and organization, K mart kept its variety store organi-

zation—the same buyers, store planners, management personnel. And this worked. Their skills and abilities were transferable and could be shared. In return, there is organizational simplicity. And this brought the advantages of better communication, coordination, and cooperation by all sectors of the corporation than normally could be expected when such functions and activities are divided. It also brought a lower overhead.

- Simplicity of store planning and layout. According to the size of the market area, five different sizes and models of K marts were constructed:
  1 40,000 square feet (for cities 8000 to 15,000 in population).
  2 65,000 square feet (for up to about 50,000 population).
  3 70,000 square feet (for the 75,000-population target).
  4 84,000 square feet (for large metropolitan markets).
  5 95,000 square feet (for still larger metropolitan markets.

  Thus, K mart was able to enter a market with the most effective competitive size for that market. In the process, the stores and the layouts were standardized to maximize the effectiveness and speed of planning, stocking, and opening.
- High-quality store management. The key factor of high-grade management differentiated K mart from most of its competitors, including the ill-fated Korvette. Kresge had long had one of the strongest college recruiting and management development programs of any chain, and this commitment was intensified with the heavy labor requirements brought about by the K mart expansion. Each manager was given considerable autonomy—far more than is customarily given to chain store managers, especially by discount firms. Responsibilities included hiring and training personnel, ordering merchandise, and controlling expenditures and inventory. To ensure their preparation for such responsibilities, store managers were given top salaries and intensive training. A 21-week orientation program began their training, followed by on-the-job experience as a manager of either a Jupiter or Kresge variety store. As the candidate passed these hurdles, the next step was comanager of a K mart unit. After approximately nine years of management experience, the successful candidates were given a K mart to manage. Compensation and further promotion was based on how well the manager handled the profit-center responsibilities and on the ability to generate a proper return on investment.
- Adaptability. K mart exhibited an adaptability to changing circumstances somewhat unusual in a large organization that had found the success pattern earlier. At least four strategy modifications can be identified:
  1 The early strategy of all discounters was a bare minimum of service, to keep costs and prices rock bottom. Consequently, they offered no credit, nor did K mart in its early years. However, by 1970 the company sensed the need for this customer service and began accepting bank

credit cards as well as issuing its own credit card. The latter was dropped four years later because of costs, but the bank credit cards are still accepted.

2 The early discounters located themselves in free-standing sites or abandoned warehouses and the like, and K mart found great success in building its own free-standing stores isolated from other stores and from the restrictions of shopping centers. But the company was flexible enough to enter its first regional mall in 1978 and now uses both types of locations.

3 The early beliefs about how close K marts could be sited to one another were to change. By the mid-1970s, it was determined that stores could be located much closer together than had earlier been thought. This paved the way for greater expansion and more density of market coverage.

4 When the first K mart store was opened, leased departments accounted for half of total sales volume. But K mart began taking over the leased departments as more experience was gained with the unfamiliar lines of merchandise. Thus, K mart management was able to exercise greater control and greater profitability over a wide-ranging array of products.

Comparison with Woolworth

Throughout most of its history, the Kresge Company had viewed Woolworth as its archrival, the firm to overtake sometime far down the road. In 1962, Woolworth had twice the sales volume of Kresge. That same year, Kresge opened its first K mart store, and Woolworth its first Woolco. Woolworth's management announced at that time that it would build the nation's largest discount store chain. However, a mere 10 years later, Kresge surpassed Woolworth in sales volume by half a billion dollars. By this time, Kresge was obtaining a 14.81 percent return on equity, compared to Woolworth's 9.25 percent—an amazing differential of 60 percent.

Woolworth in its venture into discounting used a different organizational structuring. With the benefit of hindsight, this may have been a significant flaw. The Woolco division was established as an autonomous unit, completely independent of the variety store division. This involved separate management staffs, merchandising policies, advertising efforts, and a complete separation of operations. Not only did such an organizational structuring increase fixed costs, it fragmented the efforts of the total company and certainly involved less total commitment to discounting than Kresge had.

The ''Jupiter'' idea of Kresge was eventually imitated by Woolworth as they faced the problem of long leases on unprofitable stores in decaying neighborhoods. They called their version the ''Worth Mart,'' but these were not successful and were phased out in 1966.

Some of the advertising of Woolco may have had a negative impact. The Woolco stores began to be touted as "promotional department stores"—a cross between discount and department stores. Since Woolco had been introduced as a discount store, this promotional switch undoubtedly confused some customers and gave the stores an uncertain image.

Kresge was opening an average of 45 to 50 new K mart stores a year up to the 1970s when it began opening much larger numbers, but Woolworth had not geared itself to opening even 30 stores in one year until 1980. At least part of the problems of Woolco can be attributed to too conservative a management: "They scattered their shots. Woolco would open one store in Columbus, Ohio and move on to another market, while K mart opened up three, four, and five stores in Columbus and got economics of distribution and, more important, advertising."[5]

However, Woolworth management believed that their cautious attitudes were fully justified. They felt that the "Woolworth Company was too valuable an asset to just go in one direction."[6] Although such a conservative approach and the inability to make a firm commitment may have been prudent under many circumstances, it resulted in vulnerability to an aggressive growth-minded competitor.

Despite the financial and workforce resources behind Woolco, the division continued to be a cash drain; it was never a money-maker. Yet, practically all other aspects of the Woolworth Company were short-changed as resources were plowed into the discount subsidiary. Finally, and suddenly, in September 1982, the chairman of Woolworth, Edward F. Gibbons, gave up on the discount chain that had sales of $2 billion, but no profits. He had staked his career on this operation. A $286 million aftertax writeoff was taken. One month later, Edward Gibbons died suddenly. The Woolworth adventure in discounting was over. But K mart was flying high.

WHAT CAN BE LEARNED?

As with most great successes, we come away from researching with a sense that there is nothing mysterious about their success, that no magic formula was used, or needed. Success can come simply, merely doing things better than competitors. K mart certainly followed the traditional discount store format, the same format and policies as those of Korvette, Topps, Spartan, Zayre's, and the host of others. But it did it better: a better job of planning operations and selecting locations; a better job of training and developing people, both managerial and nonmanagerial. It began to make some modifications and adaptations later, but these were not revolutionary and only better honed the discount format.

We are left with the conviction that one individual can exert an almost unbelievable influence—for good or bad—on a corporation's fortunes. In less than a

[5]"We're Moving! We're Alive!" *Forbes,* Nov. 21, 1983, pp. 66–71.

[6]"How Kresge Became the Top Discounter," *Business Week,* Oct. 24, 1970, p. 63.

decade, Harry Cunningham transformed the slipping and mediocre Kresge into an industry leader. At about the same time, another chief executive, Richard Mayer of W. T. Grant Company was leading his firm to utter disaster and liquidation, again, in less than a decade. Suppose Harry Cunningham had been mistaken in his assessment of the opportunity for Kresge in discounting. In such a scenario, the Kresge Company might have become another Grant. Aggressive decisions can lead a firm to great success or utter failure. But being prudent and conservative, as Woolworth's management was during this time, is not the answer either, although it may preserve the viability of the enterprise.

The K mart example indisputably shows that great growth is possible without jeopardizing viability—although Korvette and Grant show the perils of overextension. But great growth should be attempted only when it can be controlled, a growth that does not outstrip workforce, research and planning, and financial resources. Despite the almost unbelievable growth of K mart—opening as many as 271 huge stores in a single year—it had the trained employees to staff them effectively, and most of the funds needed were generated internally without the need of heavy outside financing.

The importance of maintaining a stable and clear-cut image and undeviating objectives is clearly demonstrated. As growth and success came to K mart, it resisted the temptation to try to become something it was not, such as upgrading to a department store, and thereby confuse its customers and blur its image. Korvette was not able to resist this temptation, and it succeeded in alienating many of its former customers; even Woolworth was not sure what it wanted Woolco to be—a full-fledged discount store or a promotional department store—and developed a fuzzy image.

We see the importance of simplicity. This may well be one of the keys to controlled growth. The organization was kept simple, indeed, it was hardly more complex than when Kresge had only variety stores. No separate organization was created for the discount operation, no separate division. And the existing organization found the challenge and opportunity of developing the new venture to be highly motivating and beckoning to greater responsibilities and advancement. Similarly, the store facilities were geared to simplicity in the planning and operating, with standardized sizes of stores, layouts, displays, and so on. The controls and the merchandise assortment plans—all were simply adaptations and modifications of those developed over decades of variety store operations.

The desirability of concentrating rather than diffusing efforts is demonstrated in this case, especially when we consider the laggard performance of Woolco. This strategy is not unlike that facing military commanders: do we concentrate our forces to secure a breakthrough—and what if that fails: how vulnerable do we then become? Or do we spread our efforts to all sectors?

No sweeping generalization is possible for this dilemma. In the case of K mart versus Woolco, the concentration of efforts worked to perfection. But if the

K mart venture had failed. . . ? At what point should you commit your full resources to a new and unproven venture? And if there is misjudgment, a full commitment may mean disaster. Perhaps the prudent approach to discounting was that of Woolworth. But a conservative and prudent approach is bound to fail against the aggressively successful approach. Risks cannot be avoided in marketing decision making.

Questions

1. The success of K mart, the imitator not the innovator, suggests that being first to the market may be less advantageous than coming later. Evaluate this reasoning.

2. Consider and evaluate other alternatives to discounting that the Kresge Company might have considered in its quest to revive its fortunes in the early 1960s.

Invitation to Role Play

You are the personnel director of the Kresge Company. The decision has just been made that the firm will shift as rapidly as possible into discounting. You face a major challenge to provide a sufficient number of trained executives at all levels. How would you propose to do this? In particular, address the issue of recruiting experienced discount executives from other organizations.

CHAPTER 14

Perdue Chickens: Differentiating a Commodity

It is 1971, and Frank Perdue, president of Perdue Farms, has too immediate concerns. He is trying to invade the lucrative New York City market with his fresh Perdue-brand chickens—has been trying to do so for two years now without great success—and now he realizes it is going to cost a lot more to have any impact, without any guarantee that the expenditure will be worthwhile or simply the reckless action of an iconoclast. But almost as bad, Frank muses, his new ad agency wants him to do the commercials. ''Wait a minute,'' Perdue, whose voice is sometimes squeaky and high pitched, said as he tried to scuttle this idea. ''I've never done anything like this before. I was never in a school play or took dramatics.''[1]

BEGINNINGS

Franklin Parson Perdue was born in 1920 on the Delmarva Peninsula, a strip of land separating Chesapeake Bay from the Atlantic Ocean. In that same year, Arthur Perdue, Frank's father, built a chicken coop, bought 50 Leghorn chickens for a total cost of $5, and entered the egg business. The business grew and when Frank was ten years old he was given responsibility for the care of some of the chickens. By the time he had graduated from high school Frank reckoned that he had had enough of chicken coops that needed daily cleaning. He enrolled at a local teacher's college, and hankered to be a big-league baseball player. But after two years he left college

[1]Grover Heiman, ''Fainthearted? Not 'Mr. Chicken,' '' *Nation's Business,* August 1982.

to go back into the family's egg business. This was 1939, and the company had three employees, including Frank and his father, and 2000 chickens.

Disaster struck when the layers became badly infected with a highly contagious chicken disease, leukosis. Losses ran high and the Perdues, discouraged, shifted to broiler production with a flock of 800 New Hampshire reds that were a hardier stock. The business grew from that point. World War II brought rocketing meat prices and the broiler boom was on. Now the Perdues were hatching 40,000 chicks a week. By 1950 when Frank became president, Perdue Farms was one of the largest chicken growers on Maryland's eastern shore. It had 40 employees; the company hatched its own birds, fed them with its own special feed mixture, grew them to maturity, and then sold them to processors.

In 1968 Frank decided to integrate the operation. He intended to market the birds himself rather than continue to sell them to processors at broiler auctions. He bought and renovated a processing plant that had belonged to the Swift Company. Now, instead of trying to raise all his own chickens, he decided to leave the growing of chickens to contract farmers. The company, 400 employees strong, for the first time began marketing fresh-dressed poultry. That same year Frank made another daring move. He put his label on his birds, giving them a brand-name status chickens had never had before. He did this initially by hanging a tag bearing his name on the wings of his processed chickens. Later the tag was redesigned in red and yellow.

Frank now faced the problems of marketing his brand-name chickens. He thought that advertising might be the key, but such an idea violated all the traditional promotional concepts, which maintained that commodity products, since they could hardly be differentiated, could not be effectively advertised. And chickens had always been as much a commodity as grain and beef, hardly brand identifiable. But Perdue was attempting to make his chickens brand identifiable. If he could do this he could command premium prices for them and avoid the price competition that besets producers and marketers of commodities, especially during those frequent times when supply outstrips demand.

Perdue was able to achieve differentiation in two ways:

1. He made his chickens somewhat different by giving them special feed. Along with high-nutritional ingredients, some marigold leaves were added. This gave the broiler a golden-yellow appearance instead of the usual pale flesh color.
2. Fresh rather than frozen birds were marketed, and these were generally perceived by consumers as being more flavorful and more desirable than competitors' frozen birds. Eventually more than 600 vehicles fanned out from Perdue facilities each day to ensure fresh produce in all the markets served.

Now Frank Perdue was on the way to fashioning a marketing strategy that would enable him to compete on a nonprice basis, and this was to lead to his great success. The Information Sidelight discusses the advantages of nonprice competition when this can be achieved.

Still, the idea of putting promotional money into a chicken business, which typically had small profit margins, seemed foolhardy. But Perdue said, "There

INFORMATION SIDELIGHT

The Attraction of Nonprice Competition

The great limitation in using price as a competitive tool, from the point of view of the seller, is that competitors may retaliate and a price war ensue. Not only might no seller benefit from such a situation, but prices may even settle permanently at a lower level with a lower profit margin. The objectives of nonprice competition are to either increase sales without cutting the price or raise the price without sales seriously dropping.

The distinction between price and nonprice competition is illustrated by the demand curves in Figure 14.1. A demand curve is simply the graphed relationship between prices and demand. For example, if a chicken producer wished to sell 500,000 broilers, the selling price could be lowered to 39¢; on the other hand, if by nonprice efforts the producer could shift the demand to the right, to D′D′, he could sell more than the 500,000 at the 39¢ price, or could sell 500,000 broilers at the higher price of 49¢. In actuality, of course, these demand curves are not so clear and can be reasonably estimated only with empirical testing.

The objectives of nonprice competition may be attained by increasing advertising and other promotional activities and/or by developing attractive product features and improving quality. Of course, a product must be capable of being brand differentiated in some positive ways in the eyes of potential customers, and Perdue was able to achieve this.

There are other advantages to nonprice efforts than simply avoidance of cutthroat price competition. Goodwill on the part of customers and dealers may be more lasting than from a price cut, which often brings only a temporary advantage. Anyone can copy a price cut, but some nonprice features are more difficult to match. For example, if enough consumers could be convinced that Perdue's golden chickens were indicative of plump, tender, high-quality birds which were worth paying a higher price for, this is not easily countered by competitors, and certainly not without a long and expensive promotional effort.

Certainly, some methods of nonprice competition are easily duplicated and mutally neutralizing in their impact. This is one of the drawbacks of trading stamps and games. Similarly, liberal guarantees and warranties are easily duplicated. But enough alternatives are possible to make nonprice competition attractive to sellers.

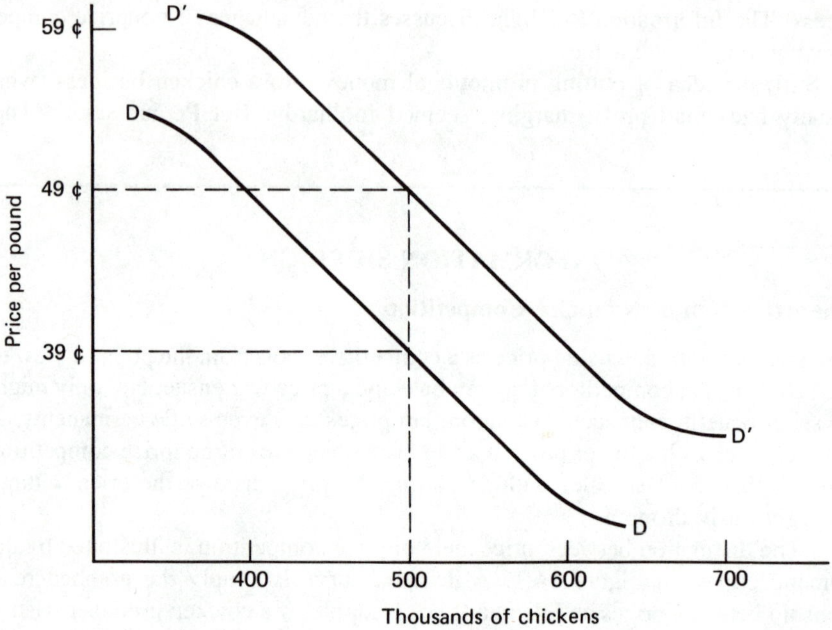

DD = original demand curve for commodity (chickens) facing price competition

D'D' = demand curve after shift due to effective nonprice efforts

Figure 14.1. Shift in demand curve from price to nonprice competition for chickens.

seemed to me to be a much greater variation in the quality of chickens than in the heavily advertised products such as detergents, cigarettes, and beer.''[2]

Perdue decided to invade the populous New York City market. In the company's first advertising campaign in 1968, $30,000 was spent on radio spots. The budget was doubled in 1969, and Perdue suggested to his advertising agency the possibility of trying television. The agency talked him out of it. In 1970, with the ad budget increased to $120,000, television was tried for the first time, but results were not very satisfactory. Meanwhile, Frank read books on advertising, talked to sales managers of radio and television stations, consulted experts, and set out to find a new agency. With a thoroughness that became legendary, he interviewed some 40 ad agencies before finally hiring the small firm of Scale, McCabe, & Sloves, which urged him to go more heavily into television. He set the budget for 1971 at $250,000—an undreamed-of budget for advertising chickens in only one market area.

[2]Reported in *Broadcasting*, June 13, 1977, p. 22.

RESULTS

Frank was persuaded to do a commercial. He flubbed his lines and extensive reshooting was required, but it was finally done, and it came out splendidly, capturing Frank's sincerity and enthusiasm for his product. Frank and his chicken commercial were so good that the commercial was ranked the best television commercial of less than 60 seconds by the Copy Club of New York, and *Advertising Age* called it "the best trade campaign of the year."

Before long, the face of Frank Perdue was appearing in full-page magazine and newspaper ads, subway posters, and the television screen. He even tried doing some commercials in Spanish. The advertising motto claimed that "it takes a tough man to make a tender chicken."

The ads evinced a sly humor. Perdue bragged about the soft life his tender chickens led in $60,000 houses, getting eight hours' sleep, and eating princely meals that included cookies for dessert. As baby chicks, the birds were chauffered about in buses, like those that school children take, only smoother and handled by nicer bus drivers ("Your kids never had it so good"). It was claimed that Perdue chickens never ate junk food and that they washed down their well-balanced meals with pure well water. The image was conveyed, with tongue-in-cheek, of soft-living superchickens.

The campaign achieved such success in New York City that Perdue chickens had captured a phenomenal 30 percent of this huge market by 1978. Perdue quickly broadened his market targets. In 1972 he entered the Philadelphia market with extensive advertising. In 1973 he pushed into Boston and Providence, Rhode Island. By 1976 he had solidly captured Baltimore, and Connecticut in 1979. By now Perdue chickens accounted for 20 percent of the entire chicken consumption of the Northeast. Market penetration of this densely populated area continued, and by 1980, expansion was targeted for the Washington, D.C. market, with Richmond, Virginia, soon to follow.

In 1970, prior to television advertising, annual sales were $50 million. By 1972, the year after Perdue first appeared on television, sales had risen to $80 million. By 1976 sales exceeded $179 million, and two years later, $270 million. For 1981 sales were $434 million, and the half-billion-dollar mark was within easy reach.

The climbing sales figures mirrored Perdue's advertising expenditures. By 1976 he was spending $1 million annually, with expenditures subsequently rising in concert with production at a rate of about 1¢ a pound.

The success of this advertising was readily apparent. In one month in 1972 advertising prompted 10,000 calls to Perdue's Maryland headquarters from New Yorkers asking where to buy his chickens. More inquiries and comments were soon received from 22,000 customers who for their interest were sent a free Perdue Cookbook instructing them how to prepare the "gourmet bird." A follow-up sur-

Table 14.1 Consumer Awareness of Perdue-Brand Poultry and the Nearest Competitor in the Various Perdue Markets, 1981 Data

	Amount of Unaided Consumer Awareness	
	Perdue	*Nearest Competitor*
New York	96	50
Philadelphia	92	23
Boston	93	26
Providence	87	25
Baltimore	86	66
Lancaster	67	19
Wilkes-Barre	65	12
Hartford	69	46

Source: Perdue: Where the Growing Is Great! company publication, n.d., p. 21.

vey in 1972 found that one out of every six chickens eaten in New York was Perdue's, and that 51 percent of those surveyed recognized the Perdue label, whereas the nearest competitive brand enjoyed a mere 5 percent awareness factor. By early 1980, Perdue chickens had a 95 percent unaided recall factor among New York housewives, meaning that 95 out of every 100 asked by marketing researchers what brand they had heard of, named Perdue. Table 14.1 shows the percentage of people in the various markets who readily named Perdue when asked to recall a brand of chicken. In all markets, Perdue easily led the nearest competitor in such brand recognition, despite the fact that it was competing with already well-established brands in each new market area. The data are based on 1981 figures.

Table 14.2 shows the growth in pounds of poultry produced by Perdue during the decade of the 1970s. In 1968 Perdue had 400 employees when the first processing plant was purchased in Salisbury, Maryland, and Perdue-brand chickens were marketed for the first time. In 1971 the company build a second, much larger processing facility in Accomac, Virginia. In 1976 a third plant was opened in Lewiston, North Carolina, followed by a fourth in Felton, Delaware. In 1979 the company opened a plant in Georgetown, Delaware, which was the only one in the United States designed solely for processing the larger five-to-seven-pound roaster chickens. By 1979 Perdue had over 4000 employees. This was to increase to 6700 by 1982. Some 4.5 million chickens per week were being processed, with every chicken shipped fresh from the Perdue plants to poultry wholesalers and chain supermarket warehouses from Boston to Richmond.

The product line by 1982 included the branded broilers, tagged pedigreed

Table 14.2 Pounds of Poultry Produced by Perdue, 1970–1981

Fiscal Year	*Pounds of Poultry*
1970–1971	119,600,000
1975–1976	263,600,000
1976–1977	327,400,000
1977–1978	376,800,000
1978–1979	431,600,000
1979–1980	568,200,000
1980–1981	644,900,000

Source: Perdue: Where the Growing Is Geat! company publication, n.d., p. 16.

parts, an ''Oven Stuffer'' roaster (a chicken large enough to feed the average family and small enough to avoid leftover problems—thus filling a void in the marketplace), fresh Cornish hens, and deboned chicken breasts.

Perdue's six commercial hatcheries were able to hatch up to 4 million chicks every week. Day-old chicks were swiftly delivered to 1600 independent growers where they remained from five weeks to a year, depending on the type of birds the grower contracted to raise. These growers were supported by Perdue health services experts, nutritionists, and other research and technical experts.

INGREDIENTS OF SUCCESS

Although the heavy expenditures for advertising are the most obvious component of the success of Perdue, this needs to be qualified. The mere spending of large sums for advertising does not guarantee success, as we have seen in earlier cases. It can help spur it, if the other ingredients are right.

The essential ingredient is Perdue's ability to develop a strong differentiation for his commodity product. Indeed, he is credited with being the first producer successfully to market a brand-name broiler.

Perdue advertised the quality of his birds and insisted that such quality be maintained; indeed, he guaranteed satisfaction with his chickens and would give a full refund to anyone complaining. He joined a strong commitment to research into genetics and nutrition with high quality control standards to ensure that the quality being so heavily advertised was real.

Not the least of the promotional success of Perdue was his personal appearance in the ads and commercials. He conveyed a sense of sincerity along with sly humor that viewers found empathetic and convincing. He sought to convey to consumers that a chicken that was good enough to bear his name was going to be a better chicken than one that was "only good enough" to be acceptable to the U.S. government. A later case, Hyatt Legal Services, is another example of the effectiveness of the owner in personally conveying the message.

The promotional efforts show the strength of a pull rather than a push strategy. Consumers, on seeing the Perdue advertising, were soon demanding this brand from their food stores. This eased entry into each new market. Before long, Perdue found that food stores in new markets were eager to stock the brand even before the first ad had been run.

Although product differentiation has been the key to the success of Perdue, he has also used segmentation effectively in his expansion efforts. Promotions featured the type of product deemed most in demand or most compatible to the particular market area. For example, in New York City where there is a "gourmet" attitude, chicken parts were featured initially. In the Pennsylvania market, where stews and country family dinners were a way of life, roasters and bigger parts were pushed. In Boston, which had more income per capita than any other market, Cornish hens were successfully emphasized.

WHAT CAN BE LEARNED?

We see that old shibboleths can be toppled and traditional cautions sometimes discarded. Perdue has shown conclusively that commodity-type products can sometimes (perhaps we cannot say always) be differentiated and marketed as something desirable and different from competing products. We have seen that such a product can be advertised effectively, that indeed it can warrant spending millions of dollars for advertising, and that the old maxim that a commodity-type product cannot be priced higher than competitors belongs to a bygone age.

The example of Perdue and his branded broilers that commanded premium prices is not quite unique in marketing annals. In the mid-1960s, United Fruit succeeded in establishing a brand image of a higher quality for its Chiquita bananas; this permitted premium prices for a product that was little different from other bananas. In the case of the Perdue chickens the quality differences and the product uniqueness was more readily apparent.

Using the owner or chief executive as the spokesperson for the company and its products appears to be better than hiring an actor or athlete. The effectiveness of such people as Lee Iacocca, Joel Hyatt, Frank Borman, and Frank Perdue has led to a popularity for this type of testimonial advertising. But let us caution that the company spokesperson must be able to convey sincerity and a good rapport with the audience. Not everyone is able to do this, despite careful rehearsals, retakes, and expert advice.

A marketing strategy based on quality can be powerful. Although it is certainly not the only strategy that can be effective in a given situation, when a quality image can be developed and scrupulously supported it can be most profitable. It permits higher prices than for competing brands, it can quickly build up a brand identification and brand loyalty, and the product is often more attractive to dealers because of higher per-unit profit margins. Any firm opting for this strategy, however, must vigorously guard its quality image and the quality standards for its brand. Otherwise, a reputation can be quickly eroded and never regained. In pursuing this strategy, a firm should consider the marketing efforts of its competitors. In Perdue's case, no competitor had attempted to achieve a significant brand identity and differentiation, much less a quality image that could command a higher price. The void was there, and Perdue filled it beautifully. However, if one or more competitors had already carved out such a strategy and image, Perdue's efforts would not have been as successful.

This brings us to the important strategic concept of *positioning*. Positioning is the development of a product image as different from most competitors and attractive to a sufficient number of consumers. Such positioning does not have to be tangible in the sense of a completely unique product. Advertising and promotional efforts can achieve an intangible positioning, that is, a perceived uniqueness on the part of customers more than a real uniqueness. One of the objectives of most positioning is to avoid direct confrontation with a strongly entrenched competitor.

A positioning map is sometimes used to determine where voids may exist in the market that might afford opportunities for positioning new brands or repositioning existing ones. Such a positioning map is shown in Figure 14.2 for the broiler industry at the time Perdue was making its big inroads in the Northeast. Note that practically the entire industry could be plotted as having little or no recognizable brand identity by consumers, whereas on the quality and price dimension it was offering average to medium quality birds at low to medium prices. Perdue, on the other hand, with its readily discernible brand identification and its strenuous efforts to convey an image of quality that was worth the higher prices, stood alone in the marketplace. Sometimes the positions of competitive firms can be ascertained simply by using expert or executive judgment. Sometimes competitive positions may not be as obvious as they were in the broiler industry, and a consumer survey may be needed to determine just how the various brands in the marketplace are viewed by customers. Generally, the more closely brands are perceived to be in their positioning, the more likelihood of brand switching. Also, products viewed as near

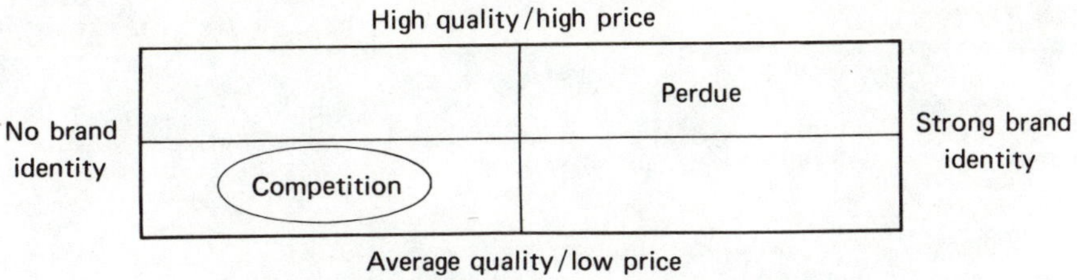

Figure 14.2. Positioning map of the broiler industry in the 1970s.

the center of the positioning map are most susceptible to brand switching and competitive inroads because, in general, they are seen as having an average or ordinary position. Conversely, those brands near the corners of the positioning map, as Perdue is, tend to have more secure positions.

Finally, a further advantage of a quality position or image needs to be mentioned. A quality image is not easy to achieve; it must be won over time. Heavy promotional efforts are usually required to convey the image of quality; and strong quality standards must be achieved and maintained if customer expectations are to be fulfilled. (Woe to the firm that through its advertising arouses great expectations among customers, only to have these dashed by a product or service that obviously does not merit the glowing promotional statements.) Such an achieved quality image is not easily duplicated or countered by competitors. Only costly and lengthy efforts usually will succeed in gaining ground against the entrenched firm in such a position. Such requirements are not very attractive to most competitors.

Questions

1. Perdue's efforts represent successful product differentiation for a product difficult to distinguish from other similar products. How would you design a marketing strategy for other such products, such as coal, corn, oranges, and pork?
2. Would Perdue achieve the same degree of success if he were to market turkeys today? Why or why not?

Invitiation to Role Play

You are a staff assistant to Frank Perdue. The success of the branded Perdue chickens has raised the possibility of expanding through company-owned or franchised fast-food chicken restaurants similar to Church's and Kentucky Fried Chicken, but featuring Perdue chickens. You have been asked to evaluate this option and present your conclusions to Frank and the executive policy committee.

PART Five

NEW DIRECTIONS FOR MARKETING STRATEGIES

As we come to the 1980s, significant advances in marketing tools and techniques seem unlikely. Perhaps we have developed all the sophisticated approaches possible to this admittedly important functional area of business operation. Of course, it would be very desirable to improve our understanding of consumer behavior, develop more precise and infallible tools of marketing research, be able to determine the best way to allocate—and the optimum commitment needed—for advertising and other promotional expenditures to achieve certain designated objectives. But such is not likely to occur in the next few decades, given the complexity of the marketplace. We know that marketing is an art, and not a science—maybe it will never be a science. So, what can we look forward to for the advancement of the discipline?

It appears that we can anticipate a broadening of marketing concepts and techniques to more and more areas of our lives—to organizations concerned with services and not products and to a host of nontraditional users and uses of marketing. Perhaps marketing may be the lubricant that can make our society more responsive to the needs of its members than anything else likely to be devised. Kotler and Levy were prescient in their landmark article, ''Broadening the Concept of Marketing'' (*Journal of Marketing,* January 1969, pp. 10–15). It has taken a long time for these ideas and predictions to come to full fruition. But now we are finding them doing so with an enthusiasm that almost arouses the question: ''What have we missed all these years?''

The new direction of marketing strategies appears to be toward use by nontraditional organizations. We examine a sampling of these new uses in some detail. In the Hyatt Legal Services we find the happy circumstance of the meeting of marketing techniques for legal services and the great need for better service to a vast segment of people who are disenchanted, skeptical, and priced out of traditional legal services. The International Management Group (IMG) has carved a fertile niche for itself in the marketing of athletic talent, beginning with Arnold Palmer and proceeding far beyond what once was envisioned as the potential for marketing of personalities.

In the last two cases in the book we describe and diagnose two of the greatest entrepreneurial successes of all time, which are still evolving: Apple Computer, and Nike, the running-shoe company. Both enterprises propelled their young founders to the dizzying heights of great wealth—some $300 million each—and into the ranks of the wealthiest individuals in the United States. In both cases, small interloper firms went head-to-head against the behemoths of their industries—IBM and Adidas respectively—and bested them.

Although marketing has matured, we are still finding many vital new uses for it. It is permeating our society and our life-style as never before, and also enriching opportunities for entrepreneurship despite the maturity of our economy and the increasing size of business firms.

CHAPTER 15

Hyatt Legal Services: New Adaptations of Marketing

In 1970 there were 355,000 lawyers in the United States. By 1984, there were 622,000. By 1995 at the present growth rate there will be over 1 million. The United States already has over twice as many lawyers per thousand people as England, about 5 times as many as West Germany, and over 25 times as many as Japan.[1] Each year over 30,000 new lawyers are admitted to the bar, but openings exist for only 20,000 new lawyers a year. The surplus of lawyers has brought about a whole new environment in the legal profession, one in which there is vastly more competition than formerly, and this arouses pressures to increase efficiency, lower prices, and tap a wider customer base. In other words, the idea of marketing the intangible product of legal services has become more and more attractive and even necessary for many law firms. Marketing techniques, previously unthinkable, are being embraced in order to keep existing clients and attract new ones. This is a revolutionary concept for the legal profession and its needs. And in the vanguard of the new breed of lawyers has been Joel Hyatt.

THE LEGAL ENVIRONMENT OF THE 1970s

Despite an ever-increasing number of lawyers and availability of legal services, many people have not availed themselves of legal help. The American Bar Association commissioned a survey in 1973 to determine if an unmet need existed for legal

[1] "Lawyers Versus the Marketplace," *Forbes,* Jan. 16, 1984, p. 74.

services. Over 2000 households across the country were interviewed, and the ABA was forced to conclude that "lawyers are consulted for slightly less than one-third of all the problems that reasonably could be called legal problems."[2] The implications were unmistakable: despite legal problems and an abundance of lawyers to service such problems, many people were not contacting lawyers.

The reason behind this situation was not difficult to ascertain. For years the legal profession had been charging premium prices for lawyers' services, even for routine procedures such as wills, uncontested divorces, and bankruptcy proceedings. It was acknowledged that "if you're rich, you can afford a good lawyer and if you're poor, there's free legal aid, but if you're in the middle, you're stuck."[3]

A few lawyers attempted to remedy this situation. Steve Meyers and Len Jacoby are credited with opening the first legal clinic in Los Angeles in 1972. By 1983, they were the nation's second largest legal clinic chain, with 75 offices in New York, New Jersey, and California. Annual revenues were more than $14 million in 1981.[4] Only Hyatt Legal Services had more offices.

While clinics such as Jacoby and Meyers, and certain smaller local affiliations of lawyers, were attempting to cater to the middle-income market, local bar associations in many communities were arrayed to thwart this growth by challenging those lawyers who advertised and insisting that all members of the bar maintain minimum fee schedules at rather high levels for various legal services. A major setback for the old guard of the legal profession, however, occurred in 1975 when the United States Supreme Court ruled that lawyers should no longer be permitted to fix prices or maintain minimum fee schedules.

The monumental Supreme Court case that paved the way for the marketing of the legal profession involved a Virginia couple who wanted to purchase a house. The couple had checked with 19 lawyers only to find that none would charge less than $522.50 to handle the closing transaction, this being the minimum fee set by the Fairfax County Bar Association. The couple sued the bar association, alleging that this practice was in violation of the Sherman Anti-Trust Act. And the Supreme Court agreed.

Another Supreme Court case in 1977 further paved the way for aggressive marketing practices and legal clinics. In *Bates* v. *State Bar of Arizona*, the Court struck down the Arizona State Bar Association rules against lawyers advertising. The Court held that such rules were in violation of the Constitution's protection of free speech, and lawyers were thus given the right to advertise.

With the Supreme Court decision, the year was not yet over when Joel Hyatt opened his first legal clinic office.

[2] "Paying Less for a Lawyer," *Consumer Reports*, Sept. 1979, p. 522.
[3] Craig Waters, "The Selling of the Law," *Inc.*, March 1982, p. 58.
[4] Ibid.

JOEL HYATT

Joel Hyatt, formerly known as Joel Hyatt Zylberberg, is from Cleveland, Ohio. He graduated from Yale Law School and then worked for a prestigious corporate law firm of Paul, Weiss, Rifkind, Wharton, & Carson in New York City. He left the firm to manage his father-in-law's successful campaign for the U.S. Senate. A few months after the Supreme Court ruling for the right to advertise, Joel and his wife Susan, daughter of Senator Howard M. Metzenbaum (Democrat of Ohio), returned to Cleveland to open the first Hyatt legal clinic.

By May of 1978, Hyatt had four clinics located around metropolitan Cleveland and was becoming a familiar figure to thousands living in the Cleveland area. Early on, Joel realized the importance of television advertising in promoting a low-cost clinic that could survive only if it had a high client volume. He himself appeared in these commercials, and his low-key, personable, and sincere manner was a powerful inducement to hundreds of viewers who had previously viewed all lawyers with suspicion.

Investment in new outlets and the advertising necessary to promote the concept of legal clinics requires substantial capital. Not every young practicing attorney has the resources needed for this. As he opened his first clinics, Joel estimated that the initial investment needed before the clinics would start to turn a profit would be in the middle to upper six figures. A large portion of this investment came from his wealthy wife.[5] By contrast, Jacoby and Meyers started small and financed most of its expansion through internally generated funds.

By the end of 1979 Hyatt had nine clinics around northern Ohio and wanted to continue expanding. In order to achieve his expansion goals, large amounts of investment capital would be needed—far more than he had used before or had readily available. The clinics were not yet generating the levels of internal funds needed for a large expansion. Some outside source of funding was needed.

THE MARKETING STRATEGY

The Target Customer

The main thrust of Hyatt, and most other legal clinics, is to provide rather routine legal services for low- and middle-income people who either need legal services but cannot afford it or who have tried to solve legal problems without the effective assistance of counsel. This market is large, estimated at some 70 percent of the total population.[6] In the past this had been a relatively untapped market except for such

[5]Steven Brill, "T. V. Pitchman for Cut-rate Legal Advice," *Esquire*, May 9, 1978, p. 87.
[6]Ibid., p. 90.

extreme cases as criminal charges or lawsuits. Consequently, all of Hyatt's marketing efforts were directed to winning this large body of potential customers.

We have to recognize that the clinic-type market was intentionally shunned by most large law firms as simply not being sufficiently profitable compared with other areas of law, especially corporate clientele. Until the emergence of legal clinics, this middle-income market was primarily serviced by sole practioners or small partnership firms, but these were too small to compete with the legal clinics that used assembly-line office procedures or generated volume through advertising.

As Hyatt continued to expand, an offshoot of this middle-income market began to look attractive—prepaid legal services. Legal insurance could be purchased in the same manner as hospital and medical insurance, with such services paid for by the employer where this could be negotiated through collective bargaining agreements. It was estimated that 20 percent of union members would have use for these services.[7]

Joel Hyatt had significant assets for reaching this market. His father-in-law had strong union support. This, and a geographical location in the heavily unionized midwest, helped propel the firm to three contracts with labor unions by 1983, including the large 160,000-member Sheet Metal Workers' International Association. Hyatt envisioned such prepaid legal insurance as the next big fringe benefit that unions would negotiate:

> It's a benefit most employers can afford to add. It represents about two to seven cents out of the hourly wage, which is a lot less than most medical benefits, and the services offered are really important to the workers' lives. If we do succeed in making prepaid legal services the next major fringe benefit, that will be terribly important. It would mean access to lawyers for hundreds of thousands of workers. And, of course, it would be financially important for us.[8]

The Product or Service

The product provided by the Hyatt Legal Clinics is a very simple one: providing low-priced consultation on routine legal matters with minimum frills. Clients enter the waiting room and await consultation from one of the lawyers at the clinic site. The accoutrements of most legal offices are lacking: no fancy artwork on the walls, no elaborate decor, not even names on the office doors.

Instead of using an extensive law library, the Hyatt lawyers use preprinted forms. These forms are titled, for example, "simple will" or "uncontested divorce."

Each Hyatt legal clinic has from one to three lawyers, and each lawyer sees

[7]"Legal Services Plan Emerges," *Wall Street Journal,* April 26, 1983, pp. 1, 5.
[8]Tamar Lewin, "Leader in Legal Clinic Field," *New York Times,* May 9, 1983, p. D.10.

about 60 clients per month. The clinics have adopted the extended hours popularized by the discount-store retailers who remained open at night and on Sundays at a time when conventional retailers were open no more than one night a week and never on Sunday. The Hyatt offices are open nights and weekends, times shunned by traditional law firms. The clinic hours offer their target customers the important convenience of not needing to take time off from work. Initial consultations usually last 20 to 30 minutes and one fourth to one third of the problems typically are solved in the initial consultation.

Pricing

To win the desired target market, pricing of the legal services is all-important. Low prices and high volume of business are key elements of the strategy. But another aspect of the pricing strategy, leader pricing, provided an extra impetus. See the following Information Sidelight for a more thorough discussion of leader pricing.

The widely promoted leader pricing of only $15 was used for the initial consultation fee.

INFORMATION SIDELIGHT

Leader Pricing

Retailers in particular have long used "leaders" to attract customers to their stores. Leaders are items intentionally offered at very low prices in order to stimulate store traffic. The expectation is that people induced to come to the store because of the advertised leaders will buy other merchandise priced more profitably. Sometimes retailers will even price certain leader merchandise at or below cost—these are commonly referred to as "loss leaders"—to make such goods particularly attractive to customers.

All items or services typically do not make good leaders. The most effective price leader should

1 Be well known and widely used.
2 Be priced low enough to attract numerous buyers.
3 Not usually be bought in large quantities and stored.
4 Enjoy a high price elasticity of demand (i.e., demand should sharply increase as prices are lowered).
5 Not closely compete with other goods in the firm's merchandise or service offerings.[9]

[9]Donald V. Harper, *Price Policy and Procedure* (New York: Harcourt, Brace and World, 1966), p. 253.

Hyatt used leader pricing very effectively and essentially met these desired characteristics. By strongly promoting a very low price for the initial consultation, he accomplished two objectives: (1) to induce prospective clients to visit Hyatt facilities at low risk, thereby being exposed to the friendly and nonintimidating environment, and (2) to cater to their specific legal needs with services that could yield a reasonable profit.

In a sense, then, Hyatt used leader pricing as a come-on—a promotional device to attract prospective clients in the best retailer tradition. The low leader price that was heavily promoted in turn gave the whole operation an aura of reasonably priced legal services, so contrary to the general perceptions of lawyers, and this was exactly what this target market was most interested in and most in need of.

The other fees were fixed in advance so that clients knew exactly what they would be paying for the various services. Any additional court costs were borne by the client.

A simple will usually cost between $45 and $65 for both husband and wife. An uncontested divorce was about $275; filing for bankruptcy about $350. Most traditional law firms handle such cases as these by the hour, and total charges would usually be much more. On more complicated matters, the Hyatt lawyers charged $40 an hour, this also being significantly lower than the $100 plus hourly fees charged by most attorneys.

The low fee structure, of course, was partly possible because of the sheer volume of business. But the operation also was kept lean, especially compared with most legal firms. Hyatt lawyers were paid from $17,000 to somewhat over $40,000, depending on their experience and managerial ability. This was much less than the compensation paid by most legal firms where even beginning lawyers can be paid over $30,000. An endemic surplus of lawyers today makes the Hyatt compensation sufficiently attractive to obtain good personnel.

The high-volume/low-profit caseload necessitates efficient office procedures. The newest computer and word-processing equipment aids this. For example, a sophisticated system allows the clinics' lawyers to prepare in a matter of minutes simple wills, dissolution agreements, trust agreements, and other standard documents geared to meet most clients' needs. For a particular type of document, the lawyers will spell out special requirements of the client into a dictaphone and then a paralegal or computer specialist will feed this information into a computer. The computer is instructed to choose, from various legal paragraphs stored in the memory, the particular phrases necessary. The computer then integrates this material along with the names and specific details supplied by the client, and produces a personalized, professionally typed document. An ordinary will, for example, can be completed in 30 minutes, including the client interview time.

Promotion

Intensive television advertising has been important in the success of Hyatt. Joel himself stars in the commercials. This personal touch enhances the ads' effectiveness because he is very photogenic and able to project sincerity. All the commercials have had the same theme: Hyatt Legal Services with their capable and qualified lawyers can handle a variety of legal problems, and initial consultations only cost $15 or $20.

Hyatt reportedly spent $2,281,800 for advertising in 1982, double the amount spend in 1981.[10] The TV commercials have been particularly effective in reaching the target market, the working-class consumer, which is the largest TV-watching group.

THE MERGER WITH H & R BLOCK

In order to finance his expansion goals, Joel Hyatt needed an outside source of funding, and he found it in H & R Block, the highly profitable tax preparation firm. Block has tax offices in every city in the United States with a population of more than 5000. The company prepares one out of every ten federal income tax returns. Although Block was highly profitable and had liquid assets of over $150 million in 1980, its founder, Henry Block, was concerned because the company's annual growth rate was down from the previous years. In addition, the new IRS short form was being used by many taxpayers without any assistance, thus eliminating some of the market for Block services. It was only natural that Henry Block should look for some diversification, especially through acquiring other service-oriented firms with high growth potential.

The match with Hyatt Legal Services seemed perfect. Block and Hyatt operations appealed to the same type of customer. These middle-income people could be easily drawn both to the tax offices and the legal clinics through mass television advertising. Hyatt certainly represented a desirable growth potential. And Block could provide Hyatt with office space, management and advertising expertise, and expansion capital.

Because of laws forbidding ownership of law firms by nonlawyers, Hyatt and Block worked out a unique format whereby Block could purchase in 1980 the tangible assets of Hyatt (i.e., the computers, office furniture, leaseholds, etc.) for $2 million under a subsidiary, Block Management Company. But Hyatt and his lawyer partners maintain the ownership of Hyatt Legal Services. Block Management provides secretarial, computer, and paralegal services, as well as advertising,

[10]Christopher C. Gilson, "How to Market Your Law Practice," *Journal of Advertising Research*, Dec. 1981, p. 36.

marketing support, and office space, and in return receives a stipulated management fee. Basically, Block provides everything but the actual legal services.[11]

The merger with Block resulted in rapid expansion. From 10 offices in northern Ohio in 1980, by the end of 1983 Hyatt had expanded to well over 100 offices in about 20 states. It employed some 300 lawyers, thus ranking among the nation's 15 largest law firms. At the present rate of growth, Hyatt expected to be the largest law firm in America by mid 1985.[12] Statistics on revenue and profitability of these operations are kept confidential and not available because Hyatt is still a privately owned law firm.

The nation's second largest clinic, Jacoby and Meyers, presents an interesting comparison with Hyatt. Jacoby and Meyers started in California and by 1983 had 75 offices, employing about 150 lawyers. Receipts per attorney in their operation have yielded profits in the range of 15 to 20 percent.[13] Despite more years of experience and proven profitability, Jacoby and Meyers have not been able to raise the capital to match Hyatt's expansion rate. The relationship with H & R Block has been a powerful spur to Hyatt's growth and potential.

INGREDIENTS OF SUCCESS

The Hyatt success exemplifies the classic textbook marketing principles taught in every beginning marketing course. These are simple:

1. Finding an untapped target market.
2. Creating a marketing strategy strictly directed to this target market.

There is nothing mysterious or arcane about this. But what makes Hyatt unique is that it does not deal with a tangible product such as toothpaste or food or a facility such as a fast-food restaurant or retail store, but with a nonproduct, a service. And we find that the same marketing principles and techniques apply to both the tangible and the intangible.

Joel Hyatt found (or really, simply recognized) a vast untapped target market, an estimated 70 percent of the total population that was turned off by traditional law firms and attorneys who were justifiably seen as catering to the rich, not only in prices but also in demeanor and opulence. Indeed, the large law firms shunned this lower income market. Joel set about changing the image of lawyers, at least as far as his firm was concerned, to one easily approachable, common in touch, and bargain priced. He then had to persuade this vast potential market that they needed lawyers, perhaps almost as much as they needed dentists or physicians.

The success of the initial Hyatt efforts paved the way for a more organized

[11] "H & R Block: Expanding Beyond Taxes for Faster Growth," *Business Week,* Dec. 8, 1980, pp. 76–78.

[12] "Lawyers Versus the Marketplace," p. 76.

[13] Waters, "The Selling of the Law," pp. 58–60.

tapping of the target market, the market of organized labor. It was not difficult to persuade union leaders that their members needed legal services as well as the more traditional medical services long negotiated in union contracts. The vast and relatively amorphous target market was assuming identifiable and very reachable customer segments.

Specifically, the marketing strategy that Joel used to tap his target market consisted of the following:

1. Mass TV advertising was used, geared to the consumer group that tends to be the heaviest user of TV. Money was budgeted for TV advertising in amounts never dreamed of before by such a service sector. And the judicial ruling of 1977 legitimatizing advertising by the legal profession created a rare opportunity for people like Hyatt who had the ''audacity'' to grasp such an opportunity aggressively. Certainly no traditional legal firms could be expected to compete vigorously with this new media tool, wedded as they were to the traditional and viewing such techniques as still anathema and incompatible with their conservative image and clientele. The attractively photogenic Joel Hyatt was a big factor in the success of this advertising. No hired actor could have engendered the same sincerity and personal interest to the audience as the young founder of such an upstart firm.

2. Instead of locating in awe-inspiring suites in prestigious office buildings, as most law firms are wont to do, Hyatt opened his legal clinics in areas convenient to the masses he was seeking to woo—in shopping centers and walk-in sites on neighborhood commercial streets. The offices themselves were simply furnished and unintimidating, where an unsophisticated client could feel comfortable and not awed. Many offices were opened as quickly as could reasonably be done and were open nights and weekends. The merger with Block, which made available many of the already operating Block tax outlets, spurred the opening of additional convenient clinics.

3. To be effective, any marketing strategy should be coordinated so that all elements are harmonious and correctly geared to the needs and wants of the target customer. Hyatt's pricing strategy was fully harmonious. Very low prices compared to those of the established competitors were offered for the routine legal transactions that could almost be mass-produced. A very low ''leader'' initial consultation fee was used to attract clients who normally would be reluctant to go to a lawyer because of the cost. Most of the general public has seen enough publicity about fabulous lawyers' fees in well-publicized court cases to fear even initial contacts as being far beyond their means. But Hyatt clearly designates prices and offers services for modest fees.

The early success of the marketing strategy of Joel Hyatt made this an attractive merger candidate. An apparently ideal suitor appeared with H & R Block, the income tax preparation people whose clientele were virtually the same as Hyatt's target market. The merger with Block brought Hyatt over the threshold to great growth. Block supplied the needed financing. Block had thousands of outlets, at least some of which could accommodate legal clinics as well as income tax preparation services. And Block had the management expertise needed to effectively control hundreds and thousands of far-flung operations.

WHAT CAN BE LEARNED?

Joel Hyatt's success in using mass marketing techniques conclusively confirms that services and nonproducts can be powerfully marketed using traditional marketing techniques. The ideas of Kotler and Levy, espoused in the pioneering article "Broadening the Concept of Marketing"[14] have perhaps never been better exemplified.

We see here an example of seizing an opportunity for innovation. An innovator looks for gaps in serving customers' needs (in this case, the general public's) by existing firms—a very obvious notion, yet its implementation tends to be disregarded or unnoticed. It is natural to assume that if all firms in a particular industry or service have operated similarly for decades or disregarded certain market segments as unprofitable, then no better way is feasible. We reason that with their years and decades of experience, different ways must have been tested and proven impractical. But this is truly fallacious thinking, the delusion of custom and size achievement.

We have to, rather gladly, come to the conclsuion that innovative opportunities are far from gone in our mature economy. They exist and will continue to exist for those who are unwilling to accept the accustomed and the ordinary. The creative mind, not in tune with stereotypical ways of doing things, should always give vitality to entrepreneurship.

Questions

1. Discuss the conditions favoring legal clinics in the 1970s.
2. In numbers the low- and middle-income consumer segment suggests enormous potential for legal services. But what are some factors that may make this potential less than it seems?

Invitations to Role Play

As a young lawyer who has just passed the bar exam, you have been approached by a Hyatt representative to join this growing organization. You are undecided whether to join Hyatt, to join an old traditional law firm, or to hang up your own shingle. What are some of the considerations that would guide your decision?

[14]Philip Kotler and Sidney J. Levy, *Journal of Marketing*, Jan. 1969, pp. 10–15.

CHAPTER 16

International Management Group: Marketing of Athletes

In the previous case, we saw how marketing techniques and concepts were applied successfully to legal services. No longer is marketing only relevant to products. It can well be applied to various kinds of services, as discussed in the accompanying Information Sidelight. It can also be applied to persons—the marketing of personalities, be they politicians, athletes, or other. A tremendous success story has evolved in the marketing of athletes. After all, the color, personality, and multifaceted dimensions of a person can produce far more exciting marketing efforts than a tube of toothpaste, a box of detergent, or a soft drink. Let us examine the notable success story in the marketing of athletes and encounter some of the most famous athletic personalities of the last several decades. As with most of our success stories, the credit must go to one individual—the shape maker, innovator, risk taker.

INFORMATION SIDELIGHT

Unique Characteristics of Marketing of Services

Table 16.1 shows the growth in number of establishments and in sale volume of certain consumer- and business-service firms in the ten-year period from 1967 to 1977. Services are playing an ever more important role in our total life-style as we have more leisure time and more discretionary income.

Marketing of services typically has several distinctive characteristics that distinguish them from product marketing and can create problems as well as opportunities.[1]

Services are *intangible*. They cannot be sampled, that is, touched, tasted, or seen, before being purchased. This means that they must be sold and bought on faith, with uncertain future benefits.

Services are *people-dependent*. That is, the persons offering them have a far more crucial role in customer satisfaction than typically is the situation with products. And there is usually a limit to how many clients or customers can be handled, since a dentist can only treat so many people, a lawyer or a financial adviser counsel so many clients.

Services usually are *unstandardized,* and as a result tend to be unpredictable. Just as dining out experiences may differ from one time to another, even at the same restaurant, so may other services vary in the degree of satisfaction and competence.

Services tend to be *perishable*. They cannot be stored and used another time. For example, an idle dentist cannot regain the lost time, nor can an underutilized financial or estate planning adviser.

Many services face *fluctuating demand*. Hotel occupancy, theater attendance, ski lifts, restaurants, tax preparers—all face wide fluctuations in demand. This situation, along with the perishability of services, poses intriguing challenges for marketers trying to reduce the extremes of demand and maximize efficiency.

Despite the unique characteristics of the marketing of services, customers' needs and wants must be catered to just as much as with product marketing. Furthermore, loyal and repeat customers are equally important to a firm whether the offering is an intangible service or a tangible product.

MARK MCCORMACK AND THE FOUNDING OF INTERNATIONAL MANAGEMENT GROUP (IMG)

When he was a young boy, Mark wanted to become a baseball player. However, he was hit by an automobile and suffered a skull fracture when he was six, and this prevented him from ever playing contact sports. Mark's father, a successful farm journal publisher, encouraged the boy to take up golf, and he immediately was taken with the game.

Among the golf partners of his youth was an elderly man who had a summer home near the McCormack family in the Dunes area of Michigan. He was Carl

[1]These distinctive characteristics of services were identified by William J. Stanton, *Fundamentals of Marketing*, 6th ed. (New York: McGraw-Hill, 1981), pp. 444–446.

Table 16.1 Number and Sales volume of Selected Consumer- and Business-Service Establishments, 1967–1977

Kind of Business	*Number of Establishments (Thousands)*		*Sales volume (Millions)*	
	1967	*1977*	*1967*	*1977*
Hotels, motels, etc.	87.0	70.7	$ 7,039	$18,453
Personal services (e.g., laundry, dry cleaning, beauty shops, barber shops, photographic, shoe repair, funeral, alterations)	498.9	512.1	11,750	18,433
Automobile repair and other automotive services	139.2	200.2	7,028	21,576
Motion picture theaters	18.8	11.8	3,476	2,606
Amusement, recreation services, except motion picture (e.g., dance halls, theatrical presentations, bowling, billiards, commercial sports)	96.0	165.0	4,827	18,537
Business services (e.g., advertising agencies, consulting firms, credit bureaus, computer services, stenographic services, research firms, employment agencies, telephone answering services, armored-car operations)	200.0	458.2	22,000	54,500

Sources: U.S. Census of Business—Selected Services, 1967 and 1977.

Sandburg. Mark spent part of a summer organizing the papers of the Pulitzer Prize winner, biographer, and poet. He did not know then the enormous stature of the man; he considered him just a good neighbor. But he had his first exposure to celebrities. Today, McCormack cherishes the books the famous man autographed for him during his adolescent and teen years.

McCormack won the Chicago prep school golf championship when he was a student at the Harvard School of Boys, and later he played on the William and Mary golf team. Among the teams challenged was Wake Forest. And playing for Wake Forest was their star, Arnold Palmer.

McCormack graduated from William and Mary in 1951 and then went on for his law degree at Yale. He joined a Cleveland law firm at an annual salary of $5400, but he found himself more interested in golf than in practicing law. He participated in four U.S. Amateur Championships and played well enough to qualify for the 1958 U.S. Open in Tulsa, Oklahoma. It was there after a practice round that pro golfer Gene Littler asked him to examine an endorsement contract. McCormack was amazed at how one-sided the contract was and began to involve himself in negotiating contracts for golfers.

In 1959, McCormack formed National Sports Management, Inc., with the objective of booking playing dates and appearances for 16 golfers, one of whom was Palmer. A year later, in 1960, Palmer asked McCormack to be his agent. Their deal was sealed with a handshake. At that time Palmer earned about $60,000 a year. However, with McCormack as his financial manager/agent, within two years Palmer was making more than $500,000 annually through licensing arrangements, books, articles, radio and TV appearances, golf franchises, exhibitions, and an array of golf-related industries. Soon after, Palmer asked McCormack to manage a relatively unknown player from South Africa, named Gary Player, and a chubby Ohioan golfer, Jack Nicklaus. In a few years, these three were to dominate pro golf.

In 1961, McCormack founded the International Management Group, and growth intensified. Soon he was representing most of the top golfers of the world. Now he realized that IMG needed to branch out into other areas if it was to grow further.

It was natural to expand into other individual sports. In tennis, such big names as Rod Laver and John Newcombe were signed up; in skiing, the famous Jean-Claude Killy; and Jackie Stewart in auto racing. Signing up athletes in team sports, such as football was a natural extension. Next the decision was made to represent nonathletes, and cartoonist Hank Ketchum, author of Dennis the Menace, as well as other talent in modeling, songwriting, and announcing, became part of the IMG stable. Going beyond individuals, IMG began representing and negotiating television and commercial rights for the sponsors of such prestigious events as Wimbledon and the British Open.

Diversification did not stop at that point. Consulting, promotional, and merchandising plans and activities were provided for purely business organizations, such as Rolex, Sears, Seagram, Wilkinson Sword, AT&T, and British American Tobacco Company. The tie-in of IMG's athletic clients with the promotional needs of such firms was a natural and mutually beneficial. "We're showing corporations how to use sports to sell their products," McCormack explains.[2] IMG further expanded into the largest independent producer and packager of sports programming in the world. Sports events, specials, and series appearing on television included The Superstars, The Superteams, Games People Play, Challenge of the Sexes, and Battle of the Network Stars.

By the early 1980s, IMG and its various divisions was managing the affairs of some 400 clients from the world of sports, business, and the professions. Annual revenues were over $200 million. And an office network had been established with 15 offices located around the world, from Hong Kong to New Zealand, from Monte Carlo to London. Such offices enabled IMG clients to stay in contact with IMG representatives at all times as they toured outside their home countries.

As a result of his successful services, McCormack attracted a wide range of famous clients. The most notable has to be Pope John Paul II, whom he obtained as

[2]IMG brochure, n.d., p. 5.

a client in the spring of 1981. The Vatican wanted somebody to handle the commercial aspects of the Pope's visit to England, Wales, and Scotland and to avoid the widespread merchandising of trashy, unofficial items. A few years before, a Papal visit to Ireland had brought the Vatican all sorts of problems from vendors selling cheap junk to ineffective sound systems for sermons and celebration of masses.

IMG was able to provide the Vatican with good quality merchandise for sale at profits to help defray the cost of the trip. Special emphasis was given to such commemorative items as books, videotapes, statues, gold watches, and bricks inscribed with "To commemorate the visit of Pope John Paul II to Great Britain 1982." This last item was bought by homeowners for $7 and used to replace a brick in their home. Now McCormack is known around the world as the Pope's agent.

SERVICES

For Individuals

The foundation of IMG's success is its variety of services tailored to meet the individual needs of its clientele. Most of these have been celebrity athletes who typically have a relatively short period of high income, and whose income may come from different activities throughout the world. IMG not only represented these clients in their particular sports, but greatly enhanced their earning power through the marketing of their names. Clients could thus earn income from commercials and various licensing agreements that far exceeded their tournament winnings.

In addition, through its subsidiaries IMG managed many financial matters for its clients such as investing their money, paying their bills, arranging for adequate insurance, legal services, tax planning and tax return preparation, and retirement advising. One of the many ways in which IMG protected an athlete's assets from erosion was through tax planning techniques such as recommending to some athletes that they move their homes from high-tax countries to lower tax countries. Tennis star Bjorn Borg, at the time the world's highest paid athlete who under McCormack's guidance was making an estimated $5 million a year, was advised to move from Sweden where taxes were as high as 85 percent to Monte Carlo where taxes were paid only on income earned in Monaco.[3] Legal services might involve collecting money from foreign sources, the use of a client's name and likeness, and the development and use of trademarks.

For Corporate Clients

Corporations quickly realized the promotional and public relations benefits of sponsoring events such as track meets, ski races, equine events, golf tournaments, and a

[3] "Choosing a Financial Planner," *Money*, April 1982, p. 52.

variety of other athletic events including the Olympics. However, every sport is not compatible with every manufacturer. For example, IMG account executive, Mary Hambrick, noted: "It would be foolish for a potato chip maker to sponsor a horse-jumping event, despite the fact that people who like horses eat snack food too. We could find a sport in which the fans eat more or even the majority of potato chips. The key is matching the sport and the product as closely as possible."[4] IMG developed the expertise to create a mutually beneficial relationship between sponsor and event.

More than 50 international companies were using IMG's services, which involved reviewing the firm's existing programs and, when appropriate, proposing ways to make them more efficient and effective. Long-term marketing and public relations plans were developed and tailored to the firm's objectives. Plans were then created for the tactical use of sports to solve individual sales, distribution, and corporate image problems. IMG "helps customers assess the potential value of sport as leisure-time opportunities presented to them from the outside. And it implements . . . and oversees the details of a promotion, right down to and including on-site supervision when it is called for."[5]

In addition to sponsoring events, IMG worked closely with businesses for corporate outings and pro-ams, which give companies the opportunity to introduce their associates and customers to well-known personalities from highly visible sports. Such activities gain exposure and credibility, and can build personal relationships with hard-to-reach customers, as well as giving the opportunity to show "you are important to us."

Fee Structure

The fees IMG charged its clients appear to have varied from person to person based on their service requirements. Published articles state a range from 20 to 50 percent of gross income for athletes, averaging $30,000, whereas corporate clients were paying a flat fee of $8000.[6] Although the fees appear high, they are normally tax deductible and this reduces the net of tax cost considerably for these high-income clients.

McCormack explains these considerable fees this way: "It's a question of how good a job you can do. If I were to pick the 25th leading tennis player in the world . . . and say to him, 'I can get you a $1 million-a-year contract with Ford Motor Company, and there is no way he can get that $1 million without me, then 90 percent might be a fair price on that deal."[7]

[4]Julie Howell Turner, "The Midas Touch," *Spur,* Sept.–Oct. 1982, p. 56.
[5]IMG brochuer, n.d., p. 26.
[6]"Choosing a Financial Planner," p. 52.
[7]Robert Cubbedge, "Is This Man Going to Take Over Pro Tennis?" *Tennis,* Feb. 1981, pp. 47–48.

INGREDIENTS OF SUCCESS

The marketing of athletes, which began with Arnold Palmer asking Mark McCormack to manage his affairs, was a new idea for the 1960s. Part of the popularity of agents for athletes today stems from the success that IMG achieved. So we have an innovative concept melded with an operational effectiveness that was mutually satisfactory. Success was not surprising because a latent need was only awaiting the proper execution.

We need to be more specific, however, about this successful marketing of athletes. Even with the latent need, a poor execution would undoubtedly have scuttled the concept or at least delayed its widening appeal. McCormack's marketing strategy involved these three facets:

1. Developing a stable (or inventory) of personalities, mostly athletes, who could provide a quality promotional offering for business customers.
2. Providing a strong incentive for the celebrity clients to be affiliated with IMG.
3. Providing integrated services for both clients and customers.

These three facets mesh together and reinforce each other. Before discussing them in more detail, let us clarify what we mean by "clients" and "customers."

The clients are the individual celebrities—mostly athletes—who use IMG as an agent to increase their income and provide financial and other services.

The customers are business firms who (1) use IMG athletes and other celebrities as promotional tools to further their public image and promote their products, and/or (2) use IMG planning and execution for various sporting events also to further the public image and promote the products of the firm.

IMG uses great care in marketing athletes and celebrities to business firms. These individuals are chosen carefully and some rather well-known people are turned down as clients. For example, Wilt Chamberlain was not accepted as a client because his promotional possibilities were seen as limited to only demonstrating the amount of leg room in a small car commercial. McCormack saw such a limited utilization as not worthwhile. Athletes in some team sports were found to be less effective and desirable as promotional entities. This was particularly true for football and basketball in which most of the athletes did not have the appeal of an Arnold Palmer, a Bjorn Borg, or a Jean-Claude Killy. Because of such selectivity, IMG's athletes have been very effective promoters for most business firms. And the amount that firms have been willing to spend to have athletes represent them multiplied greatly by the late 1970s. Arnold Palmer conveyed the charisma and great public popularity that made him particularly valuable. His low-key sincere approach and his great recognizability, although he is no longer a winner on the PGA tour, made him most effective in promoting an array of products from Cadillacs to Penzoil motor oil. By the early 1980s, Palmer reportedly was making more than Borg through his various business and personal appearance ventures: between $7 million and $10 million a year.[8] The success of some of IMG's client athletes and the increasing publicity IMG was receiving through the press and word of mouth brought great credibility and further enhanced business.

As demand for the services of IMG's individual clients increased because of corporate interest, the athletes benefited greatly in supplemental income that often far exceeded their regular earnings. And the array of financial services that IMG provided freed clients from worrying about such matters, knowing that these were in expert hands, and permitted concentration on their profession.

Although other agents have provided some of the services of IMG to their clients, IMG has been unique in the array of integrated services it can provide, both for its individual clients and for its business firm customers. Lawyers, insurance specialists, accountants, financial analysts, and investment advisers all are provided under one roof of services. For corporate customers, IMG was able to provide a complete package consisting of both the planning and the execution of sporting events and publicity efforts. Such an integrated service package, along with a history of considerable expertise in a variety of sports-related endeavors, has given IMG a powerful competitive advantage over a scattering of much smaller agents and promoters.

The initial success of McCormack in promoting his golf clients was creatively evolved and expanded. Other sports stars in both individual and team sports were a natural extension. Then other types of celebrities who were not athletes rather logically followed. Selling his clients' promotional appeal to business customers naturally evolved into providing more managerial services for such customers, notably in planning, executing, and even creating sporting events of various kinds that could be sponsored by firms.

From personal financial planning for individual clients, a major diversification effort reached beyond athletes and other celebrities to corporate executives. Most recently, IMG has inaugurated efforts to provide its financial planning to the more general public and has teamed up with a bank to form a joint venture whereby "each customer of the new service would be assigned a professional banker and a financial planner to manage the account."[9] This venture is considered a first in the financial world.

Finally we are left with the question: Is the major ingredient of IMG's success the drive and personality of Mark McCormack? Is he the vital ingredient in developing clients and customers and in keeping both happy? I think not. Despite his 18-hour working days and his travels of nearly 300,000 miles a year, and his "stamina of a marathon runner and genius for organization and detail,"[10] I do not believe that today this growing and creative venture depends on one individual, and probably it

[8]Reported in *Cleveland Plain Dealer,* March 6, 1983.
[9]*Cleveland Plain Dealer,* July 27, 1983.
[10]IMG brochure, n.d., p. 5.

has not since the early 1960s when the major golfers of the world sought him as their agent.

One individual can certainly make an impact, as we have seen time and time again in these success stories. But if the individual builds well and develops an effective organization—as McCormack seems to have done—the enterprise should be able to continue its course much as a plane on auto pilot, at least until major external changes arise.

WHAT CAN BE LEARNED?

In this case we have strong confirmation of how marketing insights and techniques can be powerfully applied to other than tangible products. This corroborates the evidence of the previous case we examined in this section, Hyatt Legal Services.

Mark McCormack has proven that athletes can be successfully marketed and that they can have great promotional, publicity, and public relations value to a business firm. For this they can be worth millions in fees. Testimonials are nothing new in advertising; indeed, testimonials have been used since the early decades of this century. But McCormack has brought the use of celebrities—especially the superstars of sports—to a level far beyond merely appearing in an advertisement or commercial and extolling a product that they perhaps never use. McCormack's athletic celebrities are involved in endorsements, public appearances in behalf of firms, apparel and related licenses, and in other ways increase the value of their services.

In particular, the superstar can help a firm in the following ways:

1. As an image builder—when a firm is identified with a well-known, successful, and popular athlete, some of the esteem and excitement rubs off on the firm and its public image. Positive associations can buttress stodgy public awareness.
2. Strengthening customer, supplier, and employee relations—by getting a famous athlete to act as a company spokesperson, a firm can strengthen its relations with its outside affiliates as well as its own employees. All can take some pride in this association. Not the least of these benefits is the powerful motivational tool that can be provided by the personal appearance of the celebrity. For example, for some $20,000 IMG will furnish a celebrity sports star such as Arnold Palmer to play a few holes of golf or a few tennis matches. Important customers, suppliers, and company personnel and executives can participate, and long afterwards they may still be saying, "Do you know what Arnie said about my chip shot?" or "When Arnie and I were teeing off. . . "[11]
3. The biggest incentive for a corporation to use high-priced athletic talent is

[11] "The Midas Touch," p. 59.

as a promotional tool. If the athlete by endorsing and recommending the product can increase sales, then this is an uncontroversial decision and well worth virtually any expenditure to obtain the endorsement. For example, in 1980, the Italian tennis wear firm, Fila, paid for a one-year advertising campaign using Borg's name and picture (including one day of his time to shoot the ad), at $50,000 per commercial. Why would a firm pay so much for a Borg endorsement? Fila eventually signed Borg to a five-year contract, and during the last three years of the agreement, Fila's sales climbed from $35 million to $53 million.[12]

We noted earlier the challenge that nonproduct marketing (i.e., service marketing) faces in gaining credibility and loyal clients and customers. Much depends on faith that the service expectations will be realized. This poses the major challenge to any firm involved with service marketing: to serve the needs of its present and potential customers sufficiently according to customer expectations, and to do so better than competitors can. An agency relationship with clients such as IMG's must provide perceived tangible benefits to its clients and customers to justify high fees. Otherwise it will easily be replaced. In general, IMG did a superlative job of this. But there were some who disputed the value. For example, Jack Nicklaus was lost as a client in 1971. Perhaps Nicklaus felt that he was not being represented as well as Palmer was. This may have been particularly disturbing to Nicklaus because by the beginning of the decade he had dethroned Palmer as the number one golfer in the world, yet Palmer was still receiving more attention. In Jack's case, then, relative tangible benefits was the criterion for acceptance or nonacceptance of the client/agent relationship.

We see the desirability of providing a unique and quality offering, in this case people. This quality strategy is by no means the only approach to marketing success because certainly some products and firms have found success with a low-priced bargain image, as we know from some previous examples. Still, uniqueness combined with a quality image may be most important for service marketing when the customer has to purchase on faith from an intangible and relatively unstandardized offering and is highly dependent on the persons offering the service. A unique and quality offering is more likely to meet with customer approval in these circumstances, especially when dealing with high-income clientele and major business firms. But the quality appeal must be maintained by scrupulous controls.

Finally, we see the opportunity and desirability of expanding a successful format to related endeavors. IMG illustrates the potency of a constantly evolving firm. Diversification and modification of a highly successful format to tap other opportunities should be the rule for any such firm. The firm that is content to rest on its laurels repudiates opportunities for transference of its marketing prowess to related areas, and eventually may find itself vulnerable to more aggressive competi-

[12] "A Word from the Sponsors," *Time*, June 30, 1980, p. 60.

tion. We are not suggesting willy-nilly diversification with the objective of growth at any cost, but a more controlled growth according to the lines of proven strength.

Questions

1. Discuss the promotional impact of using prominent athletes and other celebrities versus using ordinary people in commercials.
2. Do you see any limit of the fees that celebrities can command, as well as their effectiveness in promotional activities?

Invitation to Role Play

As an IMG executive charged with developing the promotional effectiveness of runners, how would you plan and execute this athletic sector development? Be as specific and creative as you can.

CHAPTER 17

Apple Computer: Blending Technology and Marketing

In the 1984 *Forbes* Special Edition on the Richest Four Hundred People in America, Steven P. Jobs is one of those cited:

> Apple Computer . . . 28, Single . . . College dropout . . . saw potential in fellow computer freak's home-built personal computer. With partner started production in 1976 in family garage on $1,300 from sale of calculator and VW minibus. Went public in 1980. . . . Has 7.5 million Apple shares worth $225 million.[1]

In perhaps the greatest success story of the last half a century, this young man who was 21 at the time he turned entrepreneur had become a multimillionaire and one of the richest individuals in America in just a few years. Jobs is the youngest of all those who accumulated their great wealth without inheritance.

Here is a true Horatio Alger tale, almost a fairy tale, but one that any of us, given the right timing, luck, and whatever other mystical factors might have been involved, could have achieved.

INDUSTRY BACKGROUND

In the early 1970s it had become obvious that survival in the computer industry required a larger market share and broader customer base. Computers ranged from

[1]*Forbes,* Fall 1983 (The *Forbes* Four Hundred Edition), p. 110.

small units to the very large, with prices reaching limits only affordable by the well-heeled firms. The industry was dominated by one company, IBM, which held 70 percent of the market. All the other firms in the industry were scrambling for small shares. IBM seemed to have an unassailable advantage because it had the resources for the heaviest marketing expenditures in the industry as well as the best research and development. The firm with the masterful lead in a rapidly growing industry had ever-increasing resources over its lesser competitors who can hardly hope to catch up and must be content to chip away at the periphery of the total market.

The computer industry had been characterized by rapid technological changes since the early 1960s. By the early seventies, however, the new technology being introduced generally involved peripheral accessories, and not further major changes of main units.

Before the advent of microelectronics technology, which made smaller parts possible, computers were very costly and complicated. It was not economically feasible for one person to interact with one computer. The processing power at that time existed only in a central data processing installation, and for those who could not afford to have their own computer, time-sharing services were available.

The "small" or minicomputer industry began in 1974 when a few small firms began using memory chips to produce small computer systems as do-it-yourself kits for as low as $400. These proved popular and other companies began to build microcomputers designed for the affluent hobbyist and small businessperson.

In 1975 microcomputer and small business computer shipments went over the $1 billion mark. As the mainframe market began to mature, the microcomputer industry was beginning its rocketing ascendancy. In 1975 the first personal computer reached the market.

Personal computers can be defined as easy-to-use desktop machines that are microprocessor based, have their own power supply, and are priced below $10,000. By using various software packages, these computers can be customized to serve the needs of businesses and a variety of professionals such as accountants, financial analysts, scientists, and educators, as well as the sophisticated individual at home. The big three minicomputer makers in 1977 were Data General, Digital Equipment, and Hewlett Packard. It should be noted that the minicomputer grew up without IBM, the company that dominated mainframe computers and accounted for two thirds of all computer revenues in 1976.

THE MARKET FOR SMALL COMPUTERS

By 1977 there were three identifiable segments within the microcomputer market: (1) hobbyists, (2) home users, and (3) professional and small business users. Table 17.1 shows an industry analysis of this market in 1977. At that time the biggest percentage of customers was in the hobby segment, and a complete hobby system could involve a $2000 investment or more. Such systems were sold both by mail order and through approximately 300 retail stores.

Table 17.1 Estimates of the Market for Personal Computers, 1977

Segment	*Potential Market* *Units*	*Percent Share*	*Price Range*
Hobby	40,000	57.1	$1,000 to $5,000
Home	20,000	28.6	$ 500 to $1,000
Professional/business	10,000	14.3	$5,000 to $20,000
Total	70,000	100.0	

Source: "Home Computer Sales Ready to Take off," Industry Week, Nov. 7, 1977, p. 98. Reprinted by permission of Industry Week, copyright © Penton/IPC, Inc., Cleveland, Ohio.

The home segment was basically interested in video games. During 1977 the Commodore PET priced at $495 was introduced especially for this market. National Semiconductor and Tandy's Radio Shack also had products targeted to this consumer, with distribution through computer stores, consumer electronic shops, and department stores.

For the professional and small business segment, the IBM 5100, Wang 2200, Hewlett Packard 9830 series, and the Datapoint 2200 were targeted, with prices ranging from $5000 to $20,000. At that time there was nothing lower priced that could provide the needed level of reliability. Software availability was a problem, and an inadequate network of field service offices also left the needs of this segment unmet. Because of these deficiencies, most of this segment relied on time sharing.

In summary, in 1977 as Jobs and his Apple were making the initial market entry, the hobby market was mature, with little growth. The consumer market seemed ripe for growth but lacked computer equipment simplified enough for home use to achieve mass penetration. For the professional/business sector, the potential was real, but two obstacles existed: (1) product capabilities and prices had not yet become attractive enough for this market and (2) service, support, and efficient distribution were also lacking. Computers were needed that were more user-oriented and lower priced.

STEVEN JOBS

Few multimillionaires were more unpromising youth that Steven Jobs. He was a loner in school, and his family had to move once because the boy refused to go back to his junior high school. At Homstead High School in Los Altos, California, it looked like Steven may have found himself, and he became enchanted with technology. He often went to Hewlett Packard lectures after school. One day he boldly called the president, William Hewlett, to ask for some equipment for a machine he was building. Hewlett was impressed, gave him the equipment, and helped arrange summer employment.

While at Homestead High School, Jobs became acquainted with Stephen Wozniak, who also was profoundly interested in technology. Jobs and Wozniak collaborated to build a device called a "blue box" to make long distance telephone calls for free.

After graduating from high school, Jobs went to Reed College in Oregon. But he dropped out before the first semester was over. He decided college was not for him, and he experimented for a year with fruitarinism and Hare Krishna. Next he took a job at Atari, a small electronics firm, at that time only two years old. Steve did not last long at Atari and soon left because of personality conflicts. With the money he had saved he took a trip to India and spent the rest of 1974 trying to decide what to do with his life.

Meanwhile, Wozniak had gone to the University of Colorado, then the next year to DeAnya College in Cupertino. After a year of designing software, he enrolled at the University of California at Berkeley. But he dropped out in 1975 and found a job as an engineering designer at Hewlett Packard. In his free time he worked at building a small computer, something that had fascinated him from his childhood when his father had taught him to design logic circuits.

Jobs often visited Wozniak where he was building small computers and circuits to show other computer buffs. At one such visit Jobs envisioned the potential that such Wozniak devices might have in the marketplace, and the germ of the idea was born that was to make the two college dropouts multimillionaires.

THE BEGINNING

In March 1976 Jobs and Wozniak formed a partnership and by June were selling pint-sized circuit boards. They pestered electronics suppliers for credit; they even tried to get backing from Atari and Hewlett Packard but were unsuccessful. The two young men finally raised $1300 by selling Jobs' Volkswagen bus and Wozniak's Hewlett Packard hand-held calculator. They got $10,000 in parts and credit and soon found that orders for their circuit boards outnumbered their ability to manufacture. By that summer they were well into the design of an advanced version, which they called the Apple II, a personal computer. By the end of 1976, sales were $200,000 with a 20 percent net income—all this coming from a $1300 investment.

In late 1976 and early 1977 Jobs and Wozniak made some major moves. They placed a technical article in a leading trade journal that gave them considerable visibility. They established a distribution agreement with several computer retailers. And they persuaded an attorney to provide legal services in a pay-later plan. But they still needed vastly more capital if they were to tap what seemed to them an almost unlimited potential, and they badly needed marketing expertise.

Jobs called a major semiconductor company in the area to find out who did their advertising. The agency, Regis, McKenna, at first refused to consider Apple as a client because of the insistence on a pay-later plan. But Jobs continued to pester Regis and the ad agency finally agreed to the proposition and remains the Apple agency today.

Jobs and Wozniak found the answer to their financial and marketing needs in A. C. Markkula, marketing manager of Intel Corporation, a leading semiconductor manufacturer. He was made an equal partner in return for his services and a $250,000 personal investment. (Markkula is now also one of the *Forbes*' Four Hundred, the richest people in America, thanks to this grasping of a nascent opportunity.)

Markkula helped arrange a credit line with Bank of America. The firm was beginning to look very impressive at this early stage. It was beginning to attract the attention of strong financial venture capitalists. Two such financial backers who were enticed were Venrock Associates (the Rockefeller family), and Arthur Rock. Apple now had received over $3 million, enough to begin major production.

THE CHARGE OF APPLE

In March 1977 Apple incorporated and moved out of a garage into a plant. The Apple II was introduced at a trade show in April and was an instant success. It was the first fully programmable personal computer. It was designed to function as a home system and was simple enough for a beginner but easily adaptable to the expert programmer. The name ''Apple'' was chosen because it was believed that computers intimidated the lay user, but ''apple'' conveyed a friendly and ordinary image that could be nicely targeted to the home user.

The total marketing budget for 1977 was $162,419. This was close to the total sales of the year before. And sales for 1977 surged to $774,000. The amazing growth now was causing corporate structural problems. The company leadership needed to be formalized, with a president and chairman designated. Jobs and Wozniak balked at the day-to-day operating responsibilities. They nominated Markkula as chairman and brought in Michael Scott, president of National Semiconductor, to be president. Scott saw the growth potential of Apple and took a 50 percent pay cut to come on board. Jobs became vice-chairman, and Wozniak vice-president of research and development. The firm was to remain privately held and primarily employee-owned until December 12, 1980, when it made a $96.8 million public offering. The stock was snapped up and rose quickly in market value. At that point, three years after the founding, Jobs and his colleagues became multimillionaires.

The growth burgeoned again in 1978 as the Apple II found wide acceptance among small businesses and professionals. The international market opened up as IT&T agreed to handle overseas sales of Apple computers. Sales for 1978 were $15 million.

By 1979 Apple and its major competitor, Tandy, dominated the market for personal computers. Apple had 500 retailers selling its computers in the United States, whereas Tandy with its Radio Shacks had 8000 outlets. Because of this retail network, Tandy led the personal computer industry, but Apple was second and closing fast. Many other computer makers were gearing up to invade the personal computer market, with rumors that mighty IBM might soon put in an appearance, too. Atari, a company gaining success in the video arcade market, was ready to invade, and Texas Instruments had already entered the market early in the year. By the end of 1979, approximately 30 companies were making personal computers. Apple added 100,000 square feet of manufacturing capacity to its 22,000 square feet, as it had to keep expanding to keep pace with the growing market potential and not concede position to eager competitors. Apple sales in 1979 rose to $70 million, more than a fourfold increase over the previous year. Apple was now marketing through five independent distributors who in turn sold to dealers and other customers.

In 1980 the Apple II was still selling strong at $1435 for the basic model. This same year the more expensive and heralded Apple III was introduced. This was targeted to the small business and professional market and was not really meant to be a home computer. However, this Apple was plagued with one technical flaw after another. Overheating problems in the main circuit board resulted in a lab overhaul. At the time, Apple had 850 U.S. dealers who were left empty-handed because of the unavailability of the Apple III, but fortunately many customers turned to the II. The company was forced to recall the 1400 units it had sold so that it could be reengineered. It was not brought to market again until November 1981. If the Apple II had not been held in such high esteem, the debacle with the Apple III could have jeopardized the entire company.

In March, Apple set up its own network of four regional replenishment centers. It now controlled its entire channel of distribution except the retail outlets, of which it was up to 800 stores. The marketing budget for 1980 reached $12.1 million. Some 135,000 Apple IIs were sold, with total yearly sales reaching $200 million and a $12 million net profit.

The fiasco of the Apple III brought some changes in 1981. The product manager of the Apple III resigned, as did president Scott, and some 40 employees were dismissed. The Apple III was redesigned and vigorously tested and its reintroduction met with some sales success. In the fall, IBM came into the market. Apple had recently surpassed Tandy in the race for market share and now became IBM's target. To increase customer and dealer service, Apple opened three more distribution centers. The Apple II was upgraded and named the Apple II plus. It retailed for about $1530 and about 15,000 units per month were sold through 1981. Total sales for this year were $334,783,000, again a phenomenal increase.

The next year, 1982, was again one of great increases. Net sales rose 74 percent to $583,061,000. Earnings also increased by 56 percent. Although more

Table 17.2 Market Shares (Based on Value of 1982 Shipments)

Computers	*Market Shares (%)*
Computers costing less than $1,000	
Commodore International	43
Texas Instruments	23
Atari	18
Timex	9
Tandy	3
Computers costing $1,000–$4,999	
Apple	24
IBM	17
NEC Home Electronics	11
Tandy	10
Commodore International	8
Computers costing $5,000–$30,000	
IBM	25
Tandy	17
Apple	14
Convergent Technology	7
Datapoint	7

Source: "Behind the Shakeout in Personal Computers," U.S. News & World Report, June 27, 1983, p. 59. Reprinted by permission.

than 100 manufacturers had entered the personal computer market, Apple had pulled ahead with a 24 percent market share. Table 17.2 shows the market shares for the major firms in the major categories of small computers for 1982. The retail distribution network was strengthened. Research and development expenditures were greatly increased, and marketing costs rose 117 percent. Two service centers were added to bring the worldwide total to 12. But the entry of IBM was casting shadows over the optimism of Apple. *Forbes* analyzed the situation thus:

> Apple's essential problem is that it could find itself squeezed from below by Atari, Commodore, and Tandy, and from above by the big battalions of IBM, Xerox, H-P, and others.[2]

In 1983 Apple unveiled its new computer, "Lisa." This was a $10,000 unit that Apple hoped would attract the corporate market. Late in 1983 the MacIntosh was introduced, aimed at the home and professional markets. The success of these new product offerings cannot be ascertained at this time, and they may be somewhat blunted by the aggressive efforts of IBM. Regardless, we are looking at one of the

[2]Kathleen K. Wiegner, "Tomorrow Has Arrived," *Forbes*, Feb. 15, 1982, p. 119.

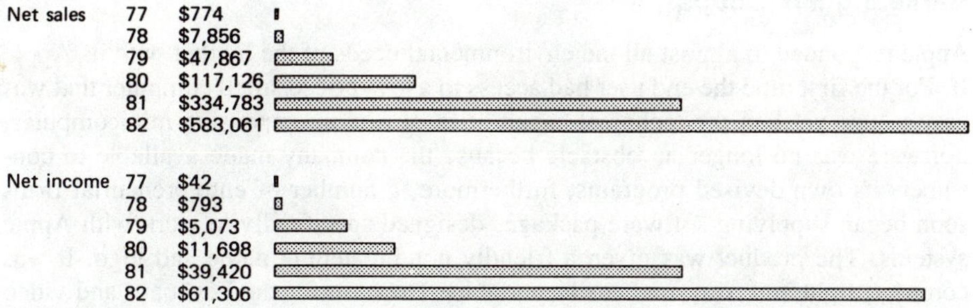

Figure 17.1. Sales and income, Apple Computer, 1977–1982 (in thousands of dollars). (*Source:* Company annual reports.)

greatest success stories. Figure 17.1 shows the fantastic growth of Apple in sales and profits in the six years from 1977 through 1982.

INGREDIENTS OF SUCCESS

Environmental

The success of Apple might be attributed to the old cliché, ''Having the right idea at the right time.'' But this is far too simplistic to be helpful in this analysis. It took no genius to recognize that there was a latent demand for a simple personal computer. But it took a young computer buff, Wozniak, to design such an innovation and an entrepreneurial whiz to maneuver the idea and the early prototypes into a half-a-billion-dollar company, wedging in through entrenched, well-heeled, experienced, and aggressive competitors. Most would have said this was an unrealistic possibility. But we know it happened.

The following were conditions that made the environment favorable to the introduction of the personal computer:

- Interest in computers was growing even among the general public, while the need to improve business productivity through better information flow and analyses was becoming ever more apparent.
- Simplified equipment that could offer the degree of reliability required by small professional and business users was just not available.
- Lack of programming knowledge was a big deterrent for many potential users. People wanted a product that would let them program without being a computer expert.
- Microcomputers were available in the market in the form of kits, so the technology and interest was emerging.
- Software was lagging behind the hardware, and manufacturers such as Commodore and Heath were entering the market unaware of this gap. This situation was aggravated by an incompatibility of language support.

Marketing Mix Coups

Apple responded to almost all the environmental needs of the market with its Apple II. For the first time the end user had access to a low-priced small computer that was easy to use yet had the technical capabilities of a more expensive minicomputer. Software was no longer an obstacle because the company made available to consumers its own devised programs; furthermore, a number of entrepreneurial firms soon began supplying software packages designed specifically to work with Apple systems. The product was given a friendly nonthreatening name and logo. It was compact, light and trim, and easily portable. The case for the keyboard and video display was light plastic instead of metal. The video display was smaller than a television but large enough to provide good resolution and clear print. The whole product was light-colored and attractive, rather than the more austere and formidable black and silver colors of such brands as Tandy. The instruction manual made it easy to understand the system and the software. This was an early key to success because these instructions added to the ease of operation, the "user friendliness." All these features reinforced the perception that the computer was easy to use: a friendly computer with a high-quality image at an affordable price.

From the beginning, the decision had been to manufacture the Apple with the highest quality control standards possible. The reputation for high quality quickly followed and Apple was able to command a price premium and maintains its market lead over a host of scrambling competitors.

Early on Apple detected the need to shift the target market from the general public and home use that most personal computer firms were trying to cater to. A lack of suitable software, a fear of machines, and a growing recognition that in many households the need for such sophisticated machines was really not all that great—except for computer games—began to disillusion many consumers. Apple quickly recognized professionals and small businesses as the main market. It accordingly shifted gears and therefore chose to emphasize software, encouraging independent software developers as well as its own developers to design software products for a vast array of needs of potential users.

Apple's pricing policies also aided this entry into the personal computing-for-profit market. For example, when Tandy was offering a 4000-character memory system for $499 as their primary product aimed at the home user, Apple II was selling for $1195 for a 16,000-character memory or $1495 for a 48,000-character memory. These products were much more suited to the computing needs of the small business firm, especially in view of the wide array of software to meet almost any demands, and were still attractively priced.

The distribution channels and strategies initially used also proved to be appropriate for the professional/business market. Apple created strong ties to 750 to 800 independent retail outlets, such as Computerland, Inc. It provided toll-free software hotlines for users, a monthly newsletter, and a magazine that focused on different applications in each issue. A cooperative advertising program reimbursed dealers for 3 percent of their dollar purchases. By using these marketing efforts directed

Table 17.3 Personal Computer Media Expenditures January through September 1982 (in Thousands)

	Total	*Magazines*	*Newspapers*	*Spot TV*	*Net TV*
Apple	3197.4	3110.3		87.1	
Commodore	650.9	650.9			
Ditgital	482.8	482.8			
IBM	3620.4	3307.0	313.4		
Osborne	1360.5	1245.5		115.0	
Sinclair	1286.9	1245.5	19.8	21.6	
Tandy (TRS80)	2027.8	652.3		2.9	1372.6
Texas Instruments	3183.8			3183.8	
Timex	2059.4	756.9		1302.5	
Wang	918.0	720.7		197.3	
Warner (Atari)	7786.1	1306.0		5819.2	660.9
Xerox	274.0	274.0			

Source: Marketing Media Decisions, February 1983, p. 143. Reprinted by permission.

primarily to dealers, Apple overturned a key computer industry marketing law established by IBM: that selling computers requires armies of direct sales people schooled in handholding of the end user.

Apple was able to keep its margins high and direct sales costs low by using this method of distribution. By 1981 it had also eliminated the intermediaries by selling directly to retailers through its own regional support centers. The objective was better inventory control. Efforts were also made to gain better access to end users. Direct training was given dealers through sales seminars entitled "Apple Means Business." Dealers were provided structured presentations that they could use to educate end users. Apple also equipped dealers to do same-day walk-in repairs and replaced equipment free if needed.

Apple's promotional efforts reinforced the other strong ingredients of the marketing mix. The theme of "user friendliness," was continually stressed. The name "Apple," of course, fostered wide recognition of the company and product. Although the mass market did not materialize as originally expected, when and if it does, Apple should be well positioned. Heavy emphasis was placed on television in the early years. A recognizable and authoritative spokesman, Dick Cavette, helped to gain the awareness of millions of people of Apple, long before any competitor had attempted to achieve such public awareness. In unaided tests in 1981, 79 percent of consumers asked to name "a company that makes personal computers" named Apple.[3] Since professionals are among the general public, this high awareness proved very effective in tapping such a market and should be all the more so if a mass market does open up. Table 17.3 shows the 1982 breakdown of advertising expenditures among Apple and its major competitors.

[3]"Apple Takes on Its Biggest Test Yet," *Business Week,* Jan. 31, 1983, p. 72.

Table 17.4 Comparisons of Growth in Sales for Kresge (K mart), McDonald's and Apple during the Six Greatest Growth Years

Year	*Sales (in Millions of Dollars)*	*Percent Change from Previous Year*
	Kresge	
1965	851.4	25
1966	1090.2	28
1967	1385.7	27
1968	1731.5	25
1979	2185.3	26
1970	2558.7	17
	Apple	
1977	0.8	286
1978	7.9	915
1979	47.1	510
1980	117.1	145
1981	334.8	186
1982	583.1	74
	McDonald's	
1965	35.4	37
1966	42.7	21
1967	53.7	26
1968	97.8	82
1969	143.3	47
1970	200.3	40

Source: Company records.

Handling Great Growth

The ability of Jobs and the organization he created to handle the phenomenal growth—from $200,000 in 1976 to $583 million in sales in 1982, only six years—has to be one of the most remarkable growth episodes of U.S. business, and all without losing control of the company or having ownership badly diluted. Table 17.4 compares the six key growth years of Apple with those of K mart and McDonald's during their most rapid growth. As can be seen, Apple's growth rate far surpassed them, despite their being outstanding successes and the dominant influences in their industries. Of course, we must recognize that a small firm can much more easily double and triple its sales year to year than larger firms that have a much greater base to exceed. But even McDonald's in its embryonic years could not come close to matching the growth of Apple.

True, Apple had some problems in handling its growth. Management of creative employees is an important and often difficult task because such people tend to be nonconformists. Jobs attempted to encourage a creative, risk-taking spirit, one in which high motivation and embracing of challenges prevailed. He used techniques that deviated from orthodox management thinking with its insistence on formal lines of authority and well-designated policies. But in-fighting and power struggles caused the departures of several key people, most notably Stephen Wozniak, co-founder of Apple, and Michael Scott, the former president. Apple was described as disorganized and incompetent in its management.[4]

The problems with Apple III, which could have scuttled the company, were perhaps caused by these loose management controls and bickering, or may simply have reflected the strains of great growth amid fantastic market potential and the eagerness to tap this before competitors could.

Not the least of the success factors for Apple was its handling of adversity. The significant failure of the Apple III was dealt with probably as well as was possible. The danger with any highly heralded product that fails because of quality problems is that a firm's image will be so badly tarnished it will tar the rest of the product line. Such a danger is especially acute for the new firm that has little tradition of quality to sustain it.

But Apple handled this quality dilemma very well. As soon as the magnitude of the problems with Apple III surfaced, it withdrew the product, despite extensive preintroductory promotional efforts. The product was not reintroduced until all the problems had been corrected, and this was many months later. A potential catastrophe was averted.

A firm shows its character not only in good times but even more so in adversity.

WHAT CAN BE LEARNED?

Perhaps the first thing we can learn from Apple's great success is that venture capital is available for the idea that can be persuasively presented to well-heeled investors. Certainly Apple could not have achieved more than limited success without the investment of outsiders convinced that it stood on the threshhold of opportunity. For any small business an aggressive and attractive concept helps in winning seed money. But some venture capitalists look more at the person than the idea: "Nearly every mistake I've made has been because I picked the wrong people, not the wrong idea," says Arthur Rock, a reowned venture capitalist.[5] So the probability of venture capital exists—some $1 billion a year is flooding into venture capital by pension funds, corporations, and wealthy individuals[6]—for innovative entrepreneurs.

Apple has proven that great growth is possible, that it can be managed without losing control, even if the organization and human relations may be a bit flaky

[4] "Building Computers Is as Easy as Apple Pie," *Industry Week,* June 9, 1980, p. 80.
[5] "Have You Got What It Takes?" *Forbes,* August 3, 1981, p. 60.
[6] Ibid., p. 61.

during some of the wildly escalating years. It poses the concept that we "need to run with the ball" when we get that rare opportunity. In other words, if a glorious opportunity arises, we should not hold back, not be conservative or cautious, but maximize the opportunity. And yes, this is what Apple did, as well as the other successes we have studied.

But are there any cautions to this solidly grasping and running with a nascent opportunity? Perhaps there are. Let us recognize that risks lie on all sides as we reach for such opportunities, and often reach quickly lest they be grabbed be competitors:

> When a market begins to boom and a firm finds that it cannot keep up with demand without greatly increasing its capacity and resources, it faces a dilemma: do we stay conservative in the expectation that the burgeoning potential will be short-lived, and thereby abdicate some of the growing market to our competitors; or do we expand vigorously, run with the ball, so as to take full advantage of the opportunity. And perhaps we will find that the euphoria was short-lived, that demand has ceased its exponential increase, and may even be tapering off. Meanwhile, we are left with greatly expanded capacity, more resource commitment than is needed, high interest and carrying costs, and perhaps even a jeopardized viability because of overextension.

This is the dilemma, and there is no firm answer or solution to it. But this makes the risk of marketing and management decision making in the chaotic times of technological breakthroughs risky, challenging, and tremendously exciting.

The great importance of guarding a quality image is vividly illustrated here. Apple had been successful in establishing itself, in only a few short years, as the quality product among its many competitors, but it stood to lose all with its inferior Apple III. Drastic action was required if the reputation was not to be tarnished, perhaps irrevocably, especially with IBM standing in the wings. Biting the bullet, Apple quickly withdrew the product and made restitution to all purchasers without delay. All firms should heed this example. To tarry, to find excuses, to try to dismiss the reality of a defective product is flirting with disaster. If the problems cannot be quickly remedied, for the sake of customer relations and the protection of the vital quality image any such product should be withdrawn immediately.

In an industry of rapidly changing technology, the importance of heavy commitments to research and development seems inescapable. In such a youthful industry, technological breakthroughs can come at any time, from any firm. The competitor who lags in research and development (R&D) faces serious problems that may well jeopardize its continuance in the industry. Technological breakthroughs may bring improvements or modifications that make existing products obsolete; or they may increase production efficiency and lower costs. Regardless, such an industry is in transition and no firm can rest on its laurels. Figure 17.2 shows the increasingly heavy expenditures for R&D by Apple from 1977 to 1982 as it sought to avoid vulnerability and achieve further breakthroughs.

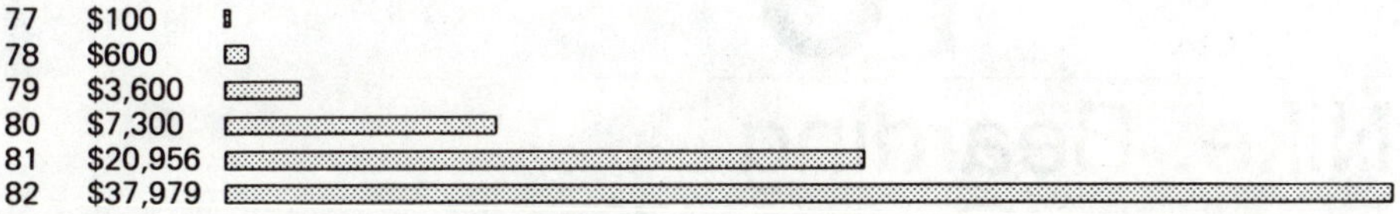

Figure 17.2. Apple research and development expenditures, 1977–1982 (in thousands of dollars). (*Source:* Company annual reports.)

Finally, we see the importance of selecting the right customer segment. In this case the segment that offered the realistic potential for personal computers was not the widely sought-after home market. Rather, it was the small business/professional market, which Apple identified earlier than its competitors and swung its marketing efforts toward.

Questions

1. Discuss and evaluate the pros and cons of a heavy growth commitment for a small innovator in
   (a) A personal computer adaptation.
   (b) Running shoes.
   (c) Discount-concept retailing.
   (d) A fast-food restaurant.
2. How would you use research to determine which target market would be best for an innovative new small computer? What criteria would you use in evaluating such a target market?

Invitation to Role Play

As an entrepreneur seeking venture capital for a new and innovative personal computer, what persuasive arguments would you propose for a $500,000 initial request for funds? How would you counter the skeptic's query of how you could possibly compete with the might of IBM?

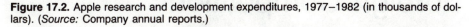

CHAPTER 18

Nike: Bearding Foreign Competition

In this last case of the book we have another remarkable success story, almost another Apple, but the product is very different. This success also produced another of *Forbes*' Four Hundred Richest Americans: Philip H. Knight, the cofounder and chairman of Nike, Inc., the athletic shoe company. Although Nike was older than Apple, and took more years to reach its takeoff point, when it occurred its growth practically matched that of Apple.

PHIL KNIGHT AND THE BEGINNING OF NIKE

Phil Knight was a miler of modest accomplishments. His best time was 4:13, hardly in the same class as the below 4:00 world-class runners. But he had trained under the renowned coach, Bill Bowerman at the University of Oregon in the late 1950s. Bowerman had put Eugene, Oregon, on the map in the 1950s when year after year he turned out world-record-setting long-distance runners. He was constantly experimenting with shoes, because of his theory that an ounce off a running shoe might make enough difference to win a race.

In the process of completing his MBA at Stanford University, Phil wrote a research paper that was based on the theory that the Japanese could do for athletic shoes what they were doing for cameras. After receiving his degree in 1960, Knight went to Japan to seek an American distributorship from the Onitsuka Company for Tiger shoes. Returning home, he took samples of the shoes to Bowerman.

In 1964 Knight and Bowerman went into business. They each put up $500, formed the Blue Ribbon Shoe Company, sole distributor in the United States for Tiger running shoes. They put the inventory in Knight's father-in-law's basement, and they sold $8000 worth of these imported shoes that first year. Knight worked by days as a Cooper & Lybrand accountant, while at night and on weekends he peddled these shoes mostly to high school athletic teams.

Knight and Bowerman finally developed their own shoe in 1972 and decided to manufacture it themselves. They contracted the work out to Asian factories where labor was cheap. They named the shoe, Nike (rhymes with psyche), after the Greek goddess of victory. At that time they also developed the "swoosh" logo, shown below, which was highly distinctive and subsequently was placed on every Nike product. The Nike shoes' first appearance in competition came during the 1972 Olympic trials in Eugene, Oregon. Marathon runners persuaded to wear the new shoes placed fourth through seventh, whereas Adidas wearers finished first, second, and third in these trials.

Nike faced severe competition in the athletic-shoe industry. This industry was absolutely dominated at that time by foreign manufacturers, particularly two German firms, Adidas and Puma, with Tiger being number 3. Knight and Bowerman realized that they had no hope for capturing a large share of the market unless they could develop a product better than what was currently available. And up to then American-made running shoes just did not match most foreign shoes, particularly Adidas.

On a Sunday morning in 1975, Bowerman began tinkering with a waffle iron and some urethane rubber, and he fashioned a new type of sole, a "waffle" sole whose tiny rubber studs made it more springy than those of other shoes currently on the market. This product improvement—seemingly simple compared to the high-tech innovations of the previous chapters—gave Knight and Bowerman an initial impetus on their way to almost the heights of success of Steven Jobs and his Apple. The marketing strategy that propeled Nike to tops in the U.S. market was more imitative than innovative, however. It was patterned after that of the very successful Adidas. But the result was that the imitator outdid the originator.

ADIDAS

The Rise to Dominance

Rudolf and Adolf Dassler began making shoes in Herzogenaurach, West Germany, shortly after World War I. Adolf, known as Adi to his family, was the innovator, and Rudolf was the marketer who sold his brother's creations. The brothers achieved only moderate success at first, but then in 1936 a big breakthrough came. Jesse Owens agreed to wear their shoes in the Olympics and won his medals in front of Hitler, the German nation, and the world.

In 1949 the brothers had a falling out and, indeed, never again spoke to each other outside of court. Rudolf took half the equipment and left his brother to go to the other side of town and set up the Puma Company. Adolf established the Adidas Company from the existing firm (''Adidas'' was derived from his nickname and the first three letters of his surname). Rudolf and his Pumas never quite caught up with Adolf's Adidas, but they did become number 2 in the world.

Adolf was constantly experimenting with new materials and techniques to develop stronger, yet lighter shoes. He tested thorny sharkskin in attempts to develop abrasive leather for indoor flats. He tried kangaroo leather to toughen the sides of shoes.

The first samples of Adidas footwear were shown at the Helsinki Olympic Games of 1952. Then in 1954 the German soccer team, equipped with Adidas footwear, won the World Cup over Hungary. The shoes were definitely a factor in the win, as Dassler had developed a special stud to screw into the shoes that allowed good footing on the muddy playing field that day; Hungary's shoes did not give the same traction.

Dassler's many innovations in the running-shoe industry included four-spiked running shoes, track shoes with a nylon sole, and injected spikes. He developed a shoe that allowed an athlete to choose from 30 different variations of interchangeable spike elements that could be adapted to an indoor or outdoor track as well as to natural or artificial surfaces.

With its great variety of superior products, Adidas dominated in the widely publicized international showcase events. For example, at the Montreal games, Adidas-equipped athletes accounted for 82.8 percent of all individual medal winners.[1] This was tremendous publicity for the company, and sales rose to $1 billion worldwide.

But competitors were entering the marketplace. Prior to 1972, Adidas and Puma had practically the entire athletic shoe market to themselves. Although this was changing, Adidas seemingly had built up an insurmountable lead, providing footwear for virtually every type of sporting activity as well as diversifying into

[1]Norris Willett, ''How Adidas Ran Faster,'' *Management Today,* December 1979, p. 58.

other sports-related product lines: shorts, jerseys, leisure suits, and track suits; tennis and swimwear; balls for every kind of sport; tennis racquets and cross-country skis; and the popular sports bag that carried the Adidas name as a prominently displayed status symbol.

Marketing Strategy

The marketing strategy originated by the Dassler brothers became the guiding influence for the entire industry, including Nike. The Dasslers had long used international athletic competition as a testing ground for their products. Many years of feedback from these athletes led to continual design changes and improvements. Agreements were entered into with professional athletes to use their products. However, Adidas' strength was in international and Olympic events in which the participants were amateurs, and such endorsement contracts were more often made with national sports associations rather than the individuals.

Following the lead of Adidas and Puma, endorsement contracts with athletes have become commonplace. For example, every player in the National Basketball Association is under contract to at least one manufacturer. The going rate for an endorsement contract ranges from $500 to $150,000. The athlete must wear a certain brand name and appear in various promotional activities. It has become an industry practice to spend about 80 percent of the advertising budget for endorsements and 20 percent for media advertising. The distinctive logos that all manufacturers have developed is key to the effectiveness of these endorsement contracts. Such logos permit immediate identification of the product; fans and potential customers can see the product actually in use by the famous athlete. These logos also permitted effective product diversification into apparel, bags, and so on.

To increase volume quickly, production facilities were sought where shoes could be made cheaply and in great quantities, in areas such as Yugoslavia and the Far East. Medium-sized firms in such countries were therefore signed up as licensees and goods were produced to specifications. Great outlays for plants and equipment were thus avoided and costs could be kept low.

Finally, Adidas led the running-shoe industry into offering a very wide variety of shoe styles—shoes to fit all kinds of running activities, from various kinds of races to training shoes. Shoes were also offered for every type of runner and running style. The great variety of offerings, more than a hundred different styles and models, was exceeded only by Nike as it charged to capture the U.S. market.

THE 1970s RUNNING MARKET

During the late 1960s and early 1970s the environment affecting the running-shoe industry changed dramatically and positively. Americans were increasingly concerned with physical fitness. Millions of previously unathletic people were searching for ways to exercise. The spark that ignited the booming interest may have been the 1972 Munich Olympics. Millions of television viewers watched Dave Wottle defeat Russian Evgeni Arzanov in the 800-meters and Frank Shorter win the prestigious marathon. But the groundwork for the running boom was laid before. The idea of fitness perhaps first came to the attention of the general public in a trailblazing book by Dr. Kenneth Cooper, *Aerobics,* which sold millions of copies and gave scientific evidence of the physical benefits of a running (or jogging) regimen. A little less than 10 years later, another book with monumental impact, *The Complete Book of Running* by James Fixx, also sold millions of copies and was on the best selling list for months.

Through the decade of the 1970s the number of joggers increased. Estimates by the end of the decade were that 25 million to 30 million Americans were joggers, while another 10 million wore running shoes around home and town.[2] The number of shoe manufacturers also increased. The original three of Adidas, Puma, and Tiger were joined by new U.S. brands: Nike, Brooks, New Balance, Etonic, and even J. C. Penney, Sears, and Converse. To sell and distribute these new shoes, specialty shoe stores such as Athlete's Foot, Athletic Attic, and Kinney's Foot Lockers sprouted up nationwide. New magazines catering to this market were springing up and showing big increases in circulation: for example, *Runner's World, The Runner,* and *Running Times.* These provided the advertising medium to reach runners with no wasted coverage.

NIKE'S CHARGE

The new "waffle sole" developed by Bowerman proved popular with runners, and this along with the favorable market brought 1976 sales to $14 million, up from $8.3 million the year before and only $2 million in 1972.

Nike stayed in the forefront of the industry with its careful research and development of new models. By the end of the decade Nike was employing almost 100 people in the research and development section of the company. Over 140 different models were offered in the product line, some of these the most innovative and technologically advanced on the market. This diversity came from models designed for different foot types, body weights, running speeds, training schedules, sexes, and different levels of skills.

Some 85 percent of Nike's shoes eventually were manufactured in 20 different overseas locations, while factories in New Hampshire, Maine, and Oregon made 15 percent of Nike's shoes. By the late 1970s and early 1980s, demand for Nikes was so great that 60 percent of its 8000 department store, sporting goods, and shoe store dealers gave advanced orders, often waiting six months for delivery. This gave Nike a big advantage in production scheduling and inventory costs.

[2]"The Jogging-Shoe Race Heats Up," *Business Week,* April 9, 1979, p. 125.

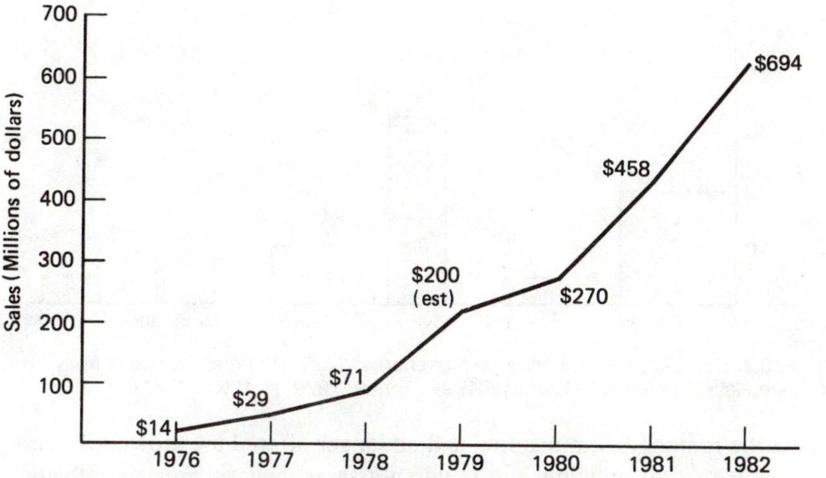

Figure 18.1. Nike sales growth, 1976–1981. (*Source:* Company annual reports.)

Figure 18.1 shows the phenomenal growth of Nike, with sales rising from $14 million in 1976 to $694 million only six years later. Figure 18.2 shows the market shares in the U.S. market for the beginning of 1979. By then Nike was the market leader with 33 percent of the market; within two years it had taken an even more commanding lead, with approximately 50 percent of the total market.[3] Indicative of the great visibility and wide appeal that Nike had achieved, in 1981 *Forbes* asked 150 junior high students in a middle-class Dallas neighborhood what their favorite athletic shoe was. All 150 listed Nike first, often citing its status as an expensive "designer" shoe.[4]

Nike continued to stay in the forefront of technology. In early 1979 it introduced the revolutionary "Tailwind." Called the "next generation in footwear," and advertised as "air travel," the Tailwind was developed by an aerospace engineer from Rockwell International and used a sole cushioned of polyurethane-encapsulated air chambers. The three-year R&D effort involved exhaustive testing by everyone from "policemen to podiatrists." At $50, it carried the highest price tag yet in the industry. Yet, demand was so great that Nike was forced to allocate it to dealers.[5]

In 1980 Nike went public, and Knight became an instant multimillionaire, reaching the coveted *Forbes*' Richest Four Hundred Americans with a net worth estimated at just under $300 million.[6] Bowerman, age 70, had sold most of his stock earlier, and owned only 2 percent of the company, worth a mere $9.5 million.

[3]"Jogging's Fade Fails to Push Nike Off Track," *Wall Street Journal,* March 5, 1981, p. 25.
[4]Reported in "Nike's Fast Track," *Forbes,* Nov. 23, 1981, p. 62.
[5]"The Jogging Shoe Race Heats Up," p. 125.
[6]"The Richest People in America—The *Forbes* Four Hundred," *Forbes,* fall 1983, p. 104.

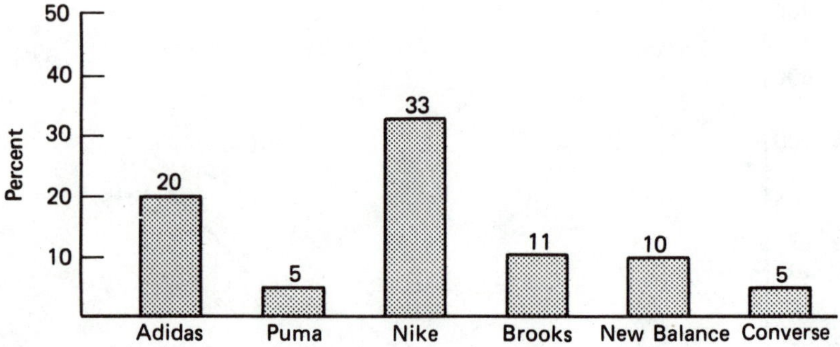

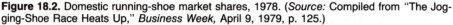

Figure 18.2. Domestic running-shoe market shares, 1978. (*Source:* Compiled from "The Jogging-Shoe Race Heats Up," *Business Week,* April 9, 1979, p. 125.)

As the running boom matured and no longer offered the growth of a few years earlier, Nike began moving into children's shoes and apparel and athletic bags. Nonshoe products especially appeared to offer considerable potential, as Adidas derived an estimated 40 percent of its sales from such products as apparel and athletic bags, which had been of miniscule value for Nike up to 1980. Nike was also diversifying into other kinds of shoes. By the end of 1980, basketball shoes accounted for 24 percent of Nike's sales, with tennis and other racquet-sport shoes adding another 18 percent. See Table 18.1 for the approximate breakdown of U.S. sales by major product types for the three years 1978 through 1980. Plans were also readied to expand into hiking and deck shoes, and Nike was gearing up to invade the overseas markets, especially Western Europe, long the domain of Adidas.

In the January 4, 1982, edition of *Forbes,* in the ''Annual Report on American Industry,'' Nike was rated number 1 in profitability over the previous five years, ahead of all other firms in all other industries.[7]

INGREDIENTS OF SUCCESS

Unquestionably, Nike faced an extraordinarily favorable primary demand in the decade of the 1970s. Jogging and keeping fit were sweeping the nation as few sports or activities had ever. Nike was positioned to take advantage of this trend, and indeed most of the running-shoe manufacturers had impressive gains during these years. But we know that Nike's success went far beyond simply coasting with a favorable primary demand. Nike outstripped all its competitors, including the heretofore dominant Adidas. Nike was able to overcome whatever aura or mystique such foreign producers as Adidas, Puma, and Tiger had.

Nike as it began to reach its potential offered an even broader product line than Adidas, which had pioneered with a great variety of shoe styles. A broad product

[7]*Forbes,* January 4, 1982, p. 246.

Table 18.1 Nike's Dollar and Percentage Sales by Product Categories, 1978–1980

	Year Ended May 31					
	1978		*1979*		*1980*	
	Dollars (in thousands)	*Percentage*	*Dollars (in thousands)*	*Percentage*	*Dollars (in thousands)*	*Percentage*
Running	39,000	55	80,500	55	107,600	43
Basketball	14,300	20	27,800	19	61,800	24
Tennis and other racquet	12,200	17	25,500	17	46,700	18
Children's	1,600	2	5,500	4	21,400	8
Apparel	1,300	2	2,200	2	8,100	3
Field sports	900	1	1,900	1	4,300	2
Leisure	1,000	2	1,200	1	1,600	1
Other	300	1	1,000	1	1,700	1
Total	70,600	100	145,600	100	253,200	100

Source: Company prospectus.

line can have its problems; it can be overdone, hurt efficiency, and greatly add to costs. Most firms are better advised to pare their product line, to prune their weak products so that adequate attention and resources can be directed to the winners. Here we see the disavowal of such a policy, and yet, this is one of the great successes of the decade. What is a prudent product mix?

Although Nike may have violated some product mix concepts, let us recognize what they accomplished and at what cost. By offering a great variety of styles, prices, and uses, Nike was able to appeal to all kinds of runners; it was able to convey the image of the most complete running-shoe manufacturer of all. In a rapidly evolving industry in which millions of runners of all kinds and abilities were embracing the idea, such an image became very attractive. The image was conveyed of a company that could provide shoes to fit every runner's needs, running styles, and special problems. And no other shoe manufacturer, not even the vaunted Adidas, could offer as much. Furthermore, in a rapidly expanding market, Nike found that it could tap the widest possible distribution with its breadth of product line. It could sell its shoes to conventional retailers, such as department stores and shoe stores; it could continue to do business with the specialized running-shoe stores. It could even be not too concerned about discounters getting some Nike shoes since there were certainly enough styles and models to go around—different models for different types of retail outlets, and everyone could be happy.

Short production runs and many styles generally add to production costs, but perhaps in Nike's case this was less of a factor. Most of the shoe production was contracted out—some 85 percent to foreign, mostly Far Eastern, factories. Short production runs were less of an economic deterrent where many foreign plants were contracting for part of the production.

Nike early on placed a heavy emphasis on research and technological improvement. It sought ever more flexible and lighter weight running shoes that would be protective but also give the athlete, world-class or slowest amateur, the utmost advantage that running-shoe technology could provide. Nike's commitment to research and development is tangibly evident in the approximately 100 employees working in this area, many holding degrees in biomechanics, exercise physiology, engineering, industrial design, chemistry, and other related fields. The firm also engaged research committees and advisory boards, including coaches, athletes, athletic trainers and equipment managers, podiatrists, and orthopedists, who met periodically with the firm to review designs, materials, and concepts for improved athletic shoes. Activities included high-speed photographic analyses of the human body in motion, the use of athletes on force plates and treadmills, wear testing using over 300 athletes in an organized program, and continual testing and study of new and modified shoes and materials. Some \$2.5 million was spent in 1980 on product research, development, and evaluation, and the 1981 budget was approximately \$4 million. For such an apparently simple thing as a shoe, this is a major commitment to research and development.

As a final point-of-sale testing, Nike maintained seven retail outlets, called "Athletic Departments." The goals of these were to bring product information to the consumer as well as provide feedback to Nike's research and development teams. These outlets served as sensors and helped Nike monitor the market and provided an additional distribution channel.

Nike attempted no major deviation from the accepted and successful marketing strategy norm of the industry. This norm was established several decades before by Adidas. It primarily involved testing and development of better running shoes, a broad product line to appeal to all segments of the market, a readily identifiable trademark or motif prominently displayed on all products, and the use of well-known athletes and prestigious athletic events to show off the products in use. Even the contracting out of much of the production to low-cost foreign factories was not unique to Nike. But Nike used these proven techniques better and more aggressively than any of its competitors, even Adidas.

For example, let us consider how Nike used athletes to promote its brand. Knight had made a rather well-publicized statement that one can pay $50,000 for a full-page advertisement in *Sports Illustrated* but it is impossible to buy the front cover. But by getting top athletes who would make the cover of *Sports Illustrated* to wear Nike shoes, Knight essentially "makes" the front cover. When such athletes are seen on television, in person, or on the cover of *Sports Illustrated* wearing the familiar Nike logo, the publicity gained for Nike is almost inestimable. Viewers will readily emulate the famous athlete by also choosing Nike for their own use. An impressive list of athletes have been under contract to wear Nike products: John McEnroe, Nolan Ryan, Alberto Salazar, Sebastian Coe, Henry Rono, half a dozen LA Dodgers, and the defensive line of the Dallas Cowboys, among others. In 1979, Coe was the first individual to hold the world records for the 800 meter, 1500 meter, and 1-mile runs. Rono was the first individual to hold world records in the 3000 meter steeplechase, and the 3000, 5000, and 10,000 meter runs.

This use of athletes was certainly followed by all such manufacturers; however, Nike was able to gain the best in many cases, partly through its R&D efforts, which placed it in the forefront of technological improvements, and also because of the momentum it had built up as the fastest growing and soon the biggest firm in the industry. "The secret to the business," explained Knight, "is to build the kind of shoes professional athletes will wear, then put them on the pros. The rest of the market will follow."[8]

Perhaps some of the accolades for the aggressive success of Nike should be tempered by the deficiencies of its competitors. Adidas began to slip in its aggressiveness; it began to coast on its laurels and certainly did not recognize the formidable inroads of Nike until rather late. Furthermore, although it had been innovative in developing improved versions of running and racing shoes, it slipped

[8]"Nike's Fast Track," *Forbes*, November 23, 1981, pp. 59–60.

a bit in the 1970s. For a time, Nike's shoes were lighter, more cushioned, and more flexible than Adidas. Even after Adidas recognized the serious threat of Nike, its efforts were weak both in its introduction of new and advanced-design products and in its promotional efforts.

Some of the U.S. companies that were traditionally strong in the lower priced athletic shoe industry, notably Converse and Uniroyal's Keds, were caught flat-footed in the race to bring new and technologically improved models to the market. These major producers of tennis shoes and sneakers (Converse made two thirds of U.S. basketball shoes) vastly underestimated the strength and the longevity of the "running boom" and did not direct strong efforts toward this market until they were completely outclassed by Nike and several other U.S. manufacturers.

And not all the U.S. manufacturers had sufficient production savvy to take advantage of the heated market. For example, Brooks, a U.S. firm that had attracted initial market success, dissipated its strength with poor quality control. Defective shoes and shoe returns destroyed its momentum both with consumers and with dealers.

Finally, a key factor in the continued success of Nike as the running market matured and began to ease slightly was its strong commitment to diversification. Children's shoes, apparel, leisure shoes, and field sport shoes exemplified the expanded product diversity. This product line expansion got underway at the peak of the running boom (about 1978–1979) and helped ensure future growth. Also, Nike began strenuous efforts to expand geographically. It began marketing shoes in Europe in 1981 and in Japan by January 1982.

WHAT CAN BE LEARNED?

We see in this case an example of a success that did not come primarily from an innovative approach to marketing, recognizing a marketing opportunity that no one else had, or plowing more resources into promotion and advertising than hapless competitors were able to muster. The key ingredient that we can identify is *effective imitation*. And yet, Nike's success almost matched that of Apple, the innovator.

Of course, imitation must be judicious. A marketing strategy to be imitated should be the most effective approach, it should be historically successful. In the case of the running-shoe market, the long-time strategy of Adidas in offering many models, in associating its brand with major athletic events and athletes themselves, in constantly seeking product improvement, in judicious and related diversification—these could hardly have been improved on, and all running-shoe manufacturers followed the same strategy; only Nike did it better.

In the effort to be imitative, a firm, of course, still needs to develop its own identity. By imitation we do not mean a slavish effort to be identical. Only the successful policies, standards, and actions are imitated. There is still room to develop the distinctive image, the trademark or logo, and an organization and management ever alert to new opportunities.

Every firm needs to react with its environment and its subtle and not-so-subtle changes. This is especially important when the product life cycle is uncertain, in both scope and duration. The following Information Sidelight discusses product life cycle uncertainties.

INFORMATION SIDELIGHT

Product Life-Cycle Uncertainties

Just as people or animals do, products go through stages of growth and maturity, that is, life cycles. We can recognize four stages in a product's life cycle: introduction, growth, maturity, and decline.

Figure 18.3 depicts representative life cycles for a typical consumer-goods product and for one that is more of a fashion or a fad item. Notice how abruptly sales peak for a fad item, and the abruptness of the decline, compared with a more standard item. Once the decline begins for a fad or fashion product, it is usually impossible to reverse or even slow it.

The life cycle for running shoes reflected on both the popularity of running and the transference of running shoe use from dedicated joggers and runners to others who bought them for their status appeal as a symbol of fitness or simply had found that running shoes were more comfortable to wear for casual use than any other type of footwear.

Regardless, a major question confronting the industry was whether this indeed was a fad that would abruptly burn out or a more long-lasting phenomenon representing a significant change in the life-style of many Americans. No one could doubt that the growth stage had to eventually level out and reach maturity. Less certain, however, was how high the life cycle would reach—how many millions of runners and others would eventually comprise the market—and how rapid the decline would be. Such uncertainties plagued running-shoe manufacturers. If they geared up for continued growth and a maintenance of high-level demand, the results could be devastating if demand fell drastically. Unless flexibility could be built into the production, and unless alternative markets were identified and targeted, a firm could find itself with so much excess capacity that its very viability might be jeopardized. On the other hand, if it did not gear its production to a sufficiently high demand, the door was open for competitors to carve out great chunks of market share. The product life cycle, its estimate and realization, was a crucial consideration.

The uncertainties about the extent and durability of the life cycle led Converse and Keds, the two biggest makers of low-priced athletic shoes, to move far too slowly into the running-shoe market, and they were never to gain much ground. Had the bubble burst, had the running boom been a short-lived phenomenon, would

Nike have been able to maintain its viability in such a greatly diminished market? We think so. Several years before the leveling-off and maturing of the market, Nike had been diversifying into related but different products. And it had kept itself flexible productionwise by contracting the greater portion fo its manufacturing to foreign factories. Consequently, a large infrastructure that would necessitate high fixed costs and vulnerability to falling demand was not built up.

Finally we see in this, as in a number of cases, the frailty of market dominance and being first in the market. No firm, market leader or otherwise, can afford to rest on its laurels, to disregard a changing environment and aggressive but smaller competitors. Adidas had as commanding a lead in this industry as IBM had in computers. But it was overtaken and surpassed by Nike, a rank newcomer, with few resources, and a domestic firm besides in an era when foreign brands (of beer, watches, cars, etc.) had a mystique and attraction to affluent Americans that few domestic brands could achieve. But Adidas let its guard down, and its aggressiveness lagged at a critical point.

A front runner tends more toward complacency in the situation we have seen here. A sharply rising primary demand is reassuring and lulling. Sales will be increasing sharply for the industry leader during such a time, and this is conducive to complacency. But such increasing sales may mask a declining market position, in which competitors are making major gains at the expense of the dominant firm. Eventually the momentum shifts to one or more of the now significant competitors.

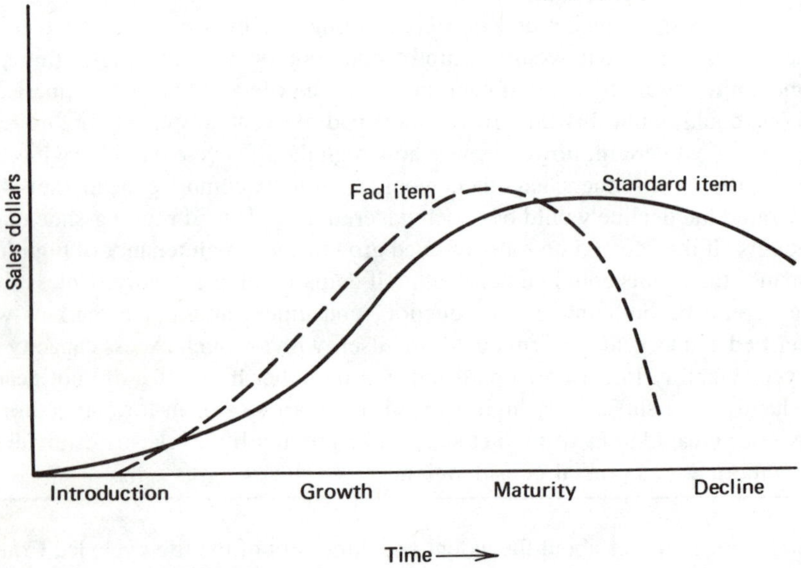

Figure 18.3. Typical product life cycles for fad and standard items.

The once dominant firm may not be able to recoup its position. Success for one firm can come from the mistakes of another, not so much of commission as omission, in which needed actions were not taken or at least not until too late.

Questions

1. "The success of Nike was strictly fortuitous and had little to do with a powerful marketing strategy." Evaluate this statement.
2. Discuss the pros and cons of optimistic versus conservative sales forecasts for a hot new product.

Invitation to Role Play

As an Adidas executive, how would you propose to counter the initial thrusts at your market share by Nike and other U.S. running-shoe manufacturers?

CHAPTER 19

Conclusions: What Can Be Learned

And now after traipsing down the corridors of historical entrepreneurial successes, what can we come away with? What can we learn that may benefit present or proposed efforts and engender worthwhile planning and idea generation?

A rather large number of generalizations can indeed be drawn from these successes. Of course, we have to recognize that marketing is a discipline that does not lend itself to laws or axioms. Examples of successful exceptions to every principle or generalization can be found. But the marketing executive does well to heed the following generalizations. After all, we should be able to learn from past experiences, both mistakes and successes. Adversity as well as success should hone the enterprise to greater effectiveness and provide models for other enterprises, not to slavishly copy but to judiciously consider.

CONCLUSIONS REGARDING OVERALL ENTERPRISE PERSPECTIVES

The Growth Perspective Needed

Many of these examples give us worthwhile insights concerning how much growth is good and how much is too much. Certainly, all of our ''successes'' have been growth firms—otherwise, they could scarcely have been successes. But an emphasis on growth for the sake of growth can be dangerous. Somehow the growth must be kept within the abilities of the firm to assimulate it. Some of our examples showed tremendous growth capability without losing control.

Our first case, the J. C. Penney Company, achieved undreamed-of growth in geographical expansion of store units. This was done without sacrificing quality of managerial resources or dissipating the financial resources of the company by simply bringing store managers intimately into the expansion process as they trained subordinates for store management and invested their own money in such new company units.

McDonald's reveals the great growth that is possible with franchised units rather than company-owned outlets. However, other franchised fast-food operations expanded too fast and either went out of business or had to drastically cut back and rid themselves of a host of marginal operations. What was the secret of McDonald's handling of rapid growth? It was achieved by very tight controls, careful screening of prospective franchisees as well as new locations, and not neglecting existing units in the excitement of opening ever more new units.

Apple and Nike show that geometric annual growth is possible without losing control of operations. Although Apple had some growing pains, it was able to overcome them and remain strong in the rapidly evolving technology of the personal computer market. Nike experienced almost as rapid growth as Apple, but it had a major problem that Apple did not: the uncertain life cycle of running shoes. It met this challenge by building an operation that could be very flexible, and it also positioned itself to move strongly into related product areas before the running bubble could burst.

Perhaps manufacturers such as Nike, Perdue, and Apple and service firms such as IMG and Hyatt can handle great growth better than retailers can. A retailer has major problems in geographical expansion in trying to maintain sufficient controls and standards with far-flung outlets. The personnel requirements for retailers in achieving great growth are far greater, also. For example, Nike was able to grow to a half a billion dollar corporation with under 3000 employees; Apple with under 4000; Perdue with 5000. International Management Group was a quarter-billion-dollar corporation, yet it had only 300 employees. A far-flung retail operation on the other hand would need tens of thousands of employees.

We saw two contrasting examples of similar types of retailers handling great growth. Korvette, the innovator and early market leader in discounting, could not handle its growth: the organization and controls were inadequate, and recruiting and training of qualified management people could not meet the growth demands. Practically at the height of its success, Korvette faltered. K mart, on the other hand, the imitator not the innovator, had the organizational strength to handle the growth, and soon became the world's largest discounter, behind only Sears among all retailers. And K mart did this while keeping its organization, its store facilities, and its merchandise plans and controls as simple as possible. It also concentrated its efforts on aggressively discounting rather than diffusing among different ventures and divisions as Woolworth did.

We can make these generalizations about the most desirable growth perspectives:

1. Great growth is possible, but this should not exceed the abilities of the organization to assimulate, control, and provide sufficient managerial and financial resources.
2. The most prudent approach to growth is to keep the organization and operation as simple and uniform as possible and to build flexibility into the expansion so that off-target sales expectations can be handled without undue stress.
3. Concentrating maximum organizational efforts on the expansion opportunity is like an army exploiting a breakthrough, and will usually win out over a competitor who more carefully diffuses efforts and resources. But such a concentration of resources is hazardous and often has a high risk/reward ratio.
4. In the quest for great growth, older aspects of the operation, such as older stores, should not be neglected.

Innovation

We have seen in these success stories that the major innovations have come from small firms, often from outsiders far removed from the traditional and accepted. But cannot large firms be innovative as well? Certainly they can be, but with size and longevity in an industry certain impediments to change tend to manifest themselves, as we will examine a little later in this chapter. Of the five major innovations described—King Kullen, Korvette, L'Eggs, Hyatt, and Apple—only one was an established firm, Hanes, which was involved with marketing higher priced hosiery, and recognized a gap in serving the lower priced sector.

King Kullen and Korvette, and later Hyatt, provide examples that opportunities can exist where traditional market structures predominate. Old customary ways of doing things may no longer be the most effective ways of serving customers, of meeting their changing needs and wants. Consequently, there is vulnerability to an innovator who can serve needs better. Both King Kullen and Korvette emerged at times when consumers were ripe for retail institutional changes that would offer them lower prices, a better assortment of goods, and more convenience of hours and parking.

In the area of service marketing Hyatt shows that opportunities exist where present firms—in this case, the conventional law firms—are disregarding or repudiating certain customers' needs. Hyatt offered lower prices and had a much wider customer appeal. Furthermore, the use of aggressive marketing techniques had a powerful impact because it was so alien to this hide-bound legal profession.

In Apple we see that product innovation can come from humble surroundings and seemingly unpromising people—in this case, college dropouts—even though they faced the resources of an IBM. Product innovation combined with aggressive marketing efforts and identification of the most potent customer segment brought great success despite the mightiest of competitors lurking on the periphery.

L'eggs illustrates how innovation can have various facets, not only in an improved product but in a highly distinctive package combined with a different method of distribution than the industry had ever known before—all combined with the sophisticated tools of marketing research and heavy advertising inputs.

We can make these generalizations regarding innovation:

1. Opportunities often exist when a traditional market structure prevails in the industry.
2. Opportunities often exist when there are gaps in serving customers' needs by existing firms.
3. Innovations are not limited to products, but can involve other elements of the marketing mix, such as the method of distribution.

Power of Judicious Imitation

Some firms are reluctant to copy successful practices of their competitors; they want to be leaders, not followers. But successful practices or innovations may need to be embraced even to survive. And sometimes the imitator outdoes the innovator.

For example, in the 1930s King Kullen was the innovator of the "revolution" to supermarkets, which threatened to sweep all before it. The major grocery chains, such as A&P, in just a few years recognized that they had to join the supermarket tide or face extinction, even if converting to supermarkets meant that thousands of their regular groceries had to be closed. K mart and Nike, on the other hand, did not have to be imitators. But they recognized an effective marketing strategy and outdid the innovators, and both were destined to dominate their markets.

But then there were certain fast-food competitors of McDonald's who disdained to adopt McDonald's successful format, even though the high standards and rigid controls were obvious to all. We can make the following generalization:

> There are good arguments for identifying those aspects of successful competitors (and even similar but noncompeting firms) that contribute most to the success and then adopting them if compatible with the resources of the imitator. Let someone else do the experimenting and take the risks of innovating. The imitator faces some risk in waiting too long, but this is usually far less than the risk of an untested product or operation failing.

Vulnerability to Competition

Time after time we have encountered the reality that marketing advantages can be short-lived, that success does not guarantee continued success, and that innovators as well as long-dominant firms can be overtaken and surpassed.

Short-Lived Market Advantages. We have seen how such firms as King Kullen, Lever and its Spry, Lestoil, and Korvette found their initial advantages rather quickly countered by competitors. The major grocery chains did adapt to the supermarket innovation; Crisco corrected its deficiencies and eventually held Spry at bay; Lestoil's product and promotional advantages were countered and surpassed by its larger competitors; and Korvette's weaknesses proved instructional to K mart.

Yet somehow the market strengths of McDonald's were not matched by most of its competitors until years after it had achieved its market dominance.

The Need to React to the Environment. The environment is dynamic. It changes, sometimes subtly, other times more violently and recognizably. This should be realized by all organizations. As we have seen so many times, to rest on one's laurels is perilous. In view of a changing environment, which opens up opportunities as well as problems, a firm can be an innovator, a leader. Not all firms are willing to accept the rewards and risks of this and, as we have seen, large, long-established organizations are most remiss here. But a firm must at least be adaptable if it is not to be wounded by the changing environment.

We saw two newcomers that successfully faced particularly dynamic and challenging environments. Nike achieved its market dominance but faced severe product life uncertainties: how long would the running boom last; would it collapse quickly or stablize? Nike reacted to this situation by keeping its operations highly flexible and by quickly moving into related diversification. Apple similarly gained initial market dominance in an environment of rapidly changing technology, with the constant threat that other firms would achieve breakthroughs; and with the behemoth, IBM, entering the market the uncertainties were greatly increased. Apple reacted by a heavy commitment to research and development in efforts to keep itself in the forefront. As this is written, it has succeeded in doing so.

Following are generalizations regarding vulnerability to competition:

1. Initial market advantage tends to be rather quickly countered by competitors.
2. Countering by competitors is more likely to occur when an innovation is involved than when the advantage involves more commonplace effective management and marketing techniques.
3. Long dominant firms tend to be vulnerable to upstart competitors because of their complacency, resistance to change, and myopia concerning a changing environment.
4. All firms need to recognize that the environment is dynamic and changing,

and to react to such changes, either by capitalizing on newly arisen opportunities or by adapting to the new problems created by change.

SPECIFIC MARKETING STRATEGY CONCLUSIONS

Importance of the Target Market Decision

The target market, that is, the customers the firm chooses to direct its efforts toward, can play a vital role in the success. This is especially true when the target has previously not been well served by competitors. With Hyatt we saw a marketing target—working-class Americans—that had been disdained by most law firms, although in numbers it was large. But it could be appealed to only with attractive prices and convenient (i.e., walk-in and unpretentious) sites. Apple correctly identified the key target market for minicomputers, as not the home market but the small business and professional user. McDonald's attained its greatest growth momentum by appealing to families, and particularly children (although it is now attempting to broaden its target market). Remember, Ronald McDonald was second only to Santa Claus in recognizability among children. Pepsi recognized that it had to discard its original target market—the poor who were interested only in getting the biggest drink for their money in the 1930s and 1940s—to the growing and affluent middle class; only then was it able to think of making a comeback. And Miller after its acquisition by Philip Morris began appealing to different segments or target markets with its different brands of beer. In particular, it revolutionized the beer industry with its Miller Lite by appealing not to women and light drinkers, but to the heavy drinker who previously had considered light beers "sissy" drinks.

The Paradox of Positioning

How a product is to be placed or positioned in the market in relation to competitive offerings has shown no consistent pattern for success. At the one extreme we saw the J. C. Penney Company for almost 50 years eschewing any direct competition with the major retailers of the East and those in the bigger cities. It stuck primarily with small towns, for the most part west of the Mississippi. Certainly Joel Hyatt positioned his firm far from the traditional law firms. On the other hand, Lever's Spry and Nike positioned themselves practically head-to-head against their entrenched major competitor. Frank Perdue and his chickens and Hanes with its L'eggs positioned themselves solidly in the higher price, higher quality ends of their markets. We conclude that how a firm positions itself is not always a major factor in success, but for most smaller and newer firms a position somewhat different from that of competitors will generally be more conducive to success than head-to-head confrontation with a bigger and more well-heeled competitor.

The Necessity of Differentiation or Uniqueness

In practically all the cases we have studied, strong efforts were exerted to maintain a distinctive brand and presence. Coca-Cola in its early days zealously guarded the integrity of its name from those who would encroach on it. The cigarette makers were willing to spend millions, even in the very early days of advertising, in order to develop and maintain a psychological (more than a physical) differentiation for their brands. Nike, although it may have imitated the marketing strategy of Adidas, certainly went to great pains to show its "swoosh" logo on all its products and advertising. Of course, McDonald's and its "golden arches" has long been identifiable from blocks away. And we saw the strenuous efforts of Frank Perdue to attain differentiation with his commodity product, chickens. By so doing, he gained the key to success.

The Desirability of Nonprice Competition. Closely akin to differentiation is non-price competition. The more a firm is able to establish either a tangible or a psychological uniqueness for its product, the more it is insulated from cut-throat price competition. Perdue, of course, was able to achieve this once he established his distinctive chickens as superior to all other chickens. L'eggs is another classic example of a very successfully differentiated product that could maintain itself above the prices and price-cutting tactics of the other brands marketed through self-service stores. On the other hand, Joel Hyatt achieved success by waging severe price competition on established lawyers, and constantly stressing this idea in all his promotional efforts.

Concentration on Customer Satisfaction

Customer satisfaction is taken for granted by many firms. They assume that as long as sales, profits, and market share are satisfactory, customers must be well satisfied. But this can be a delusion. Sales and performance statistics may mask a deteriorating situation in which customer loyalty is eroding but enough new customers are being gained to offset the dissatisfied. Or customers may be disgruntled but there are as yet no suitable alternatives to which they can switch their business. We will identify four of the cases that showed above-average efforts geared to customer satisfaction.

Jim Penney had customer satisfaction uppermost in mind. This was a powerful advantage over many other retailers in the early decades of this century. Penney's sought to give customers honest values and full satisfaction, or money back.

Mark McCormack's International Management Group emphasized a strong client commitment. The athlete and celebrity clients received the best personal and financial attention. In IMG's case, this emphasis on customer satisfaction was vital because of the agency relationship in which the client could easily drop IMG if the perceived benefits were deemed inadequate. And Jack Nicklaus did, indeed, drop

IMG because he thought Arnold Palmer was being given disproportionate attention. Hyatt also strongly emphasized customer satisfaction. Among its lower income clientele who were skeptical of most lawyers this emphasis on customer satisfaction was also crucial.

Lever found a niche in the marketplace dominated by Crisco and was able to capitalize on the somewhat dissatisfied customers of Crisco with its new product, Spry. The vulnerability of Crisco because of such customer dissatisfaction, though it was only mild, shows the need for any firm to keep apprised of how satisfied its customers are and not take this for granted because sales and other operating statistics appear satisfactory. Periodic customer surveys—feedback from the marketplace—seems desirable to detect any erosion of customer satisfaction.

Strengths and Limitations of Advertising

We have seen a diversity of results following the growing use of mass media advertising over the last 70 to 80 years. Certainly we have to conclude that sheer expenditures for advertising do not ensure success.

For example, although advertising was certainly a factor in the growth of Coca-Cola, it was used in conjunction with other aspects of the marketing strategy such as the distinctive bottle, creative uses of premiums and dealer displays, and very strong dealer relationships. Coca-Cola was a heavy user of advertising, but the major expenditures occurred after it was already well established. And it sought an effective slogan for decades until finally coming up with the "The pause that refreshes" in 1929. The cigarette firms in the early decades were heavy users of advertising for that day, but the advantage went to the brand that stumbled onto a more effective theme than its competitors. The turnaround of Pepsi in the 1950s and the inroads it made against Coca-Cola can largely be attributed to a more effective theme while Coke was groping.

The cigarette industry in the 1920s and 1930s showed the power of mass media advertising in accelerating existing social trends, particularly in turning women to smoking by making the cigarette a symbol for the "new women" who broke from traditional subservience and turned toward independence and assertiveness. Cigarette advertising also showed the potency of psychological differentiation and its advertisability. Despite their similarity, the various brands came to be perceived as different through their advertising themes. George Washington Hill showed once for all the power of repetition in advertising with his ads repeating the slogan, "LS/MFT" ("Lucky Strike means fine tobacco"), ad nauseum for more than a decade. Though many people might be turned off by such repetition, Luckies dominated the market. (We can wonder today, however, whether a more sophisticated consumer would provide the same positive impact to "ad nauseum" repetition.) Finally, we see that sheer magnitude of advertising expenditures can be countered by competitors with different marketing strategies. For example, the low-priced brands such as Wings based their success on lower prices and minimum advertising. And brands such as Philip Morris tapped the higher price/quality market also without resorting to the massive advertising expenditures of the Big Three.

Lestoil shows the power of the newly emerging medium, television, for saturation advertising on a limited market-by-market basis. Lestoil's eventual success in gaining market entry suggests that an important objective of advertising can be to impress dealers with the manufacturer's commitment, and thereby make them more willing to stock and support the product.

In several cases we have seen the effectiveness of celebrity advertising and testimonials. The cigarette firms, again, heavily relied on sports figures and entertainers to provide role models for the common folk. Half a century later, International Management Group built its success on the demand for athletes to promote products in diverse ways, from radio and television commercials to sales rally presentations, public appearances, and trade promotions. And Nike, Adidas, and the other athletic shoe makers geared their successes to persuading famous athletes to wear their brand-identifiable shoes and clothing.

Finally, we have seen how effective the owner or chief executive of a firm can be in TV commercials. Joel Hyatt and Frank Perdue can credit a substantial part of their advertising success to their own personal appearances. Chief executives of some other firms have also been effective, notably Lee Iacocca of Chrysler and Frank Borman of Eastern Airlines. But not every owner or chief executive can project the sincerity needed for success in this type of testimonial advertising.

Enlightened Dealer Relations

Several firms showed extraordinary efforts in furthering their dealer relations. Even before the turn of the century, Coca-Cola was breaking new ground in gaining rapport and great support with its dealers and bottlers. In no small way did such relations spur the success of Coca-Cola. Pepsi-Cola in the 1950s also went to great lengths to enlist the enthusiastic support of its bottlers, often by hoopla and wide recognition. Later, Hanes made it almost impossible for any self-service retailers to resist placing the L'eggs selling display on their premises. And finally, McDonald's provided such a highly successful format that millionaire franchisees became commonplace provided they did not deviate from its standards for operational excellence.

The Role of Marketing Research

Perhaps surprisingly, we have seen a rather subdued role for marketing research, even in the most recent cases. True, Lever used marketing research very effectively in uncovering the weaknesses of Crisco. So did both Philip Morris for its Miller Beer and Hanes. (We might even question whether Hanes took too long in its research and test marketing of L'eggs: an aggressive competitor might have beaten the cautious Hanes in the race for overall market dominance.) But most of the other successes, at least in their origination, used little formal research.

For example, the great successes of Nike and Apple relied on entrepreneurial hunch instead of sophisticated research. So did Frank Perdue, flying in the face of traditional thinking. Mark McCormack moved into the marketing of athletes more by happenstance than as a result of formal studies. Ray Kroc of McDonald's recognized a good thing when he saw it, although McDonald's later became a strong user of research, especially for its site selections. Kresge's major move into its K mart also came without formal research: Harry Cunningham on his own conducted a two-year investigation, but this was a far cry from a formal and sophisticated marketing research study.

Why have we not seen a more extensive use of marketing research by these notable successes? After all, this too is usually proposed as the mark of sophisticated management and the way to make better marketing decisions. A common perception is that the more money spent for marketing research the less chance there is for a bad decision. Yet marketing mistakes have occurred despite extremely heavy uses of marketing research: for example, the Edsel and DuPont's Corfam.[1]

We can deduce the following major reasons for the lack of marketing research:

1. Most of the founding entrepreneurs did not have marketing backgrounds and therefore were not as familiar and confident with such research as others would have been.
2. Available tools and techniques do not provide valid research conclusions for some problems and opportunities. There may be too many variables. They may be intangible and incapable of precise measurement. Also, much research consists of collecting data of past and present. Although this can be helpful in predicting a stable future, for revolutionary new ventures it may be of little help. The risks for such ventures can hardly be delegated or abdicated to a research function. They must be faced by the entrepreneur in the quest for the great rewards.

Generalizations Regarding Marketing Strategy

Following is a summary of the generalizations regarding specific aspects of marketing strategy that we can derive from the cases we have studied:

1. The target market decision, if correct, can play a vital role in the success of the venture. This is particularly true if
   a. The selected target market has not been well served by competitors, or
   b. A different and attractive appeal can be made to an important target market.

[1]These cases are described and diagnosed in *Marketing Mistakes*.

2. Success has come to firms who have both (a) sought to position themselves far from competitors and (b) have gone head-to-head against entrenched competition. But for the smaller firm with limited resources, a positioning somewhat different from powerful competitors seems more prudent.
3. Product differentiation or uniqueness is basic to marketing success. Such can be psychological rather than physical and can be built by advertising.

   Such uniqueness permits nonprice competition, which is usually preferable to cut-throat price competition. However, if a firm has a clear and relatively lasting advantage pricewise, then price competition is certainly warranted.
4. Every firm should closely monitor how satisfied its customers are, in order to detect emerging problems that may make it vulnerable to competition. Normally, sales, profits, market share, and other operating statistics do not provide a sufficient monitoring of customer satisfaction. Periodic customer surveys provide better feedback.
5. Advertising generalizations:
   a. Sheer expenditures do not guarantee success. An effective and distinctive theme or message is the vital ingredient but is not easily found amid the plethora of advertising.
   b. Advertising can be especially effective in accelerating existing social trends.
   c. Ads can be effective in promoting psychological differentiation, even when little or no physical differentiation actually exists.
   d. Heavy use of repetition in advertising proved successful around the midcentury; whether this same extreme of repetition would be a positive influence today may be questioned.
   e. Despite competitors who advertise heavily, other firms can counter successfully with different strategies, such as lower prices or better quality and service positioning.
   f. For the small firm attempting to gain market entry, consumer advertising can be important in influencing dealers.
   g. Athletes and other celebrities, as well as high-level company executives, can be effective in testimonials. The effectiveness, however, depends on the sincerity and credibility they are able to project.
6. Extraordinary and even creative efforts in dealer relations have been the hallmark of some of these successful firms.
7. Marketing research has not been a key factor in many of these successes. Its role has been minor in innovative entrepreneurship.

GENERAL CONCLUSIONS

Marketing Technology Powerfully Applied to Nonproducts

In the Hyatt and International Management Group cases we see evidence of how effective marketing techniques and strategies can be when applied to nonproducts.

This opens new vistas for marketing, certainly increasing the importance of marketing in our society and giving marketing-trained people diverse opportunities and wide scope for their careers.

Difficulty of Gaining Market Entry for the Small Firm

The Lestoil example shows how extremely difficult it can be for the small unknown firm, even with a recognizably superior product, to gain market entry against entrenched and powerful competitors. It is only natural that the better dealers and intermediaries already have strong relationships with established producers. They consequently are reluctant to take on a competitive brand, and an unknown one at that. Furthermore, for items distributed through self-service retailers limited shelf space may shut out the new firm from some of the market. Yet, Lestoil showed that entry can be achieved, even against the most powerful competitors of all, Procter & Gamble, and Lever Bros. Although creative approaches may be necessary to gain market entry, less innovative approaches may be effective if the product is superior in some advertisable way, and if an additive approach to the market is used. In such an additive approach, a firm concentrates all of its meager resources on a single market or part of a market, gaining a solid foothold there before directing any efforts to another market area.

Conditions Favoring Transferability of Marketing Prowess

Several cases showed the effective transference of marketing expertise to other ventures. Miller Beer in particular epitomized the successful transference of the marketing expertise developed by Philip Morris with its cigarettes. We can identify these conditions that increase the probability of successful transference:

1. An industry that is somewhat backward in using aggressive marketing techniques, or one composed of small firms with limited resources.
2. Similarity of products.
3. Similarity of customer demographics such as age, sex, income, educational level, or family situation.
4. Availability of similar media to readily reach the customers in the new market or industry.
5. Similarity of price.
6. Similarity of distribution.

Although effective transference is possible without all of these factors being positive, the more that are the more likely a successful industry invasion. The brewing industry matched these criteria ideally for the transference of Philip Morris' talent and experience.

We also saw International Management Group and Nike expanding their successful formats to related endeavors. And earlier, Lever Bros. invaded the shortening market with five of the six conditions being favorable (only the first condition, i.e., an industry backward in using aggressive marketing techniques, was not met).

Impact of One Person

In almost all of these cases we have seen the powerful impact that one person had on the organization and its success. We will mention just a few here.

Harry Cunningham of Kresge completely turned this mediocre and conservative variety-store chain into the most aggressive and largest discounter, with a growth almost unparalleled in retailing.

Ray Kroc of McDonald's had the vision and energy to convert a successful small hamburger stand into the world's largest fast-food franchised operation, and maintained its successful format against all comers.

Alfred Steele turned the faltering Pepsi-Cola completely around in just a few short years so that it was steadily taking market share away from the renowned Coca-Cola. This case is particularly intriguing for the speed with which a sick operation was turned around.

One person can also have a negative impact on an organization. We saw a hint of this with Eugene Ferkauf and Korvette. Although he was the force behind the development and growth of Korvette, and was even heralded as one of the outstanding merchants in U.S. history, he could not adapt himself or his organization to the challenges of large size, and it faltered and became a sick and worsening operation. In a sequel to this book, *Marketing Mistakes,* we describe a number of other instances in which the failure of an operation, and even the demise of a firm, can be blamed on one person. The impact of one person, for good or ill, is one of the marvels of history, whether business history or world history.

Prevalence of Opportunities for Innovation Today

By considering the most recent successes—Hyatt, IMG, Apple, Nike—we have to conclude that opportunities for entrepreneurship were never better. Despite the maturing of our economy and the growing size and power of many firms in many industries, there is still abundant opportunity. Such opportunity exists not only for the change maker or innovator, but even for the entrepreneur who only seeks to do things a little better than existing, and complacent, competition.

The availability of venture capital to support promising new businesses was never better—some $1 billion a year. And by the mid-1980s we are in the midst of the greatest boom in new stock issues and new company formations since the late 1960s.

Of course, we know that not all of us have what it takes to be an entrepreneur. It takes more than the "great idea." Nolan Bushnell, founder of Atari in 1972 with $500, says: "A lot of people have ideas, but there are few who decide to do something about them now. Not tommorow. Not next week. But today.''[2] Dreamers do not make entrepreneurs; doers do. The great venture capitalists look at the person, not the idea. Typically they distribute their seed money to resourceful people, those who are courageous enough to give up security for the unknown consequences of their embryonic venture, who have great self confidence, and who demonstrate a tremendous will to win.[3]

SOME CONCLUSIONS REGARDING THE EVOLUTION OF MARKETING

We have examined various successful enterprises covering a span of almost a century. It is worthwhile to consider how marketing strategies and tools have changed during this time, and we are forced to conclude—not as much as we would have thought.

Certainly more tools and techniques are available today than 50 or more years ago. In particular, mass media advertising, especially television, has given firms a new offensive weapon. But this can be powerful or relatively impotent depending on the judgment and the creativity used in designing and placing the message. All too often the great potential tool of advertising is blunted with nondistinctive and mundane copy that can consume millions of dollars of ad expenditures but have little impact. Mass media advertising has thus become a most expensive tool, but not always a very effective one.

Tools and techniques— and their utilization—of marketing research have changed greatly in the last 50 years, particularly since the *Literary Digest* fiasco of 1936 when sampling was just coming of age. But we have seen that this tool is not relied on as much as we would have expected. Despite decades of development of more sophisticated research tools and techniques, many decisions still are not much aided by marketing research, for example, in seeking an optimum allocation for marketing efforts. When is the optimum reached? How can it be obtained? And even, how is it to be measured? Other analyses rest on the shaky foundation of subjectivity. For example, consumer preference statements often are not translatable into actual sales without judicious imagination.

Other ingredients of effective marketing strategies are not new, even though the names have been coined in the last several decades. The marketing concept with its consumer orientation was adhered to before the turn of the century by certain enlightened retailers who saw the need to maximize customer satisfaction. Good dealer relations and the development of push efforts were initiated by Coca-Cola in the late 1800s. Even franchising is far from new, having originated also before 1900. The impact of point-of-purchase displays, promotional deals, psychological

[2]''Have You Got What It Takes?'' *Forbes,* August 3, 1981, p. 60.
[3]Ibid., p. 64.

differentiation, packaging, missionary salespeople—all of these originated decades ago.

We are left with the conclusion that perhaps marketing has not evolved as much as we thought. It still remains an art and not a science, and maybe this is what makes it so intriguing—it does not lend itself to formularizing. Perhaps the greatest change in marketing has been our increasing awareness, with evidence to support it, that marketing has potential uses far beyond products, that it can be useful in the furthering of services, institutions, causes, and personalities. Marketing is undeniably becoming a more and more important part of our society and endeavors.